D0169326

FERGUSON

CAREER COACH

MANAGING YOUR CAREER IN

Education

The Ferguson Career Coach Series

MANAGING YOUR CAREER IN

Education

Shelly Field

Ferguson
An imprint of Infobase Publishing

Ferguson Career Coach: Managing Your Career in Education

Copyright © 2008 by Shelly Field

Ferguson
An imprint of Infobase Publishing, Inc.
132 West 31st Street
New York NY 10001

Library of Congress Cataloging-in-Publication Data

Field, Shelly.
  Ferguson career coach : managing your career in education / Shelly Field.
    p. cm. — (The Ferguson career coach series)
  Includes bibliographical references and index.
  ISBN-13: 978-0-8160-5362-9 (hardcover : alk. paper)
  ISBN-10: 0-8160-5362-6 (hardcover : alk. paper) 1. Teaching—Vocational guidance—United States. I. Title.
  LB1775.2.F54 2008
  370.23—dc22   2008026047

Ferguson books are available at special discounts when purchased in bulk quantities for businesses, associations, institutions, or sales promotions. Please call our Special Sales Department in New York at (212) 967-8800 or (800) 322-8755.

You can find Ferguson on the World Wide Web at http://www.fergpubco.com

Text design by Kerry Casey
Cover design by Takeshi Takahashi

Printed in the United States of America

VB Hermitage 10 9 8 7 6 5 4 3 2 1

This book is printed on acid-free paper and contains 30% post-consumer recycled content.

CONTENTS

1

INTRODUCING YOUR CAREER COACH

Have you decided that you want a career in education? Great! You've just chosen to work in an industry that has the potential to impact the world.

If you are lucky, sometime in your life you have had a teacher who made a positive difference in your life. Perhaps he or she instilled a love of reading or taught you something new that changed the course of your life. Maybe a teacher made you feel important, helped you see your self worth, gave you confidence, or made you feel that you could do anything that you wanted.

Possibly a teacher made such an impact in *your* life that you have decided that you want to be a teacher too and do the same thing for others. If so, this book is for you.

Throughout the ages, there have been teachers and scholars. These people who shared information with others were always held in high esteem. They were the people who others looked to for answers.

The importance of education is clear. Without it our world would not be the one we know today. We would not have the advancements we have in technology, in health care, or in most other things that make our lives easier and better.

When you think of education what professions come to mind? If you're like most people, teachers are the first. While teachers are the most prominent profession in the field of education, the industry encompasses a wide variety of career options. These include, among others, those in counseling, business, administration, and support services.

But that's not all. There are also a large number of careers on the periphery for people who create the learning materials, write the textbooks, and develop testing materials.

One of the wonderful things about choosing a career in education is that there are so many diverse opportunities. You might choose to teach children, young people, or adults in an array of subject areas in private or public settings. You might choose a career in higher education, continuing education, or even in the education area of business or industry. You might choose a career in the supervision or administrative segment of education. The choice is yours.

Do you have a strong desire to teach others? Do you want to be a role model? Do you want to motivate and encourage others? Do you want to make a difference?

If so, you've chosen the right field. As a schoolteacher, you play a vital role in the development of children and older youngsters. You will be in the position to make a difference in the lives of others.

Do you have a strong belief in the education system and want to work to make it better? Do you have great communication skills? Do you have good management skills? Are you a strong leader? Do you have a vision? Can you not only share it with others, but also motivate them to work with you to bring it to fruition? If so, a career in administration might be perfect for you.

Some parts of the industry are easier to enter. Some are more competitive. Can you make it? Can you succeed?

I'm betting you can, and if you let me, I want to help you get where you want to be. Whether you've just decided that you want to work in some aspect of education, it's been your dream for some time, or you already work in the industry and you want to move up the career ladder, this book is for you.

Whether you want a career teaching in elementary schools, secondary schools, vocational technical schools, colleges or universities: this book is for you. Whether you want to teach children, teenagers, young adults, or senior citizens, this book is for you.

Whether you want a career in the business or administration segments of the industry, in teaching or any other area of education, in support services or any of the peripherals of the education industry, this book can be your guide to success.

I have been where you are; perhaps not in your specific career choice, but that doesn't matter. I know what it's like to want to have the career of your dreams so badly you can taste it. I know what it's like to want to experience success. I know what it's like to have a dream.

It doesn't matter if your dream is exactly like my dream or my dream is like yours. It doesn't even really matter exactly what you want to do. What matters is that if you have a dream—whatever it is—you can find a way to attain it.

I grew up in a family that not only stressed the importance of education, but also was very involved in it both as a vocation and on a volunteer basis.

My mother started her career as a teacher, teaching high school business classes. After leaving teaching to start a public relations business with my father, she stayed involved in education as a member of the local board of education, a seat she held for many years. Her involvement stemmed from discontent with the way the education process worked and the options for children.

With her strong interest for improving education, it was no surprise that a number of years after her terms as a school board member ended, she was appointed to the position of chairperson of the board of directors of the State University of New York at New Paltz.

After a successful career as president of his own public relations firm, my father also became involved in education. He decided that it was time to go after one of his dreams. He, too, wanted to teach in some manner. He went back to school to complete his bachelor's degree and then went on to become the first graduate of the master's program at Empire State College–State University of New York. Fulfilling his dream, he became a part-time business instructor in a number of different colleges. As both my mother and father were well known in the field of hospital and health care marketing, they were asked to teach a class together covering that subject matter for the New School for Social Research, which they did for a number of semesters.

One of my sisters is currently the superintendent of a large school district. My other sister frequently gives continuing education courses for attorneys at one of the law schools in the area in which she practices.

After college, while not a licensed teacher but on my way to *my* dream career, I substituted three or four times a week for a year. During that time the principal of one of the schools I was subbing in liked my teaching style and I was asked to become a permanent teacher. (If I agreed, while I would still have to get a license, a number of the other requirements would be waived in lieu of experience.) I turned down the offer.

While I would love to tell you working in education was my dream, at the time, I had another dream and I wasn't about to give it up. Although it wasn't related to education, I'm going to share it with you for a number of reasons.

Why? To begin with, I want to illustrate to you that dreams can come true. I want to show you how perseverance in your career (or anything else for that matter) can help you achieve your dreams and goals. Furthermore, you also might find it interesting to see how sometimes things you do in your career are stepping-stones to the career of your dreams.

I've done a lot of things in my life while pursuing *my* dreams. Some worked out, and some didn't. What I can say, however, is that I never will have to look back at my life and say, "I wish I had done this or that," because when I wanted to try something I always did. My hope is that you will be able to do the same thing.

Do I work in education now? While I am involved in many things, part of my career *is* on the periphery of education. As a career expert, through seminars, workshops, and classes, I often teach people how to find, enter, and succeed in their *perfect* career.

As a stress management specialist, I also teach people how to deal with stress, how to manage stress, and how to reduce stress. I teach people how to use humor to feel better and how to find ways to laugh. These segments of my career, however, came after I had done a lot of other things and lived a lot of dreams. This might happen to you as well.

It's important to remember that dreams can change, but as long as you keep going toward your goals you're on the right road.

With that in mind, here's my story. For as long as I can remember I wanted to be in the music industry, probably more than anything else in the world. I struggled to get in. Could I find anyone to help? No. Did I know anyone in the business? No. Did I live in one of the music capitals? No. The only thing I had going for me was a burning desire to be in the industry and the knowledge that I wasn't going to quit until it happened.

At the time I was trying to enter the industry I wished there was a book to give me advice on how to move ahead, to guide me toward my goals and give me insider tips. Unfortunately there wasn't. I wished that I had a mentor or a coach or someone who really knew what I should be doing and could tell me what it was. Unfortunately, I didn't have that either.

Did anyone ever help me? It wasn't that no one wanted to help, but most of the people in my network just didn't have a clue about the music industry. Did they know that the music industry was a multibillion-dollar business? Did they know that it offered countless opportunities? It really didn't matter, because no one I knew could give me an edge on getting in anyway.

A couple of times I did run into some music industry professionals who did try to help. In one instance, a few months after I had started job-hunting, I finally landed an interview at a large booking agency. I arrived for my appointment and sat waiting for the owner of the agency to meet with me. I sat and sat and sat.

A recording artist who was a client of the agency walked over to me after his meeting with the agent and asked how long I had been there. "Close to three hours," I replied. My appointment was for 1 p.m. and it was almost 4 p.m. "What are you here for?" he asked. "I want to be in the music industry," was my answer. "I want to be a tour manager."

"Someday," he said, "you'll make it and this joker [the agency owner] will want something from you and you can make *him* wait. Mark my words, it will happen." He then stuck his head inside the agency owner's door and said, "This woman has been sitting out here for hours, bring her in already." As I walked into the office I had a glimmer of hope. It was short lived, but it was hope just the same.

The agency owner was very nice. During our meeting he told me something to the effect of, if he ever needed someone with my skills and talents, he would be glad to give me a call, and that I should keep plugging away. In other words, "Thanks for coming in. I talked to you, now please leave. Don't call me, I'll call you."

He then explained in a hushed voice, "Anyway, you know how it is. Most managers don't want *girls* on the road with their acts." Not only was I being rejected because of my skills and talents, but now it was because I was a *girl*. (Because my name is Shelly, evidently many people incorrectly assumed I was male instead of female when their secretary's were setting up appointments. The good news is that this got me into a lot of places I probably wouldn't have had a chance to get in. The bad news? Once I got there they realized I was not a man.)

I smiled, thanked the agent for meeting with me, and left, wondering if I would ever get a job doing what I wanted. Was it sexual discrimination? Probably, but in reality the agent was just telling me the way it was at that time. He actually believed he was being nice. Was it worth complaining about? I didn't think so. I was new to the industry and I wasn't about to make waves before I even got in. The problem was, I just couldn't find a way to get in.

On another occasion, I met a road manager at a concert and told him about how I wanted to be a tour manager. He told me he knew how hard it was to get into the industry so he was going to help me. "Call me on Monday," he told me Saturday. I did. "I'm working on it," he said. "Call me Wednesday." On Wednesday he said, "Call me Friday." This went on for a couple of weeks before I realized that while he was trying to be nice, he really wasn't going to do anything for me.

I decided that if I were ever lucky enough to break into the music industry, I would help as many people as I possibly could who ever wanted a job doing *anything* to fulfill their dreams. I wasn't sure when I'd make it, but I knew I would get there eventually.

⭐ Tip from the Top

During that interview I learned two important lessons. One, use what you have to get your foot in the door. If someone thought I was a man because of my name, well, my idea was not to correct them *until* I got in the door. At least that way I could have a chance at selling myself.

The second lesson is choose your battles wisely. Had I complained about sexual discrimination at that point, I might have won the battle, but I would have lost the war.

Tip from the Coach

As big as the world is, it really is small. Always leave a good impression. Remember what the recording artist at the agency told me? A number of years after I broke into the industry his words actually did come true. At the time I was working on a project booking the talent for a big music festival overseas and the booking agent heard about it. He put in a call to me to see if I'd consider using his talent for the show. "Hi, Shelly, it's Dave. It's been a long time," said the voice mail. "I heard you were booking a new show and wanted to talk to you about having some of my acts appear on the show. Give me a call." As soon as I heard his name the words of that recording artist came flooding back into my mind. This was a true "mark my words" moment.

I was busy so I couldn't call him right away. He kept calling back. He really wanted his acts on the show. I finally took his call and told him we'd get back to him. He must have called 25 times in a two-day period to see if we'd made up our mind. He finally said, "How long do you expect me to wait?"

I then reminded him of the day I sat in his office and waited and waited for him to see me. He, of course, didn't even remember the moment, but to his credit, he apologized profusely and promised never to have me wait again. I accepted his apology and told him, he'd only have to wait . . . a little bit longer.

While like many others I dreamed about standing on a stage in front of thousands of adoring fans singing my number one song, in reality I knew that was not where my real talent was. I knew that I did have the talent to make it in the business end of the industry.

I did all the traditional things to try to get a job. I sent my resume, I searched out employment

agencies that specialized in the music industry, I made cold calls, and I read the classifieds.

And guess what? I still couldn't land a job. Imagine that. A college degree and a burning desire still couldn't get me the job I wanted. I had some offers, but the problem was they weren't offers to work in the music industry. I had offers for jobs as a social worker, a newspaper reporter, a teacher, and a number of other positions I have since forgotten. Were any of these jobs I wanted? No! I wanted to work in the music business, period. End of story.

Like many of you might experience when you share your dreams, I had people telling me I was pipe dreaming. "The music industry," I was told, "is for *the other people*. You know, the *lucky ones*." I was also told consistently how difficult the music industry was to get into and once in, how difficult it was to succeed. In essence, I was being told not to get my hopes up.

Want to hear the good news? I eventually did get into the industry. I had to "think outside of the box" to get there, but the important thing was I found a way to get in. Want to hear some more good news? If I could find a way to break into the industry of my dreams and create a wonderful career, you can find a way to break into the industry of your dreams and create a wonderful career too! As a matter of fact, not only can you get in, but you can succeed.

Coming full circle, remember when I said that if I got into the music business I would help

Words from the Wise

In addition to not leaving a bad impression, try not to burn bridges. The bridge you burn today might just be the bridge you need to cross tomorrow.

every single person who ever wanted a job do-ing anything? Well, you want to work in some aspect of the education industry and I want to help you get there. I want to help you succeed. And I want to help you live your dreams.

I am a career expert and have written nu-merous books on a wide array of different career-oriented subjects. I give seminars, pre-sentations, and workshops around the country on entering and succeeding in the career of your dreams. I'm a personal coach and stress man-agement specialist to people in various walks of life, including celebrities, corporate executives, and people just like you who want a great career and a great life. Unfortunately, much as I wish I could, I can't be there in person for each and every one of you.

So with that in mind, through the pages of this book, I'm going to be your personal coach, your cheerleader, and your inside source to not only finding your dream career, but getting in and succeeding as well.

A Personal Coach—What's That?

The actual job title of *personal coach* is relatively new, but coaches are not. Athletes and others in the sports industry have always used coaches to help improve their game and their performance. Over the past few years, coaches have sprung up in many other fields.

There are those who coach people toward better fitness or nutrition, vocal coaches to help people improve their voices, acting coaches to help people with acting skills, and etiquette coaches to help people learn how to act in ev-ery situation. There are parenting coaches to help people parent better, retirement coaches to help people be successful in retirement, and time management coaches to help people better manage their time.

There are stress management coaches to help people better manage their stress; executive business coaches to help catapult people to the top; life coaches to help people attain a happier, more satisfying life; and career coaches to help people create a great career. Personal coaches often help people become more successful and satisfied in a combination of areas.

"I don't understand," you might be saying. "Exactly what does a coach do and what can he or she do for me?" Well, there are a number of things.

Basically a coach can help you find your way to success faster. He or she can help moti-vate you, help you find what really makes you happy, get you on track, and help you focus your energies on what you really want to do. Unlike some family members or friends, coaches aren't judgmental. You, therefore, have the ability to freely explore ideas with your coach without fear of them being rejected. Instead of accept-ing your self-imposed limitations, coaches en-courage you to reach to your full potential and improve your performance.

Coaches are objective, and one of the impor-tant things he or she can do for you is to point out things that you might not see yourself. Most of all, a coach helps *you* find the best in you and then shows *you* ways to bring it out. This in turn will make you more successful.

As your coach, what do I hope to do for you? I want to help you find your passion and then help you go after it. If a career in some segment of the education industry is what you want, I want to help you get in and I want you to be successful.

Is your career aspiration to be a teacher? Do you want to teach elementary school stu-dents? Do you want to teach special education students? Do you want to teach middle school or high school students? Is your dream to teach in a college or university? Do you want to help prepare others for their career? Do you want to be a guidance counselor?

Do you have a passion you want to share with others? Perhaps you want to teach in a conservatory. Maybe you want to teach dance. How about acting? Or maybe you want to teach at a vocational or technical school.

Do you want to teach in a less formal setting? Maybe you want to be a tutor. Perhaps you want to teach students who are starring in films on Hollywood sets. Maybe you want to teach youngsters who are starring in television shows. What about teaching teenaged recording artists on tour? If you think outside of the box, the possibilities are endless!

"But I don't want to be a teacher," you say. "What if I want to work in another segment of the industry? What if I want to work in business or administration?"

If you want to be in the business or administrative end of the industry, I'm going to help you find ways to get in. Then we'll work on finding ways to catapult you to the top there, too. If you're already in, we'll work on ways to help you climb the career ladder to your dream position.

Whatever you're dream is, we'll work together to find a way to help you get in and achieve your dreams.

Look at me as your personal cheerleader and this book as your guide. I want you to succeed and will do as much as possible to make that happen. No matter what anyone tells you, it is possible to not only get the job of your dreams, but to succeed at levels higher than you dare to dream. Thousands of people have done so and now one of them can be you!

Did you ever notice that some people just seem to attract success? They seem to get all the breaks, are always at the right place at the right time, and have what you want. It's not that you're jealous, but you just want to get a piece of the pie.

"They're so lucky," you say.

Well, here's the deal: You can be that lucky too. Want to know why? While a little bit of luck is always helpful, it's not just chance. Some people work to attract success. They work to get what they want. They follow a plan, keep a positive attitude, and they know that they're worthy of the prize. Others just wait for success to come, and when all you do is wait, success often just passes you by.

The good news here is you can be one of the lucky ones who attract success if you take the right steps. This book will give you some of the keys to control your destiny; it will hand you the keys to success in your career and your life.

Through the pages of this book, you'll find the answers to many of your questions about a career in education. You'll get the inside scoop on how the industry works, key employment issues, and finding opportunities.

You'll find insider tips, tricks, and techniques that have worked for others who have succeeded in the industry. You'll discover secrets to help you get in the door and up the ladder of success as well as the lowdown on things others wish they had known when they were first beginning their quest for success.

If you haven't attended any of my career seminars, my workshops on climbing the career ladder and succeeding in your dream career, my stress management seminars, or any of the other presentations I offer, you will get the benefit of being there. If you have attended one, here is the book you've been asking for!

Change Your Thinking, Change Your Life

Sometimes, the first step in getting what you want is just changing the way you think. Did you know that if you think you don't deserve something, you usually don't get it? Did you know that if you think you aren't good enough, neither will anyone else? Did you know that if you think you deserve something, you have a much better chance of getting it? Or, if you think you are good enough, your confidence will shine through?

When you have confidence in yourself, you start to find ways to get what you want and guess what? You succeed!

And while changing your thinking can change your life, this book is not just about a positive attitude. It's a book of actions you can take.

While a positive attitude is always helpful in order to succeed in whatever part of the industry you're interested in pursuing, you need to take positive actions too.

If all it took for you to be successful was for me to tell you what you need to do or even me doing it for you, I would. I love what I do and my career and I truly want to help everyone live their dreams too.

Here's the reality of the situation: I can only offer advice, suggestions, and tell you what you need to do. You have to do the rest. Talking about what you can do or should do is fine, but without you taking action, it's difficult to get where you want to go.

This is your chance to finally get what you want. You've already taken one positive step to getting your dream career simply by picking up this book. As you read through the various sections, you'll find other actions to take which will help get you closer to the great career you deserve.

One of the things we'll talk about is creating your own personal action plan. This is a plan which can help you focus on exactly what you want and then show you the actions needed to get it.

Your personal action plan is a checklist of sorts. Done correctly it can be one of the main keys to your career success. It will put you in the driver's seat and give you an edge over others who haven't prepared a plan themselves.

We'll also discuss putting together a number of different kinds of journals to help you be more successful in your career and life. For example, one of the problems many people experience when they're trying to get a new job, move up the career ladder, or accomplish a goal is that they often start feeling like they aren't accomplishing anything. A career journal is a handy tool to help you track exactly what you've done to accomplish your goals. Once that is in place, you know what else needs to be done.

Is This the Right Career for Me?

Unsure about exactly what part the of the education industry in which you want to become involved? As you read through the book, you'll get some ideas.

"But what if I'm already working at a job in another industry?" you ask. "Is it too late? Am I stuck there forever? Is it too late to get a career in education?"

Here's the deal: It is never too late to change careers, and going after something you're passionate about can drastically improve the quality of your life.

Thousands of people stay in jobs because it's easier than going after what they want. You don't have to be one of them.

We all know people who are in jobs or careers that they don't love. They get up every day

The Inside Scoop

A few years ago the executive director of a not-for-profit organization I was involved with spoke to me about her career dreams. She told me that while she always wanted to be a home economics teacher, because of a number of circumstances she was never able to finish college.

At an age when many teachers are retiring, the woman in her 50s decided to quit her job, go after her dream, and go back to school. She applied to college, was accepted and moved to start school. I spoke to her a number of times and found that while there were some challenges along the way as an older student, she loved school and did well. Before long she did her student teaching. The last time I spoke to her, she was excited to tell me that she found a job and was looking forward to her first teaching job and living out her dream.

Words from the Wise

Always carry business cards with your phone number and other contact information. Make it easy for people to find you when an opportunity presents itself.

waiting for the workweek to be over. They go through the day, waiting for it to be over. They waste their life waiting and waiting. Is this the life you want to lead? I'm guessing it's not.

You now have the opportunity to get what you want. Are you ready to go after it? I'm hoping you are.

As we've discussed, there are countless opportunities in education. In addition to the traditional ones most people think of, there are an array of others for you to explore. No matter

Tip from the Coach

Don't procrastinate. Every day you wait to get the career you are passionate about is another day you're not living your dream. Start today!

what your skill or talent, you can almost always find a way to parlay them into some aspect of a career in education if you think creatively.

Don't be afraid to put your dreams together.

"Like what?" you ask.

Let's say you're a teacher and you also want to work around the film or television industry. You might be able to find a job working on a movie or television set, teaching youngsters starring in a film or television show.

Let's say you're a teacher and you also want to work around the music business. You might be able to create a job going on the road with touring recording artists who have children on the road with them.

"Really?" you ask.

Definitely. Every child is required to get an education. Child stars are no exception. Generally, there are classrooms on the set. You might have to get creative to find a position like this, but it can be done.

A Job versus a Career: What's the Difference?

What do you want in life? Would you rather just have a job or do you want a career? What's the difference? A job is just that. It's something you do to earn a living. It's a means to an end. A career, on the other hand, is a series of related jobs. It's a progressive path of achievement, a long-term journey. A career is something you build using your skills, talents, and passions.

You might have many jobs in your career. You might even follow more than one career path. The question is, what do you want?

If all you want is to go to work—day after day, week after week—just to get paid, a job is all you need, and there is nothing wrong with that. On the other hand, if you would like to fill your life with excitement and passion while getting paid, you are a prime candidate for a great career.

How can you get that? Start planning now to get what you want. Define your goals and then start working toward them.

Not everyone starts off with a dream job. If you just sit and wait for your dream job to come to you, you could be sitting forever. What you can do, however, is to take what you have and make it work for you until you get what you want. What does that mean?

It means that you can make whatever you do better at least for the time being. The trick in this whole process is finding ways to give the job you have some meaning. Find a way to get some passion from what you're doing. If you get that mind set you'll never have a bad job. Focus on your ultimate career goal and then look at each job as a benchmark along the way to what you want.

How to Use This Book to Help You Succeed in Education

Ideally, I would love for you to read this book from beginning to end, but I know from experience that that's probably not the way it's going to happen. You might browse the contents and look for something that can help you *now*, you might see a subject that catches your eye, or you might be looking for an area of the book that solves a particular problem.

For this reason, as you read this book, you might see what appears to be some duplication of information. In this manner, I can be assured that when I suggest something that may be helpful to you in a certain area you will get all the information you need even if you didn't read a prior section.

You should be aware that even if you're interested in a career in teaching, knowing about the business or administrative segment of the industry will be helpful to succeeding in your career. Conversely, if your career aspirations are in the business or administrative segment of education, understanding how other parts of the industry work will be useful as well.

You might have heard the saying that knowledge is power. This is true. The more you know about the education field and how it works, the better your chances are of succeeding. This book is full of information to help you learn everything you need to know about the field and how it works. I'm betting that you will refer back to information in this book long after you've attained success.

As you read through the various sections you'll find a variety of suggestions and ideas to help you succeed. Keep in mind that every idea and suggestion might not work in every situation and for every person. The idea is to keep trying things until one of them works. Use the book as a springboard to get you started. Just because something is not written here doesn't mean that it's not a good idea. Brainstorm to find solutions to barriers you might encounter in your career.

My job is to lead you on your journey to success in the education industry. Along the way you'll find exercises, tasks, and assignments that will help get you where you want to be faster. No one is going to be standing over your shoulder to make you do these tasks. You alone can make the decision on the amount time and work you want to put into your career. While no one can guarantee you success, what you should know is that the more you put into your career, the better your chances of having the success you probably are dreaming about.

Are you worth the time and effort? I think you are! Is a career in education worth it? Everyone needs education. If you have the passion and desire to work in this field, it can be one of the best in the world in which to work. Aside from the opportunity to make a living and fulfill your dreams, you have the opportunity not only to impact the lives of others, but to help them to impact others as well.

No matter what level you're currently at in your career and whatever capacity, this book is for you. You might not need every section or every page, but I can guarantee that there are parts of this book that can help you.

Whether you're just starting to think about a career in education or have been in the field for a while; whether you're going through college, are a student teacher, or are newly licensed; whether you're an up and coming administrator, are in the business end of the industry, or are anywhere in between, this book can help you experience more success in your career and a help you have a happier, more satisfying, and stress-free life.

A Sampling of What This Book Covers

This informative guide to success in education is written in a friendly, easy to read style. Let it be your everyday guide to success. Want to know how a segment of the education industry works? Want to learn how to focus on what you really want to do? Check out the book!

Want to learn how to plan and prepare for your dream career? Do you want to focus on job search strategies geared especially for the education industry? How about tips for making those important industry contacts? Need some ideas on how to network? How about how to create the ideal education-oriented resume or cover letter? Check out the book!

Do you need to know how to develop your action plan? Do you want to get your portfolio together? Want to know what business cards can do for you and your career? Check out the book!

Want to learn how to get your foot in the door? How about checking out tried and true methods to get people to call you back? Do you want to learn the best way to market yourself and why it's so important? Do you want to learn how to succeed in the workplace, deal with workplace politics, keep an eye out for opportunities, and climb the career ladder? You know what you have to do. Check out the book!

Want to know how to succeed as a teacher? How to move up the ladder? You got it. You need to read this book.

Do you need important contact information so you can move your career forward? Check out the listings of important organization, unions, and associations included at the end of this book. Want some Web sites to get you started looking for a great career? Check out the appendix of the book.

While this book won't teach you how to teach reading, writing, or arithmetic, it won't teach you how to succeed with every student, or how to run a school district, it will help you to find ways to garner success wherever your passion lies.

Anyone can apply for a job and hope they get it. Many people do just that. But I'm guessing you do not just want a job. You want a career you can be passionate about. You want a career you love. You want a career that gives you joy! Take charge of your career now and you can have all that and more.

If you dream not only of working in some aspect of education, but also of having a suc-cessful career and don't know how to make that dream a reality, this book is for you. Have fun reading it. Know that if your heart is in it, you can achieve anything.

Now let's get started.

2

FOCUSING ON A GREAT CAREER IN EDUCATION

Focusing on What You Really Want to Do

Do you know what you want to do with your life? Do you daydream about working in some aspect in education? Do you wonder how you're going get in to the industry? Do you wonder how you can succeed?

Unless you're independently wealthy or just won the megamillion-dollar lottery, you, like most people, have to work. Just in case you're wondering, life is not supposed to be miserable. Neither is your job.

Life is supposed to have a purpose. That purpose is not sleeping, getting up, going to a job that you don't particularly care about, coming home, making dinner, and watching TV, only to do it all over again the next day.

In order to be happy and fulfilled you need to enjoy life. You need to do things which give you pleasure. As a good part of your life is spent working, the trick is to find a career that you love and that you're passionate about—the career of your dreams.

This is not something everyone does. Many people just fall into a career without thinking ahead of time about what it will entail. Some-

one may need a job, hear of an opening, answer an ad, and then go for it without thinking about the consequences of working at something for which he or she really has no passion. Once hired, it's either difficult to give up the money, just too hard to start job-hunting again, or they don't know what else to do and so they stay. They wind up with a career that is okay but one they're not really passionate about.

Then there are the other people. The ones who have jobs they love; the lucky people. You've seen them. They're the people who have the jobs and life you wish you had.

Have you noticed that the people who love their jobs are usually successful not only in their career but in other aspects of their life too? They almost seem to have an aura around them of success, happiness, and prosperity. Do you want to be one of them? Well you can!

⭐ Tip from the Coach

Okay is just that—it's okay. Just so you know, you don't *want* just okay, you don't *want* to settle, you want *great*! That's what you deserve and that's what you should go after.

19

Finding a career that you want and love is challenging but it is possible. You are in a better position than most people. If you're reading this book, you've probably at least zeroed in on a career path. You likely decided that you are passionate about some segment of the education. Now all you have to do is determine exactly what you want to do within the industry.

What's *your* dream career? What do you really want to do? This is an important question to ask yourself. Once you know the answer, you can work toward achieving your goal.

If someone asked you right now what you really wanted to do could you answer the question? Okay, one, two, three: "What do you want to do with your life?"

If you're saying, "Uh, um, well . . . What I really want to do is . . . well, it's hard to explain," then it's time to focus in on the subject. Sometimes the easiest way to figure out what you want to do is to focus on what you don't want to do.

Most people can easily answer what they don't want to do. "I don't want to be a doctor. I don't want to be a nurse. I don't want to work in a factory. I don't want to work in a store. I don't want to sell. I don't want to work with numbers. I don't want to work in a job where I have to travel." The list goes on. The problem is that just saying what you don't like or don't want to do doesn't necessarily get you what you want to do. You can, however, use this information to your advantage.

It may seem simple, but sometimes just looking at a list of what you don't like will help you see more clearly what you do like.

Sit down with a sheet of paper or fill in the "Things I Dislike Doing/Things I Don't Want To Do" worksheet and make a list of work-related things you don't like to do. Remember that this list is really just for you. While you can show it to someone if you want, no one else really has to see it so try to be honest with yourself.

Here's an example to get your started. When you make your list, add in things *you* don't want to do. Add in your own personal dislikes.

◎ I hate the idea of being cooped up in an office all day.
◎ I don't want to teach in a traditional school setting.
◎ I don't want to be stuck in one classroom all day.
◎ I hate the idea of having to work with numbers.
◎ I don't want to teach in a big city.
◎ I don't want to teach in a public school.
◎ I don't want to have to do a lot of reports.
◎ I don't want to have to go to work early in the morning.
◎ I don't want to have to work evenings.
◎ I don't want to have to travel for my job.
◎ I don't want to work in a large university.
◎ I don't want to have to commute for an hour each way every day.
◎ I don't want to teach young children.
◎ I don't like working with teenagers.
◎ I don't like making decisions.
◎ I don't want to work in sales.
◎ I don't like doing the same thing day after day.
◎ I don't like being in charge.
◎ I don't like taking risks.
◎ I don't like working under constant pressure.
◎ I don't like not knowing where my next paycheck is coming from.
◎ I don't like being under constant deadlines.
◎ I don't like having a boss working right on top of me.
◎ I don't like someone telling me what to do every minute of the day.
◎ I don't like working where I don't make a difference.

Things I Dislike Doing/Things I Don't Want to Do

We now know what you don't like. Use this list as a beginning to see what you do like. If you look closely you'll find that the things you enjoy are the opposite of the things you don't want to do.

You might make another list as well as using the "Things I Enjoy Doing/Things I Want to Do" worksheet. Here are some examples to get you started. Remember that the reason you're writing everything down is so you can look at it, remember it, and focus in on getting exactly what you want.

◎ I don't want to teach in a traditional school setting.
   ▫ But I really want to teach. I want to share knowledge and help other people learn. Perhaps I can find a job as a tutor.
◎ I don't want to be stuck in one classroom all day.
   ▫ But I would really like to teach. Maybe I can teach children who can't go to school. Maybe I can find a teaching job where I move from one room to another or even one school to another.
◎ I hate the idea of having to work with numbers.
   ▫ But I really like writing and creating with words. And I really want to work on a college campus. I love that environment. I think I would really enjoy a career as a publicist, public relations director, or marketing director for a college. Perhaps I could even become an education reporter.
◎ I don't want to teach in a big city school.
   ▫ But I really want to teach. I would love teaching in a rural area where everyone knows everyone.
◎ I don't want to teach in a public school.
   ▫ But my dream is to work in a small, prestigious private school.

◎ I don't want to have to do a lot of reports. The thought of it bothers me.
◎ I don't want to do reports because I'm not confident in my writing skills. Perhaps if I take some writing classes I'll begin to feel more confident. Then I can go after the job I really want in administration.
◎ I don't want to have to go to work early in the morning.
   ▫ But I really want to teach in a college. Maybe I can find a job teaching at night. Maybe I can teach adult education.
◎ I don't want to have to work evenings.
   ▫ I'm so lucky I want to teach elementary school. Teaching elementary school gives me a really great schedule.
◎ I don't want to work in a large university.
   ▫ But I would really like working in a community or junior college. I think I would really like to find a job working in student affairs in a smaller college.
◎ I don't want to have to commute for an hour each way every day.
   ▫ I'm going to focus my job search on schools within 20 minutes from here. If that doesn't work, I'm going to consider moving closer to where I find my job.
◎ I don't want to teach young children.
   ▫ But I really like working with teens and other young people. I want to teach English in a junior or high school.
◎ I don't like working with teenagers.
   ▫ But I really want to teach young children. I'm going to get my degree in early childhood education.
◎ I don't like working where I don't make a difference.
   ▫ I really want to make a difference. And I really want to make a difference working with young children. My dream job will be working in an inner-city school with children just starting to read.

Things I Enjoy Doing/Things I Want to Do

_____

_____

_____

_____

_____

_____

_____

_____

_____

_____

_____

_____

_____

_____

_____

_____

As you can see, once you've determined what you don't like doing, it's much easier to get ideas on what you'd like to do. It's kind of like brainstorming with yourself.

You probably know some people who don't like their jobs. There are tons of people in this world who don't like what they do or are dissatisfied with their career. Here's the good news. You don't have to be one of them.

You and you alone are in charge of your career. Not your mother, father, sister, brother, girlfriend, boyfriend, spouse, or best friend. Others can care, others can help, and others can offer you advice, but in essence, you need to be in control. What this means is that the path you take for your career is largely determined by the choices you make.

The fastest way to get the career you want is by making the choice to take actions now and going after it! You *can* have a career you love and you *can* have it in education. And when you're doing something that you love, you'll be on the road to not only a great career but to a satisfied and fulfilled life.

The next section will discuss how to develop your career plan. This plan will be your road map to success. It will be full of actions you can take not only to get the career in education you want, but to succeed in it as well. Before you get too involved in the plan however, you need to zero in on exactly what you want your career to be.

At this point you might be in a number of different employment situations. You might still be in school planning your career, just out of school beginning your career, or in a job that you don't really care for. You might be in your late teens, 20s, 30s, 40s, 50s, or even older.

"Older? Did you say older?" you ask. "Can I start a career in education even if I'm older?"

Yes! If you have a dream it is never too late not only to pursue it, but also to succeed in it. And it doesn't matter what segment of education in which you're interested.

As a matter of fact, if you're interested in teaching in one of the areas of education in which there is a shortage, such as math or the sciences, and you have a background in either of those areas, you will be an attractive candidate.

You might also be interested to know that the Age Discrimination In Employment Act of 1967 specifically prohibits discrimination against people who are 40 years of age or older.

What does that mean to you? If you are a career changer, it means that you have just as much chance of getting a job as anyone else.

The Inside Scoop

Over the years, I've seen many adults go back to school to continue or finish their education so that they could fulfill their dream of a career in education. These include a woman in her mid 40s who went back to school to become an elementary school teacher after years of working as housekeeper, a social worker with a master's in social work, who went back to school in her 50s to complete the education necessary to become a high school administrator, a woman in her 50s who went back to school after raising her son as a single mom because she had a life-long dream to become a high school home economics teacher, and my father, who went back to school in his 60s to first finish his bachelor's and then earn his master's so he could become a college business instructor.

Age didn't stop any of these people and it shouldn't stop you. If you have a dream to work in education that you have not yet fulfilled, no matter what your age, go after your dream.

Of course, you need to make yourself the best candidate possible, but we're going to cover that later in the book.

Whether you start off choosing a career in education, you're a career changer, or you are into your second career, it's never too late to go after your dreams.

Perhaps you always wanted to work in some segment of education or maybe you've done some research on various career areas and decided education is for you. With so many options to choose from in education, do you know what your dream career is?

There are hundreds of exciting career choices in education, whether you want to be a classroom teacher, a teacher or educator in a different setting, or an administrator. Options exist in public and private educational institutions.

Opportunities are available in the business segment of the industry, technology, consulting, sales and communications. Opportunities are available in educational administration and management as well as research and development. There are additional options in educational governance and more. It's up to you to decide which you want to pursue.

So let's focus for a bit on exactly what you want to do.

What's Your Dream?

I bet that you already have an idea of what your dream job is and I'm sure that you have an idea of what it should be like. I'm also betting that you don't have that job yet or if you do, you're not at the level you want to be. So what can we do to make that dream a reality?

One of the challenges many people often have in getting their dream job is that they just don't think they deserve it. They feel that dream jobs are something many people talk about and wish they had, but just don't. Many people think that dream jobs are for the lucky ones.

Well, I'm here to tell you that you are the lucky one. You *can* get your dream job—a job you'll love—and it can be in education.

If I had a magic wand and could get you any job you wanted what would it be? Do you want a career in some aspect of classroom teaching? Do you want to teach preschool? What about kindergarten? How about elementary school? Is it your dream instead to teach in a middle or junior high school? What about a high school?

Have you always dreamt of teaching special education? What about teaching gifted children? Would you like to teach English as a second language? How about becoming a bilingual teacher? Do you want to be a teacher's aide?

Is it your dream to teach in a vocational or technical situation? What about some area of adult or continuing education? Or has it been your dream to be a professor or instructor in a college or university?

Is it your vision instead to work in the educational support area? Do you want a career as a school librarian? An academic librarian? How about a media specialist?

Is your passion a career as a guidance or school counselor? How about a college career counselor? What about an employment counselor?

Are you dreaming about a career in some aspect of high school or collegiate sports? Do you want to pursue a career as a high school or college coach? What about scouting out the best high school athletes for a collegiate sporting program?

Do you want to teach outside of a traditional school setting? Would you like to be an aerobics instructor? What about a personal trainer?

Is teaching fashion design your passion? What about teaching cooking? How about teaching Web design or computer technology. It's all up to you!

Do you want to work in the business area of a college or university? Are you interested in handling their public relations? Their fund-raising? Do you want to work in the human resources department? What about registration? Is your dream career putting together special events or handling student activities? Is it workforce development? There are literally hundreds of different opportunities in colleges and universities. You just need to find where you fit.

Do you want to be an education reporter? The editor of an education-oriented Web site? A textbook author? Your dream job can be a reality if you prepare.

Not sure what you want to do? Then read on!

Determining what you really want to do is not always easy. Take some time to think about it. Throughout this process try to be as honest with yourself as possible, otherwise you stand the chance of not going after the career you really want.

Tip from the Coach

What are your dreams? Are you ready to turn them into reality? You increase your chances of success if you have a deep belief in yourself, your vision, and your ideas.

Words from the Wise

The only thing we have to fear is fear itself.

—Franklin Delano Roosevelt

Let's get started with another writing exercise. While you might think these are a pain now, if you follow through, you will find it easier to attain your dream.

Get a pad of paper and a pen and find a place where you can get comfortable. Maybe it's your living room chair. Perhaps it's your couch or even your bed. Now all you have to do is sit down and daydream for a bit about what you wish you could be and what you wish you were doing.

"Why daydream?" you ask.

When you daydream your thinking becomes freer. You stop thinking about what you *can't* do and start thinking about what you *can* do. What is your dream? What is your passion? What do you really want to do? Admit it now or forever hold your peace!

Many people are embarrassed to admit when they want something because if they don't get it they fear looking stupid. They worry people are going to talk badly about them or call them a failure. Is this what you worry about?

Do you really want to be a teacher, but you're afraid you'll fail? Is your dream to be a school administrator but you're not sure you'll make it? Do you want your own call-in radio show focusing on all aspects of education, but you're worried everyone will think it's a stupid idea? Do you want to be a corporate trainer, but you're not sure anyone will think you're good enough?

First of all, don't ever let fear of failure stop you from going after something you want. While no one can guarantee you success, what I can guarantee you is that if you don't go after what you want, it is going to be very difficult to get it.

One thing you never want to do is get to the end of your life and say with regret, "I wish I had done this or I wish I had done that." Will you get each and every thing you want? While I would like to give you a definitive "yes," that probably wouldn't be true.

The truth of the matter is, you might not succeed at everything. But, and this is a major *but*, even if you fail when you try to do something, it usually is a stepping-stone to something else. And that something else can be the turning point in your career.

"How so?" you ask. "What do you mean?"

At one point in my life I wanted to become a professional comedienne and do stand-up comedy. The reason I bring it up here is to illustrate the point that while I certainly didn't turn into a megastar stand-up comedienne, performing comedy was certainly a major stepping-stone for me to do other things I wanted to accomplish in my career. Had I not done stand-up, I probably would never have ended up teaching stress management, becoming a motivational speaker, doing corporate training, or even coming up with ideas about doing something in those areas.

Had I been too scared to try it, or not wanted to take the risk for fear I would fail, I would have missed out on important opportunities which helped shape my career. I also would have always looked back and said, "I wish I had."

Your dreams are probably totally different from mine. That is okay. What you need to take from the story is the concept that taking risks and pursuing your dreams can lead to wonderful things.

Let's get started. Think about things that make you happy. Think about things that make

> ### ★ Tip from the Coach
>
> If there is something that you want to do or something that you want to try in your career or your life, my advice is go for it. No matter what the risk, no matter how scared you are, no matter what. Your life and career will benefit more than you can imagine and you'll never look back with regrets. Even if it doesn't work out, you'll feel successful because you tried.

you smile. Continue to indulge your passions as you daydream. As ideas come to you, jot them down on your pad. Remember, nothing is foolish, so write down all the ideas you have for what you want to do. You're going to fine-tune them later.

Here's an example to get you started.

◎ I want to be a high school math teacher. I want to make math easy and help every student understand math concepts.

◎ I want to be a write a best seller on improving the education system.

◎ I want to be the state commissioner of education.

◎ I want to be a first grade teacher. I want to help mold children's love of learning.

◎ I want to teach people how to become great teachers.

◎ I want to have a Web site dedicated to everything education. As a matter of fact, I want the most successful educational Web site in the world.

◎ I want to be a tutor for children on movie and television sets.

◎ I want to be a director of development for a large, prestigious university.

◎ I want to be the headmaster at a prestigious private school.

◎ I want to be the president of a big university.

◎ I want to work in the public relations department of a college. As a matter of fact, I want to be the director of the department. I can't wait to put together a public relations campaign for the university that hires me.

◎ I want to be work in a high school and teach young people about science.

◎ I want to become tutor. I think I want my own tutoring business.

◎ I want to be a corporate training consultant in the gaming industry.

◎ I want to be a corporate sales trainer.

◎ I want to be on a team that turns around schools in trouble.

Do you need some help focusing on what you really want to do in education? In order to choose just the right career you should pinpoint your interests and what you really love doing. What are your skills? What are your personality traits? What are your interests? Fill in the following worksheet to help you zero in even more.

What Is Stopping You From Getting What You Want?

Now that you have some ideas written down about what you want to do, go down the list. What has stopped you from attaining your goal?

The Inside Scoop

When you write down your ideas you are giving them power. Once they are written down on paper, it makes it easier to go over them, look at them rationally, and fine-tune them.

Tip from the Coach

Start training yourself to practice finding ways to turn *can't*s in your life into *can*s.

Is it that you told people what you wanted to do and they told you that you couldn't do it? Did they tell you it was too difficult and your chances of making it were slim? Did they tell you that you were too old to go after your dreams?

Is it that you don't have the confidence in yourself to get what you want? Or is it that you need more education or training?

Perhaps it's because you aren't in the location most conducive to your dream career? If you can identify the obstacle, you usually can find a way to overcome it, but you need to identify the problem first.

Do you know exactly what you want to do but can't find an opening? Do you, for example, want a career as a marketing director of a university, but can't find a job? Do you want to be a high school art teacher, but there are no openings? Have you trained for your dream job as a guidance counselor and can't find a position?

Sometimes, while you know what type of job you want, you just can't find a job like that which is available. Don't give up. Keep looking. Remember, you may have to think outside of the box to get what you want, but if you're creative, you can succeed. Try to find ways to get your foot in the door and then once it is in, don't let it out until you get what you want.

Have you found the perfect job and interviewed for it, but then the job wasn't offered to you? While at the time you probably felt awful about this, there is some good news. Generally when one door closes, another one opens.

Focusing on the Job of Your Dreams

Finish the following sentences to help you pinpoint your interests and find the job of your dreams.

In my free time I enjoy

_____

In my free time I enjoy going

_____

My hobbies are

_____

Activities I enjoy include

_____

When I volunteer the types of projects I enjoy most are

_____

When I was younger I always dreamed of being a

_____

My skills are

_____

My talents are

_____

My best personality traits include

_____

My current job is

_____

Prior types of jobs have been

_____

The subjects I liked best in school were

_____

If I didn't have to worry about any obstacles, the three jobs I would want would be

_____

What steps can I take to get one of those jobs?

_____

Hard to believe? It may be, but if you think about it, you'll see it's true. Things work out for the best. If you lost what you thought was the job of your dreams, a better one is out there waiting for you. You just have to find it!

Perhaps you're just missing the skills necessary for the type of job you're seeking. This is a relatively easy thing to fix. Once you know the skills that are necessary for a specific job, if you don't have them, take steps to get them. Take classes, go to workshops, attend seminars, or become an apprentice or intern.

"But," you say, "I'm missing the education necessary for the job I want. The ad I read said I need a master's degree and I don't have one."

Here's the deal. In certain cases educational requirements may be negotiable. Just because an ad states that a job has a specific educational requirement doesn't mean you should just pass it by if your education doesn't meet the requirement. First, advertisements for jobs generally contain the highest hopes of the people placing the ads, not necessarily the reality of what they will settle for. Second, organizations often will accept experience in lieu of education. Lastly, if you're a good candidate in other respects many organization will hire you while you're finishing the required education.

Is a lack of experience what's stopping you from your dream career? Depending on the career area you're pursuing, this can be easily fixed.

Of course, if your dream is to become a teacher you will be doing student teaching. Need more experience? Consider volunteering at a local school or an after-school program.

As a matter of fact, if you can't get experience in the workplace, volunteering is one of the best ways to get experience for any type of job. How do you get experience? Take every op-portunity that presents itself to get the experience you need. Depending on what you want to do and where you live, you might need to get creative, but you can definitely find a way to do it.

For example, do you need experience doing publicity for a career in the public relations department of a college or university? Experience is transferable. What about getting some experience by volunteering to do publicity for a community or civic organization. What if that doesn't pan out? See if you can find an internship with a business or organization.

Is one of the obstacles you're facing that you just aren't in the geographic location of the opportunities you're looking for? Do you, for example, want to work in one of the support services areas of a large university, yet you don't live anywhere near a large university?

There's no question that living in an area that doesn't have the opportunities you're looking for makes your job more difficult. If this obstacle is what is holding you back, put some time into developing a solution and find a way to move forward. If you're not prepared to move and don't want to give up your career dreams, you might want to start your career working in a smaller college closer to where you live. After a year or two, perhaps you will be ready to move on.

Is what's holding you back that you don't have any contacts? Here's the deal. You have to find ways to make contacts. Take classes, seminars, and workshops in subject areas related to the segment of education in which you're interested.

Volunteer. Make cold calls. Network, network, and network some more. Put yourself in situations where you can meet people in the industry and sooner or later you will meet them.

Tip from the Coach

While you're working on your day-dreaming exercise, don't get caught up in thinking any of your ideas are foolish or stupid. Let your imagination run freely. If these negative ideas come into your head, consciously push them way.

What else is standing between you and success? "The only thing between me and success," you say, "is a big break." Getting your big break may take time. Keep plugging away. Most of all, don't give up. Your break will come when you least expect it.

Are you just frightened about going after what you want? Are you not sure you have the talent or the skills? Are you not sure you can make it? If you start doubting yourself, other people might do the same. As we just discussed, do not let fear stop you from doing what you want.

Most importantly, don't let anyone chip away at your dream, and whatever you do, don't let anyone burst your bubble. What does that mean?

You know how it is when you get excited about doing something and you're so excited that you just can't keep it to yourself. You might share your ideas of what you want to do with your family and friends. And while you want them to be excited too, they start trying to destroy your dream by pointing out all the possible problems you might encounter.

It's not that they're trying *not* to be supportive, but for some people it seems to be their nature to try to shoot other people's dreams apart.

Why? There are a number of reasons. Let's look at a few scenarios.

Scenario 1—Sometimes people are just negative. "Oh," they might say to you. "You don't want to get involved in education. Kids are not what they were years ago. Teaching can be a horrible experience now. You don't want to get involved."

"Well," you tell them, "I do. I think teaching can be very rewarding. I want to help instill a love of learning in young people. I want to help people learn. I'm excited."

Their response?

"It's hard work. You don't really want to do that. You'll hate it. Kids bring guns to school; it's dangerous. Find some other way to help people."

Scenario 2—Sometimes people are jealous. They might hate their job and be jealous that you are working toward finding a great career. They might have similar dreams to yours and be jealous that you have a plan and they don't. Some might just be jealous that you might make it before them.

Scenario 3—Sometimes people are just scared of change. In many cases friend or family are concerned about your well-being and are just scared of change. "You have a job," your girlfriend may say. "Why do you want to go back to school? It's going to take years to get your doctorate and then you might not even be able to get a job. Why don't you think about it for a while?"

Scenario 4—Sometimes people just think you're pipe dreaming. "You're a pipe dreamer," your family may say. "What you need is a dose of reality. You never are going to find a publisher who will buy your book on education. And if you do find one, who is going to listen to your advice? No one knows you. The odds are not good."

Scenario 5—Sometimes people really think that it's not realistic to think you should make a living doing something you love. "Nobody likes their

> ⭐ **Tip from the Coach**
> Almost everything you can wish for in life, including your career, starts with a dream. Go after yours!

job," a family member may tell you. "Work is just something you have to do."

Scenario 6—Sometimes people think that you are just too old to change careers or go after your dream. "You're 45 years old," your friend says. "Who is going to hire a 45-year-old teacher? And that doesn't even take in to account that you *still* have to finish school and do your student teaching. You're actually going to be older than 45 when you are ready to get a job. Give up before you fail."

Whatever the scenario, there you sit, starting to question yourself. Well, stop! Do not let anyone burst your bubble. No matter what anyone says, at least *you* are trying to get the career you want. At least *you* are following your dream.

While I can't promise that you will definitely achieve every one of your dreams, I can promise that if you don't go after your dream, it will be very difficult to achieve. What I want you to do is not listen to anyone negative and keep working toward what you want.

What Gives You Joy? What Makes You Happy?

Let's zero in further on what you want to do. Let's talk about what gives you joy. Let's talk about what makes you happy. Did you ever notice that when you're doing something that you love, you smile? It's probably subconscious, but you're smiling. You're happy inside. And it's not only that you're happy—you make others around you happy.

Let's think about it for a few minutes. What makes you happy? What gives you joy? Is it helping others? Is it teaching others? Is it writing? Is it putting together events? Is it organizing things? Is it developing things? Is it a combination?

Does the thought of teaching a young child how to read make you smile? What about teaching a student with special needs? When you close your eyes can you see yourself as the administrator of a high school? What about the dean of a prestigious university? Can you almost hear yourself giving a lecture to students?

Can you see yourself standing at the podium at a major educational conference delivering a paper on helping children succeed in school?

Are you smiling as you think about seeing the word *superintendent* and your name on a sign outside of your new office? Are you smiling as you think about seeing your name as the author on the cover of a series of books on education? Are you smiling as you imagine yourself on your very first day of teaching? Then maybe that's your dream—that is what would make you happy.

Keep dreaming. Keep asking yourself what makes you happy? What gives you joy? Are you having a hard time figuring it out? Many of us do. Here's an idea to help get your juices flowing.

Take out your pad and a pen again. Make a list of any jobs or volunteer activities you've done, things you do on your "off time," and hobbies. If you're still in school, you might add in extracurricular activities in which you've participated.

Note what aspects of each you like and what you didn't like. This will help you see what type of job you're going to enjoy.

What are your special talents, skills, and personality traits? What gives you joy and makes you happy?

Do you truly enjoy teaching someone something new? Are you patient? What about creative? A career where you are working hands-on with students in some capacity might be just what you should look for.

Have you always been good at motivating others? Are you inspiring? Are you a good teacher? Perhaps a career in corporate training might be for you.

Is your special talent singing? What about playing an instrument? How about dancing? What about acting? Do you want to use these talents for a career in some aspect of education? Perhaps you want to be a vocal coach. What about an elementary school music teacher? How about a high school band teacher? What about teaching in a conservatory? The choice is yours.

Maybe you want to teach acting in a theater arts program in a college. Perhaps you want to be a private acting coach. Maybe you want to teach in a private school in New York City or Hollywood. What is going to give you joy? What are your aspirations?

Is your special talent writing and crafting words? What about taking photographs? Can you see the pictures that most people wish they could? There are dozens of ways you can parlay these talents into a wonderful career in education, from teaching English and writing to teaching photography, from handling the public relations and marketing at a college or university to writing textbooks, from developing the content for an education-oriented Web site to editing a book on education. There are traditional options as well as less tradition ones. The choice is yours.

Are you the one who is always volunteering to do the publicity for a charity or community organization? If you love doing that, you probably would really love doing the publicity for a college, university, or school system. You most likely would also really enjoy a career as a publicist for an association related to some aspect of education.

Are collegiate sports your passion? Your choices are vast, from coaching to recruitment, from fund-raising to program development, and more.

Are your special skills in administration? You need only decide what area of educational administration you want to pursue. Perhaps it would give you joy to become an elementary school principal? Maybe your passion is to use your skills and talents in a middle school or high school. Perhaps it is to administer an entire school district. Some use their administrative skills and talents to become department heads or supervisors. Some decide, instead, to use their skills and passions as administrators of institutions of higher learning.

A few years ago I was doing some radio interviews for a book I wrote about hot careers. I was explaining that any career could be a hot career if it was your passion. During one of those shows a woman called in to ask some questions regarding a career working at a university.

"I really love being in an academic atmosphere," the woman said. "A hot career to me would be one working in a university. There is always so much going on around a campus. I think I would love just being part of it."

"What do you want to do on campus," I asked. "What type of job do you want to pursue?"

"That's the problem," she said. "I'm not a professor. I can't really teach anything. Can you think of something?"

"What are you doing now?" I asked her.

"I'm the executive director of a really small, not-for-profit organization which deals in animal rights. I believe in the cause, but there isn't a lot of room for career growth. Generally I do a lot of fund-raising."

"Do you enjoy fund-raising?" I asked her. "Are you good at it?"

"I do like it," she said. "I especially like running special fund-raising events. I wish I could do the same kind of job at a college. That would make me happy I think."

"Have you tried to get a job doing fund-raising in a college?" I asked her.

"No, not really. I didn't even know there was a job possibility doing fund-raising at a college."

"You might find a position doing fund-raising or development for a university or for their foundation," I told her. "Sometimes schools also have a position doing fund-raising and development in the collegiate athletics department. There are a lot of options. Why don't you get a list of schools in your area or the area in which you want to live and start by calling them and sending your resume. You might also do a search on the Internet to see if you can locate any openings."

"Thanks," she replied. "I'm going to give it a try."

While I don't always hear back from people who call during radio interview shows, I did hear back from that woman. She e-mailed me a few months later to thank me and tell me that as soon as she hung up, she went to the Web

---

Words from the Wise

The first requisite for success is the ability to apply your physical and mental energies to one problem incessantly without growing weary.

–Thomas Edison

---

sites of a number of colleges and looked at their career opportunities section. And she found an opening just like she was looking for at a college located 45 minutes from her home. She interviewed, got the job, and loves working on campus.

What Are Your Talents?

It's important to define what your talents are. Sometimes we're so good at something that we just don't even think twice about it. The problem with this is that often we don't see the value in our talent. What does this mean? It means that we may overlook the possibilities associated with our talents.

It is also important to know that you can have more than one talent. Just because you are an inspirational teacher does not mean you can't be a talented artist. Just because you're a talented writer, doesn't mean you can't be a great speaker. Just because you are great working with numbers, doesn't mean you're not good at organizing. Just because you're creative, doesn't mean you can't make people laugh. Most of us have more than one talent. The trick is making sure you know what *your* talents are and using them to your advantage.

Do you know your talents? Can you identify them? This is another time you're going to have to sit down with a pad and start writing. Write down everything that you're good at.

Tip from the Coach

If you dream large and reach high, you can have a life and career that is better than you can ever imagine. If, on the other hand, you just settle, you will never feel fulfilled.

Write down all of your talents; not just the ones you think are related to the area of education in which you're interested.

This is not the time to be modest. Remember, that this list is for you, so be honest with yourself.

Can you finish this sentence? "I am a talented (<u>fill in the blank</u>)." You might be a talented teacher, administrator, writer, publicist, caregiver, writer, photographer, salesperson, etc.

Now finish the sentence, "I am talented in _____." You might be talented in organizing, supervising, cooking, or baking. You might be talented at negotiating, teaching, making people feel better about themselves, writing, persuasion, painting, drawing, decorating, or public speaking. Whatever your talents, there usually is a way you can use them to help your career.

How? Let's say you want to be a college public relations director. Your talents are creativity and writing, among others. You also are very persuasive and a great negotiator. While creativity and writing are the talents that can help you become a successful public relations director, having the talent to persuade the media to give stories a certain spin or the talent to negotiate to get your press release in the paper or reporters to your press conference can be priceless.

Let's say, instead, you want to be an elementary school teacher. Your talents are, among others, creativity, organization, and leadership. You also are very good at problem solving and are a very talented cook. In addition, you have a natural ability to relate to children and are a great listener. While having a natural ability to deal well with children is paramount to being a good teacher, being creative and organized helps a lot. The ability to solve problems is also helpful in finding ways to deal with classroom challenges. How might you use your talents as a cook to make you a better teacher? You might teach children how to follow instructions or how to measure.

I know a very well-liked and respected teacher who is also a very talented artist. He often shows his work at art shows in his area and has won some regional awards. Does he *need* to do this? Not really, but he *enjoys* doing it. Not only that, he has inspired his students to get involved in showing their work. Many have gone on to careers in graphics and fine arts.

I also know a number of schoolteachers who also are amateur gourmet chefs. One frequently gives cooking classes to her students and their parents to illustrate that you can cook healthy gourmet meals quickly. Another takes part in an annual "Men Who Cook" fund-raiser put on by the local hospital. Another volunteers to give vegetarian cooking lessons at the local community center. Still another donates his services to cook a gourmet meal for the winner of a prize given in a school fund-raiser. Generally when these things occur, there is media coverage. The end result is the teachers get a ton of publicity, and it brings his or her name to the eyes of the public and school administrators in a positive way. These teachers also are doing something they really enjoy.

Use every talent you have to catapult you to the top. Don't discount those you feel are not "job" related. Whether your extra talent gets you in the door, helps you standout, or climb the career ladder, it will be a useful tool in your career.

Getting What You Want

You hear opportunity knocking. How do you get what you want? How do you turn your dream into reality? One of the most important things you need to do is have faith in yourself and your dream. It is essential that you believe that you can make it happen in order for it to happen.

As we've discussed, you need to focus on exactly what you really want. Otherwise you're going to be going in a million different directions. Remember that things may not always come as fast as you want. No matter how it appears, most people are not overnight successes.

Generally, in life you have to "pay your dues." What's that mean? On the most basic level it means you probably have to start small to get to the big time. Before you get to ride in the limo, you're going to have to drive a lot of Chevys. (There's nothing wrong with a Chevy—it's just not the same as having a chauffeured limo.)

Depending on your situation, it might mean working in smaller schools before getting a job in larger, more prestigious facilities. It might mean being assigned the less desirable times slots for classes instead of the more desirable slots. It might mean working as a coordinator before you become a director. It might mean teaching without the security of tenure before you become tenured.

Paying your dues means you may have to pound on a lot of doors before the right one opens. It means you may have to take jobs that are not your perfect choice to get experience so you can move up the career ladder and get the job of your dreams. You may have to do a lot of the grunt work and stay in the background while others get the credit. While all this is going on you have to be patient with the knowledge that everything you do is getting you closer to your goal.

If you look at every experience as a stepping-stone to get you to the next level of your career, it's a lot easier to get through the difficult things or trying times you may have to go through.

Setting Goals

Throughout this whole process it's essential to set goals. Why? If you don't have goals, it's hard to know where you want to end up. It's hard to know where you're going. If you don't know where you're going, it's very difficult to get there.

It sometimes is easier to look at *goals* as the place you arrive at the end of a trip. You can also look at *actions* as the trips you take to get to your destinations.

What's the best way to set goals? To start with, be as specific as you can. Instead of your goal being, "I want to be a teacher," your goal might be, "I want a career teaching first or second grade in a school in the suburbs." Instead of your goal being, "I want to be a student activities director," your goal might be, "I want to be a successful student activities director in a large, prestigious four-year university in the eastern part of the country." Instead of your goal being, "I want to be a principal," your goal might be, "I want to be the principal of a mid-sized high school in the tri-state area." Instead of your goal being, "I want to be an administrator in education," your goal might be "I want to be a superintendent of a rural school system where I can truly help to make a difference."

Instead of, "I want to be a college president," your goal might be, "I want to be a well-respected college president of a large, presti-

> ### Tip from the Top
> Successful people continue setting goals throughout their career. That ensures their career doesn't get stagnant and they always feel passion for what they do.

Tips from the Top

Goals are not written in stone. Just because you have something written down does not mean that you can't change it. As you change, your goals might change as well. This is normal.

gious university. As a matter of fact, down the line, I want to be the college president of an Ivy League university."

You should also try to make sure your goals are clear and concise. You'll find it easier to focus on your goals if you write them down. Writing down your goals will help you see them more clearly. Writing down your goals will also give them power and power is what can make it happen.

Take out your pad or notebook and get started. As you think of new ideas and goals, jot them down. Some people find it easier to work toward one main goal. Others find it easier to develop a series of goals leading up to their main goal.

To help you do this exercise, first develop a number of long-term goals. Where do you think you want to be in your career in the next year? How about the next two years, three years, five years, and even 10 years?

Need some help? Here is an example of the goals for someone who is still in school and pursuing a career as an elementary school teacher.

First-year goals:
◎ I want to complete my student teaching.
◎ I want to finish my coursework and get my bachelor's degree with a major in early childhood education. .
◎ I want to take and pass the state teachers certification exam and get licensed.

Second-year goals:
◎ I want to find a job teaching in an elementary school within an hour of here—hopefully teaching first or second grade.
◎ I want to teach children using innovative and creative teaching strategies.
◎ I want to continue my education and begin working on my master's degree in education.
◎ I want to network and start getting known in my field.
◎ I want to join and get involved in some trade associations.

Five-year goals:
◎ I want to start working on getting my Ph.D. in education.
◎ I want to be tenured.
◎ I want to continue networking and doing volunteer projects that help me hone my skills.
◎ I want to get involved in curriculum development.

Long-term goals:
◎ I want to complete my Ph.D.
◎ I want to become an elementary school principal.
◎ I want to be recognized as a talented and innovative professional by my peers.

Once you've zeroed in on your main goals, you can develop short-range goals you might want or need to accomplish to reach your long-range goals. Feel free to add details. Don't concern yourself with situations changing. You can always adjust your goals.

When focusing on your goals, remember that there are general work-related goals and specific work-related goals. What's the difference? Specific goals are just that. Look at the following examples:

◎ General Goal: I want to get a promotion.
  ▫ Specific Goal: I want to become the math department head by the end of the school year.
◎ General Goal: I want to work in some segment of education.
  ▫ Specific Goal: I want a career as an elementary reading specialist.
◎ General Goal: I want to be a teacher.
  ▫ Specific Goal: I want to be a junior high school biology teacher.
◎ General Goal: I want to work in educational administration.
  ▫ Specific Goal: I want a career first as a principal and then as a superintendent of schools.
◎ General Goal: I want to work at a college or university.
  ▫ Specific Goal: I want to work as an admissions director at a large university.

Visualization Can Help Make It Happen

Visualization is a powerful tool that can help you succeed in all aspects of your career and your life. Visualization is "seeing" or "visualizing" a situation the way you want it. It's setting up a picture in your mind of the way you would like a situation to unfold.

How do you do it? It's simple. Close your eyes and visualize what you want. Visualize the situation that you long for. Think about each step you need to take to get where you want to go in your career and then see the end result in your mind. Want to see how it's done?

What do you want to be? How do you want your career to unfold? Do you want to be an elementary school teacher? A guidance counselor? How about a preschool teacher? Do you not only want to be a high school English teacher, but also the director of the department? Perhaps you want to be the next commissioner of education?

Do you want to be the dean of a medical school? How about the president of a large, prestigious university? Do you want to be an elementary school principal? How about the principal of a middle school? What about the principal of a high school?

Do you want a career as a school psychologist? An ESL teacher? How about the dean of workforce development at a college? A university athletic director? The head coach for a winning NCCA basketball team? A university marketing director? A high school math teacher? A middle school home economics teacher?

Do you want a career as school nurse? A school librarian? A high school physical education teacher? What about an online instructor?

Do you want to teach art? Music? What about theater arts? Do you want to teach aspiring chefs how to be the next Wolfgang Puck? Do you want to teach corporate executives how to deal more effectively with the media? How about teaching salespeople how to increase their sales? Do you want to be a corporate trainer? Do you want to be the director of consumer education for a beauty product? How about teaching guests on television shopping networks how to do their demonstrations? What about teaching people how to do better on the SATs?

Is it your dream to be a professor in a large university? What about the registrar? How about the director of marketing? What about the director of workforce development? How about the director of continuing education?

The options are endless. The decision is yours. Whatever your dream career is, visualization can help you get there!

How so? Visualize driving up to a school and parking in the space that says, "Reserved for _____, Principal," with your name on the sign. You walk into the school and hear your name being paged. As you're walking down the hall to your office, students and teachers are greeting you.

You get to a door and see a sign outside your office. Do you see your name? "Chris Prime, Principal." Wow! You can hardly believe you are living your dream.

Now visualize yourself standing on the stage in an assembly. See yourself leading the school in an assembly. Hear the applause when you are introduced. Visualize looking at the students sitting in the auditorium. Imagine telling them about a new exciting program the school is embarking on. Can you almost hear the students cheering? It is a good day.

Now visualize yourself going to a meeting with the superintendent of schools. You walk in and shake her hand and she tells you that you are doing a great job. As a matter of fact, she called you in for the meeting because she was wanted to congratulate you. It seems she was just notified that you have been named Principal of the Year.

Your heart is pounding in a good way. You are doing what you prepared for and trained to do. What a feeling.

It's a good day and it's only one of many. You're a high school principal living your dream. Got the picture? That's visualization!

Are you getting the idea? You need to visualize your life and your career the way you want it to be. Visualize yourself as you would like others to see you.

No matter what you want to do you can visualize it to help make it happen. Visualize the career you want. Visualize the career you deserve. See yourself going for the interview, getting the job, and then sitting at your desk. Visu-

---

The Inside Scoop

Visualization works for more than your career. Use it to help you make all your dreams come true in all facets of your life.

---

alize speaking to coworkers, going to meetings and doing your work.

The more details you can put into your visualization, the better. Add in the colors of things around you, the fragrance of the flowers on your desk, the aroma of the coffee in your mug, the color of the suit you're wearing; even the bright blue sky outside. Details will help bring your visualization to life.

Whatever your dreams, concentrate on them, think about them, and then visualize them. Here's the great news: If you can visualize it, you can make it happen! No one really knows why, but it does seem to work, and it works well. Perhaps it's positive energy. Perhaps you're just concentrating more on what you want.

One of the tricks in visualizing to get what you want is actually visualizing all the actions you need to take to achieve your goal. If you don't know what these actions are or should be, an easy exercise that might help you is called reverse visualization. In essence what you're going to do is play the scenes in reverse.

Tip from the Coach

Make a commitment to your dream and stick to it. Without this commitment, your dream will turn into a bubble that will fly away and burst in mid air.

Start by visualizing at the point in your life where you want to be and then go back to the point where you are currently. So what this means is if your dream is to be a curriculum director at a large, prestigious school, that's where you're going to start. If you are currently in college finishing up your bachelor's, that's where you're going to end up.

If your dream is to be a department head, that's where you're going to start. If you have just graduated from college and you're looking for a job, that's where you're going to end up.

In the same vein, if your dream is to be a kindergarten teacher, that is where you're going to start. If you are just finishing your student teaching, that is where you're going to end up.

Let me show you how it works. Go back to your dream of being a teacher. As we just did a moment ago, start visualizing that you have what you want. You have a great job as a teacher. Now visualize the school you work in, its location, what it looks like from the outside, what it looks like once you walk in the door. Now visualize your classroom. Think about what it looks like. Visualize your desk, the setup of the room, the books and other learning materials. Even the blackboard with the chalk dust!

Now visualize the students in your class. Imagine saying, "Good morning, class." And then interacting with them. Imagine them asking you questions about your current lesson.

Now, take one step back. Right before you got to that point in your career, what did you do? There were probably a number of things. Let's make a list of how events might have unfolded in reverse.

◎ You answered the phone. You got the job! You will be working in the Big City Elementary School teaching kindergarten.

◎ You interviewed for the job. The hiring committee asked hard questions, but you knew all the right answers. It seems like a good match.

◎ You drove to the interview.

◎ You got dressed in your blue suit for the interview and made sure your resume and supporting materials were perfect.

◎ You prepared for the interview.

◎ You went to the school's Web site, downloaded an application, filled it in, wrote a cover letter, and forwarded it all with your resume via e-mail.

◎ You saw an advertisement in the newspaper for a job teaching kindergarten.

◎ You took and passed your state's test and fulfilled the requirements necessary to get a provisional teaching license.

◎ You graduated from college with a bachelor's degree.

◎ You loved absolutely everything about student teaching. Every day was like an adventure.

◎ You decided that you wanted to fulfill your dream of becoming a teacher and finished your student teaching. (This is the point where you are now.)

Here's a different example of the same reverse visualization exercise you might do if you were interested in a career working in the business area of a college. It's the same concept, just a slightly different way of doing it. Let's say you want to pursue a career in the fund-raising and development area of a college. Think about where you'd like to work. Think about your job title. Visualize that you are the director of fund-raising and development for the college or university of your choice.

Add in your office environment, the office décor. Now add in your coworkers. Next, put yourself in the picture. Remember to visualize what you're wearing, your accessories, even the color of your suit.

Visualize yourself speaking to colleagues, supervisors, and the board of directors. Create a picture in your mind of major fund-raising events. Visualize speaking to donors. Visualize getting a million-dollar donation. Feel the excitement of the day.

Now go backward. Visualize yourself driving to work your first day. Keep visualizing. Now you're thinking about getting dressed that morning. Keep going. Remember hearing the alarm buzzing and how you just couldn't wait to get up to go to work.

Keep visualizing in reverse. Hear your cell phone ringing and remember the feeling you had when the voice at the other end told you that you got the job. Going back, visualize the feeling that you had waiting for that call. Visualize the thank you note you wrote to the human resources director at the college. See the letter in your mind. Now, remember leaving the interview. Visualize in detail what you wore, what the experience was like, the questions that you were asked, and the feelings you had at that moment. Remember how much you hoped you would be hired.

Visualize filling out the application and developing and sending in your resume with your

> ### ⭐ Words from the Wise
> I have learned this at least by my experiment: that if one advances confidently in the direction of his dreams, and endeavors to live the life which he has imagined, he will meet with a success unexpected in common hours.
>
> –Henry David Thoreau

perfectly tailored cover letter. Now visualize seeing the job advertised and the excited feeling you had.

Recall all the preparation you did to find that job. The skills you updated. The people you spoke to; the networking. Visualize the internship you went through.

You are now back at the position in the visualization process where you currently are in your career. You now have an idea of the steps needed to get where you want to go. This might not be the exact way your situation unfolds, but maybe it can get you started on the visualization process.

Paint a picture in your mind of what you want to achieve, detail by detail. Whether you're using a reverse visualization or a traditional visualization technique, this powerful tool can help you get what you want. Give it a try. You'll be glad you did.

3

PLAN FOR SUCCESS IN EDUCATION

Take Control and Be Your Own Career Manager

You might have heard the old adage that if you want something done right, you need to do it yourself. While this might not always hold true for everything, there's a shred of accuracy in relation to your career.

It's important to realize that no one cares about your career as much as you do. Not your mother, your father, your sister, or your brother. Not your best friend, girlfriend, boyfriend, or spouse. Not your colleagues, your supervisors, your business partner, or even your mentor. It's not that these people don't care at all, because in most situations they probably not only care but they also want you to be successful. But no one really cares as much as you do.

If you want more control over success in your career, a key strategy to incorporate is becoming your own career manager. What does this mean? It means that you won't be leaving your career to chance. You won't be leaving your career in someone else's hands. You will be in the driver's seat! *You* will have control and *you* can make your dream career happen!

Will it take a lot of work? Yes. Being your own career manager can be a job in itself. The payoff, however, will be worth it.

If you look at successful people in almost any industry you will notice that most have a tremendous dedication to their career. Of course, they may have friends, colleagues, professionals, and others who advise them, but when it comes to the final decision-making, they are the ones who take the ultimate responsibility for their career.

Now that you've decided to be your own career manager you have some work to do. Next on the list is putting together an action plan. Let's get started!

What Is an Action Plan?

Let's look at success a little closer. What's the one thing successful people, successful busi-

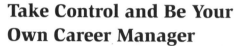

⭐ Words from the Wise

Always keep control of your career. Even at the height of your success make sure *you* oversee things. This doesn't mean you can't delegate tasks. It just means that you should be aware of what is going on, whom you are dealing with, how much money is coming in and going out, and where your money is going.

nesses, and successful events all have in common? Is it money? Luck? Talent? While money, luck, and talent certainly are all part of the mix, generally, the common thread most share is a well-developed plan for success. Whatever your goal, be it short range or long range, if you have a plan to achieve it you have a better chance of succeeding. With that in mind, let's discuss how you can create your own plan for success.

What can you do with your plan? The possibilities are endless.

People use all types of plans to help ensure success. Everyone has a version of what is best. To some, just going over in their mind what they're going to do and how they're going to do it is plan enough. Some, especially those working on a new business, create formal business plans. And some people develop action plans. That's what we're going to talk about now.

What exactly is an action plan? In a nutshell, an action plan is a written plan detailing all the actions you need to and want to take to successfully accomplish your ultimate goal. In this case, that goal is success in your chosen career.

During my seminars, while going over the section on action plans, there are always some people who ask if they really need them.

"Why do I need a plan?" someone often asks. "All I want is a job."

The answer is simple. You don't just want a job. You want to craft a great career. An action plan can help you do that.

How an Action Plan Can Help You Succeed

Success is never easy, but you can stack the deck in your favor by creating your own personal action plan. Why is this so critical? To begin with, there are many different things you might want to accomplish to succeed in your career. If you go about them in a haphazard manner, however, your efforts might not be as effective as they could be. An action plan helps define the direction to go and the steps needed to get the job done. It helps increase your efficiency in your quest for success.

Another reason to develop an action plan is that sometimes actually seeing your plan in writing helps you to see a major shortcoming, or it simply makes you notice something minor that may be missing. At that point you can add in the actions you need to take and the situation will be easily rectified.

With an action plan you know exactly what you're going to be doing to reach your goals. It helps you focus so that everything you need to do is more organized.

Many of us have had the experience of looking in a closet where everything is just jumbled up. If you need a jacket or a pair of pants from the closet, you can probably find it, but it may be frustrating and take you a long time. If you organize your closet, however, when you need that jacket or pair of pants, you can reach for them and find them in a second with no problem.

One of the main reasons you develop a plan is to have something organized to follow, and when you have something to follow things are easier to accomplish and far less frustrating. In essence, what you're creating with your action plan is a method of finding and succeeding in your dream career no matter what segment of the education industry you are interested in pursuing.

Tip from the Coach

When you break up large projects into smaller tasks they seem more manageable. It's kind of like spring-cleaning. If you look at cleaning the entire house at one time it can seem impossible. Yet, if you break up the job into cleaning one or two rooms at a time it seems easier to accomplish. When you look at the ultimate task of finding the perfect career and then becoming successful, it too, can seem like a huge undertaking. Breaking up the tasks you need to accomplish will help you reach your goal more effectively.

When you put that plan into writing, you're going to have something to follow and something to refer to, making it easier to track your progress.

"Okay," you say, "how do I know what goes into the plan? How do I do this?"

Well, that depends a lot on what you want to do and what type of action plan you're putting together. Basically, your action plan is going to consist of a lot of the little, detailed steps you're going to have to accomplish to reach your goal.

Some people make very specific and lengthy action plans. Others develop general ones. You might create a separate action plan for each job you pursue, a plan for your next goal, or even a plan that details everything you're going to need to do from the point where you find yourself now up to the career of your dreams. As long as you have some type of plan to follow, the choice is yours.

Your Personal Action Plan for Success in Education

Now that you've decided to be your own career manager, it's up to *you* to develop your personal action plan for success in your career in education. Are you ready to get started?

A great deal of your action plan will depend on what area of the industry you're interested in and exactly what you want to do. Let's start with some basics.

Take a notebook, sit down, and start thinking about your career and the direction you want it to go. Begin by doing some research.

What do you want to find out? Almost any information can be useful in your career. Let's look at some of the things that might help you.

Your Market

One of the first things to research is your market. What does that mean? Basically it means that you need to determine what jobs and employment situations are available and where they are located. Who will your potential employers or clients be? Where will they be located?

While jobs in education can be located throughout the country, in some situations you might have to relocate to find the perfect job. Where are the best opportunities for the area of education you're interested in pursuing? With a bit of research, you can start to find the answers.

Remember that the clearer you are in your goals, the easier it will be to reach them, so it's important when identifying your goals to clarify them as much as possible.

Let's say you've decided you want to teach. While most positions are located in public schools, they are not the only places to work. If you do some research you'll find a variety of other situations. What about private schools? What about a position as a private teacher?

Do you want to teach elementary school? Middle school? High school? What subject do you want to teach? English? History? Math? Biology? Are you interested in becoming a specialist?

Are you interested in teaching adults instead of children? What about teaching in some area of continuing education? What about teaching in a vocational or technical situation?

Perhaps you are interested in a career in higher education? Depending on your education and experience, you might teach at a junior or community college, a state school or a private college. You might work at a large university or a small college. Where are the colleges in which you are interested in working located? These are your markets.

Maybe you're interested in a career in administration. What type of situation interests you? Do you want a career as a principal in a public school? Do you want to be a headmaster at a private school? Is your goal to be a superintendent of schools? Where are job openings? Where are the opportunities?

If you want to work in the business or corporate side of education, you might consider a position as a corporate trainer or a training

consultant. Who will your potential clients be? Who will your employers be? What industry within the corporate world are you interested in? The choice is yours.

Do you want a career in sales? Do you think you would like to sell textbooks? What about equipment or supplies used in schools? If you love sales, your options are unlimited.

Do you love writing and want to work in some aspect of education? You have so many options! What about writing textbooks? What about writing other educational materials? How about a position as a publications director for a college or university? What about a job as a copywriter or education writer for a Web site, newspaper, or periodical? Would any of those careers be possibilities for you? If so, where specifically, could your markets be located?

Why do you have to research your market now? Why do you need this information at all? Because information is power! The more you think about your potential options and markets now, the more opportunities you may find down the line.

What Do You Need to Do to Get What You Want?

Next, research what you need to do to get the career you want. Do you need additional skills? Training? Education? Experience? Do you need to move to a different location? Make new contacts? Get an internship? Do you need to get certified? Licensed? What do you need?

Would it help to take some writing classes? How about taking a class in a new computer software program? Do you need to take a seminar on grant writing? What about a workshop in teaching special skills? Would a public speaking workshop help?

Tip from the Top

With a bit of creativity, you can weave your passions together in your career. If you want to be around the music industry and you are a teacher, you might find a position going on tour with a teenage recording act, teaching the young performers on location. If you wish you could be around the glitz and glamour of Hollywood and you are also a teacher, you might want to search out a position as a private tutor on the set of television shows or films featuring school-aged children or teens.

Do you need to get your bachelor's degree? What about your master's degree? Do you need your doctorate? Would additional continuing education help you get where you want to go?

Do you need to join a union? Would joining a trade association help you? Do you need to find new ways to network? Do you need more contacts?

What you need to determine is what is standing in between you and the career you want. What obstacles do you face?

If you are already working in education in some capacity, you need to determine what is standing between you and the success you are looking for. How can you climb the career lad-der of success and perhaps even skip a few rungs to get where you want to go?

Take some time thinking about this. If you can determine exactly what skills, qualifications, training, education, licensing, certification, or experience you're missing or what you need to do, you're halfway there.

It often helps to look at exactly what is standing between you and what you want on paper. What barriers do you face? Here's a sample to give you an idea.

Use this form to help you clarify each situation and the possible solution you feel is standing between you and the career success you want.

What Stands Between Me and What I Want?	Possible Solution
I need my degree.	I'm going to finish college.
I need experience in administration.	I'm going to see if there are any positions in administration in a summer school program.
I can't find a teaching opening.	I'm going to go on the Web and check out school Web sites and newspaper want ads to see what types of opportunities are available.
I don't know how to find a job as a corporate trainer.	I'm going to cold call and send out letters to see if there are jobs available or I can create my own job. I'm going to check out the Web and browse to find some possibilities.
I need to be bilingual.	I'm going to look into an immersion course to see if I can learn another language quickly.
I need a master's degree to succeed and keep my teaching license.	I'm going to start by taking a couple of classes. I can afford both the time and money to do this.
I need to find a way to advance my career and can't get a promotion because my supervisor isn't going anyplace.	I'm going to start to actively find a better job.

What Stands Between Me and What I Want?	Possible Solution

How Can You Differentiate Yourself?

No matter what area in which you want to be involved in education, I can almost guarantee that there are other people who want the same type of job.

There are thousands of people who want to be teachers, thousands who want to be professors, and thousands who want to work in the administration segment of education as department heads, principals, superintendents, or other administrators.

There are also thousands of people who want to work in different areas on the business side of education. And don't forget all the people who want to work in the peripheral segments of the education industry, including journalism, communications, retail, wholesale, and more.

I can almost hear you say, "That is a lot of competition. Can I make it? Can I succeed? "

To that I answer a definitive "yes!" Lots of people succeed in all aspects of education. Why shouldn't one of them be you?

Here's the challenge. How can you standout in a positive way? What attributes do you have or what can you do so people choose you over others?

"I don't like calling attention to myself," many people tell me. "I just want to blend into the crowd."

Unfortunately, that isn't the best thing to do if you want to make it. Why? Because the people who get the jobs, the ones who succeed, the ones who make it, are the ones who have found a way to set themselves apart from others. And if you want success, you are going to have to find a way too.

How? Perhaps it's your personality or the energy you exude. Maybe it's your sense of humor or the way you organize things. Perhaps it's your calm demeanor in the eye of a storm. Maybe it's your smile or the twinkle in your eye. Some people just have a presence about them.

It might be the special way you have of dealing with students. Perhaps you have a way of explaining something difficult in an easy to understand manner. Maybe it's the way you calm down a situation or make people feel better. Possibly it's the way you make others feel special.

Perhaps it's the way you write grants, which bring in huge sums of money. It might be the way you can look at an accounting ledger and

⭐ The Inside Scoop

Successful people usually have something special about them, something that sets them apart from others. Sometimes it is related to their career; sometimes it isn't. Noted psychologist Dr. Joyce Brothers first gained fame in the 1950s when she went on the popular game show of the day, *The $64,000 Question.* Brothers's specialty was boxing. She answered the questions and not only won *The $64,000 Question*, but then followed with a win on the *$64,000 Challenge*. She parlayed her experience into a position as a co-host of a show on NBC called *Sports Showcase* before snagging appearances in a series of syndicated television programs as a psychologist, the field in which she had trained. Today, Dr. Joyce Brothers still appears on radio and television as well as writing columns and articles for leading magazines. Had she not originally taken advantage of her expertise in boxing, she might never have gained the fame and recognition she has enjoyed over the years.

Tip from the Coach

If you don't know what makes you special, take a cue from what others tell you. You know those conversations where someone says something in passing like, "You're so funny, I love being around you," or "You always know just what to say to make me feel better," or "You have such a beautiful voice that I love listening to you sing," or "You always are so helpful," or "You make it so easy to understand, the most difficult things." Listen to what people say and always take compliments graciously.

see the error that everyone else has been trying to find.

Maybe it's the way you motivate people or inspire them. Maybe it's the way you can take a complicated project and make it easier to understand. Perhaps it is that you are not only a visionary, but have the ability to bring your visions to fruition.

Everyone is special in some way. Everyone has a special something they do or say that makes them standout in some manner. Most people have more than one trait. Spend some time determining what makes you special in a positive way so that you can use it to your advantage in your career.

How to Get Noticed

Catching the eye of people important to your career is another challenge. How are you going to bring your special talents and skills to the attention of the people who can make a difference to your career? This is the time to brainstorm.

First, instead of waiting for opportunities to present themselves, I want you to actively seek them out. You are also going to want to actively market yourself. We're going to discuss different ways to market yourself later, but at this point you need to take some time to try and figure out how to make yourself and your accomplishments known to others.

Consider joining a not-for-profit or civic organization with a mission you believe in. And don't just join; get involved. How? That depends what your passion is and where your talents lie. You might, for example, offer to do the marketing, publicity, or public relations for a nonprofit organization or for one of their events. You might volunteer to do fund-raising for a nonprofit or even suggest a fund-raising idea and then chair the project.

You might volunteer with a literacy program and teach adults to read or children to read better. You might volunteer to work at a food bank or at a library. You might volunteer with abused or neglected children, or perhaps abused or neglected animals.

Why volunteer when you're trying to get a job? Why volunteer when you're trying to climb the career ladder? What's the point? Aside from doing something for someone else, it can help you get noticed.

"I can see volunteering in something related to the education area," you say, "but what will volunteering for an unrelated industry and not even getting paid for it do for my career?"

It will give you experience. It will give you exposure. And maybe, just maybe, someone else involved in that not-for-profit or civic group for which you're volunteering may have some contacts in the area of the education industry in which you are seeking a job.

Need some other ideas? Think creatively. What about giving a class in preparing healthy snacks? How about teaching a workshop on helping kids do homework? Don't forget to call the media and send out a press release about your activities.

What about coordinating a fund-raiser for the PTA? How about offering to develop a newsletter for the local hospital auxiliary? What about volunteering to put together a community cookbook for a not-for-profit organization?

Just keep coming up with ideas and writing them down as you go. You can fine-tune them later.

Why are you doing this? You want to get your name out there. You want to call attention to yourself in a positive manner. You want to set yourself apart from others. You want people in education not only to know you exist, but to think of you and remember you when opportunities arise.

Have you won any awards? Have you been nominated for an award (even if you didn't win)? Honors and awards always set you apart from others and help you get noticed.

Have you presented a paper at a conference? Have you spoken at a conference or convention? These events can help set you apart from others as well.

What have you done to set yourself apart? What can you do to accomplish this goal? Think about these possibilities. Can you come up with any more? As you come up with answers, jot them down in a notebook. That way you'll have something to refer back to later. Once you determine the answers, it's easier to move on to the next step of writing your plan.

What Should Your Basic Action Plan Include?

Now that you've done some research and brainstormed some great ideas, you are on your way. It's time to start developing your action plan.

What should your basic action plan include?

Career Goals

One of the most important parts of your action plan will be defining your career goals. Are you just starting your career? Are you looking for a new job or career? Are you already in the industry and want to climb the career ladder? Are you interested in exploring a different career in education other than the one you're in now?

Are you a teacher who is interested in becoming an administrator? Do you want to teach elementary school? Do you want to teach art? Music? Physical education? Do you want to be a reading specialist? What about a guidance counselor?

Is it your dream to be a high school principal? How about a superintendent? Do you want to be a college dean? Do you want to be the public relations director of a college? How about the marketing director?

Do you want to be an education correspondent for a television or radio station? What about a journalist for a newspaper or periodical? Do you want to be the human resources director of a large university?

What is your dream? The sky is the limit once you know what your goals are.

When defining your goals try to make them as specific as possible. So, for example, instead of writing in your action plan that your goal is to be a teacher, refine your goal to be a respected, tenured high school English teacher or perhaps even the head of the English department (if that's what you want to do).

Instead of writing that your goal is a career in school administration refine your goal to be the superintendent of a large school district in the location of your choice. Instead of defining your goal to be the marketing director for a college, you might define your goal to be the marketing director for a prestigious university in the northeast. Instead of defining your goal as working in some aspect of counseling, you might define it as being a guidance counselor in a high school, helping at-risk teens find their niche.

It's important when thinking about goals to include your short-range goals as well as your long-range ones. You might even want to include mid-range goals, that way you'll be able to track your progress, which gives you inspiration to slowly but surely meet your goals.

For example, let's say you're interested in pursuing a career as a high school English teacher. Your short-range goals might be to go to college, finish your student teaching, and get your bachelor's degree with a major in education. You mid-range goals might be to get a job as a high school English teacher and get tenured. Your long-range goals might be to become the head of the English department at a large high school.

Keep in mind that goals are not written in stone and it is okay to be flexible and change them along the way. The idea is that no matter what you want, moving forward is the best way to get somewhere.

What You Need to Reach Your Goals

The next step in your action plan is to put in writing exactly what you need to reach your goals? Do you need some sort of training or more education? Do you need to learn new skills or brush up on old ones? Do you need to move to a different geographic location? Do you need to network more? Do you need to make more contacts?

Your Actions

This is the crux of your action plan. What actions do you need to attain your goals?

- Do you need to get a bachelor's degree?
  - Your actions would be to identify colleges and universities that offer that degree, apply, go through the program, and gradate with the degree you need.
- Do you need to continue your education? Do you need a master's? Do you need to get your doctorate?
  - Your actions would be to locate schools offering the degree you are seeking, apply, and continue your education.
- Do you need to take some classes or attend some workshops?
  - Your actions would be to identify, locate, and take classes and workshops.
- Do you need to find seminars and attend them?
  - Your actions would be to investigate potential seminars to see if they will assist in accomplishing your goals, and if so, attend them.

◎ Do you need to learn how to write better? Do you need better written-communications skills?
  ▫ Your actions would be to find classes to help you hone your skills.
◎ Do you need to find a way to feel more comfortable speaking in public?
  ▫ Your actions would be to find and take a course in public speaking.
◎ Do you need to move to another geographic location?
  ▫ Your actions would be to find a way to relocate.
◎ Do you need to attend industry events, conferences, and conventions?
  ▫ Your actions would be to locate and investigate events, conferences, and conventions, and then attend them.
◎ Do you need to find more ways to network or just network more?
  ▫ Your actions would be to develop opportunities and activities to network and follow through with those activities and opportunities.
◎ Do you need more experience?
  ▫ Your actions might include becoming an intern, volunteering, or finding other ways to get experience. Talk to people who might be able to help you find opportunities to volunteer.
◎ Do you need to join a union?
  ▫ Your actions would be to call the specific union you need to join and check out the requirements.
◎ Do you need a teaching license?
  ▫ Your actions would be to call the specific state you live in and check out the requirements.
◎ Do you need to find a headhunter to help you locate the perfect job?
  ▫ Your actions would be to talk to people in the industry, get suggestions and then contact a number of headhunters.

Your Timetable

Your timetable is essential to your action plan. In this section you're going to include what you're going to do (your actions) and when you're going to do them. The idea is to make sure you have a deadline for getting things done so your actions don't fall through the cracks. Just saying "I have to do this" or "I have to do that" is not effective.

Remember there is no right or wrong way to assemble your action plan. It's what you are comfortable with. You might want yours to look different in some manner, have different items, or even have things in a different order. That's okay. The whole purpose of action plans is to help you achieve your career goals. Choose the one that works for you.

Let's look at a couple of examples. First, let's look at an example of what a basic action plan might look like. Then look at sample plans first for someone who wants to teach high school English, someone who wants to teach elementary school, and someone interested in a career in school administration.

After reviewing these samples, use the blank plan provided to help you create your own personal action plan. Remember, you can start your action plan at whatever point you currently are in your career. Feel free to change the chart or add in sections to better suit your needs.

⭐ **Tip from the Coach**

Try to be realistic when setting your timetable. Unrealistic time requirements often set the groundwork for making you feel like you failed.

Example 1

My Basic Action Plan

Career Goals

Long-range goals:
Mid-range goals:
Short-range goals:

My market:

What do I need to reach my goals?

How can I differentiate myself from others?

How can I catch the eye of people important to my career?

What actions can I take to reach my goals?

What actions do I absolutely need to take now?

What's my timetable?
   Short-range goals:
   Mid-range goals:
   Long-range goals:

Actions I've taken: Date completed:

Example 2

My Basic Action Plan

Career Goals

Long-range goals: To teach at-risk teens high school English; to help them not only get through the class, but excel; to make a difference in the lives of students; to create a method of teaching that helps change and impact at-risk teens' lives in a positive way; to get my doctorate in education.

Mid-range goals: To get a job at a high school in the inner city, teaching English; to get my master's degree in education.

Short-range goals: To finish college and go through student teaching; get my bachelor's degree in education.

My market (short term): Colleges and universities with majors in education.

My market (long term): High schools in the inner cities in the northeast.

Possibilities for employment (after getting my teaching degree): Public high schools, private high schools.

Possibilities for employment long-range: Public high schools, private high schools.

What do I need to reach my goals?
Graduate from college; go through student teaching.
Volunteer in schools working with at-risk youth.
Get involved in extra-curricular activities and volunteer projects.
Get licensed.
Search out opportunities.
Get a job.
Get master's degree.
Network in the industry.
Learn as much as I can; continue my education.
Find nontraditional methods of teaching.
Market myself.
Look for other opportunities.
Get doctorate in education.
Write a book on nontraditional methods of teaching at-risk youth.

How can I differentiate myself from others? I have a 4.0 GPA. I volunteer in a program for at-risk youth. I received an award for one of the projects I developed using theater to get at-risk youth excited about school. I've networked and have a number of good contacts I interview well.

How can I catch the eye of people important to my career? Continue my involvement in some not-for-profit projects such as the theater project.

What actions can I take to reach my goals? Explore seminars and workshops in teaching at-risk teens, continue my education, talk to a number of people involved in this area to make sure this is the path I want to follow.

What actions do I absolutely need to take now? Graduate from college and get my undergraduate degree, continue volunteering and working with at-risk youth, network, develop my resume.

What's my timetable?
  Short-range goals: Within the next two years.
  Mid-range goals: Within the next three years.
  Long-range goals: Within the next eight years.

Actions I've Taken
Finished two years of college toward my bachelors degree.
Spoken to my advisor about my goals.
Talked to Dr. Johansen about teaching at-risk teens.
Worked with the "Theater For Us" program.
Started developing my resume.
Looked into schools with special programs for at-risk teens.
Found seminars on using the arts to develop English skills and took them.
Volunteered with a number of school programs.
Continue on with actions.

★ The Inside Scoop

Don't start panicking when you think you are never going to reach your career goals. Just because you estimate that you want to reach your long-range goals within the next five years or seven years or whatever you choose does not mean that you can't get there faster. Your timetable is really just an estimate of the time you want to reach a specific goal.

Example 3

My Basic Action Plan

Career Goals

Long-range goals: To become a tenured elementary school teacher. I want to make a real difference in the lives of students.

Mid-range goals: To get a job as an elementary school teacher, preferably teaching first or second grade. Continue my education; get my master's degree in education. Get tenure.

Short-range goals: To finish my bachelor's degree in education, go through student teaching, and get my teaching license.

Possible employers: Public elementary schools, private schools.

What do I need to reach my goals? Finish college, go through student teaching, get teaching license.

How can I differentiate myself from others? I was valedictorian in high school. I volunteer in a number of programs with children. I have a great sense of humor. I'm empathetic, compassionate, and patient. I am creative. I relate well to children.

How can I catch the eye of people important to my career? I volunteer in the local school. I take part in a number of volunteer activities involving children in my community. I volunteer with a literacy program.

What actions can I take to reach my goals? Go through student teaching program. Contact my school's career center to see if they know of any job openings. Register with career center in case they hear of any openings. Speak to supervisors of volunteer programs to get letters of reference.

What actions do I absolutely need to take now? Contact my advisor to make sure I am meeting the requirements to graduate. Finish student teaching. Find out what I need to do to get licensed in the states I hope to work.

What's my timetable?
    Short-range goals: Finish college in the next year
    Mid-range goals: Within the next 18 months
    Long-range goals: Within the next three years I want to be a tenured elementary school teacher in a job I love. I eventually hope to have the children of my students as students too.

Actions I've taken: (Short-term)
1. Spoke to my supervisor at volunteer program. Asked for letter of recommendation.
2. Completed three years of college toward my bachelor's degree.
3. Attended a number of seminars on "out of the box" teaching methods.
4. Continue on with actions.

Example 4

My Personal Action Plan

CAREER GOALS (Long-range): High School Principal

CAREER GOALS (Short-range): Assistant Principal

ACTION TO BE TAKEN	COMMENTS	TIMETABLE/ DEADLINE	DATE ACCOMPLISHED
SHORT RANGE			
Finish master's degree in educational administration.		December	December
Speak to Dr. Lyons, superintendent	Discuss goals and get suggestions.	Within the month	September
Look for seminars, workshops, etc., related to education and school administration.	Contact American Association of School Administrators, National School of Secondary School Principals and other industry associations for leads. Look on Internet.	ASAP	
Read industry periodicals and visit Web sites to get familiar with trends in education and education administration.	See if library or college library subscribes to any education and education administration periodicals.	This week and continually.	
Look into industry conferences and conventions to network.	Try to attend one or two.		
Read books about education and education administration.	Do search on Amazon then go to library to borrow books.	Browse through at least one a week.	
Look into licensing requirements.		Now	

(continues)

Example 4, continued

Action To Be Taken	Comments	Timetable/ Deadline	Date Accomplished
Start working on resume.		Finish first draft by end of next month.	
Start building career portfolio.		Start now and keep going.	
Find networking events.	Call chamber of commerce.	Start now and continue.	
Make up business cards.	Find printer, check out other people's business cards for ideas.		
Contact school districts to see about openings.	Send letters and resumes asking about openings.		
Contact industry associations.	Check to see if there are any networking events or career fairs.	Start now.	
Check out trades for job openings.			
Continue on with actions.			

Specialized Action Plans

What things might be in your specialized action plan? Once again, that depends on the area in which you're interested in working and the level you currently are in your career.

Let's first look at some actions you might take. Remember, these are just to get you started. When you sit down and think about it you'll find tons of actions you're going to need to take.

- ◎ Identify your skills.
- ◎ Identify your talents.
- ◎ Identify your passions.
- ◎ Look for internships.

(continues on page 60)

My Personal Action Plan

CAREER GOALS (Long-range):

CAREER GOALS (Short-range):

Action To Be Taken	Comments	Timetable/ Deadline	Date Accomplished
Short Range			
Long Range			

◎ Develop different drafts of your resume.

◎ Develop cover letters tailoring them to each position.

◎ Network.

◎ Go to industry events.

◎ Make contacts.

◎ Volunteer to get experience.

◎ Obtain reference letters.

◎ Get permission to use people's names as references.

◎ Develop your career portfolio.

◎ Attend career fairs.

◎ Look for seminars, workshops, etc., in your area of interest.

◎ Take seminars, workshops, and classes.

◎ Get a college degree.

◎ Make business cards.

◎ Perform research online.

◎ Learn about industry trends.

◎ Make cold calls to obtain job interviews.

◎ Read books about education.

Now look at some actions you might have if your career aspiration is to become a teacher. Specific actions will, of course, be dependent on the particular area of teaching you are targeting. Remember, this list is just to get you started thinking. It is by no means a complete list.

◎ Do student teaching.

◎ Explore steps necessary to get state licensed and certified.

◎ Take state licensing exam.

◎ Take continuing education courses.

◎ Subscribe to trade journals.

◎ Join trade associations.

◎ Join appropriate unions.

Now let's say you might be interested in a career as a corporate trainer. What other actions might you add in?

◎ Take courses, seminars, and workshops in training and techniques.

◎ Take courses in public speaking and facilitating.

◎ Make up business cards.

◎ Research companies.

◎ Send out cover letters and resumes to companies and corporations asking about openings.

◎ Place cold calls to human resources directors of corporations.

◎ Find relevant trade magazines and read them on a regular basis.

◎ Get experience in training.

When developing your own action plan, just keep adding in new actions as you think of them.

Using Action Plans for Specific Jobs

Action plans can be useful in a number of ways. In addition to developing a plan for your career you might also use action plans when looking for specific jobs. Let's look at an example.

Copy the blank plan provided to use when you find specific jobs in which you're interested to keep track of your actions.

Fill in this worksheet for any of the jobs you apply to. Feel free to change the chart or add in sections to better suit your needs.

How to Use Your Action Plan

Creating your dream career takes time, patience, and a lot of work. In order for your action plan to be useful you're going to have to use it. It's important to set aside some time every day to work on your career. During this time you're going to be *taking actions*. The number of actions you take, of course, will depend on

Action Plan Looking for Specific Job

Job title: School Counselor

Job description: Help students to understand and deal with social, behavioral, and personal problems; assist students in evaluating their abilities and interests; advise students on educational issues; advise students on college admission requirements and financial aid.

Company name: Some Town High School

Contact name: Michael Jardine

Secondary contact name: Sue Nessin

Company address: 342 Bridgeville Road, Some Town, NY 11111

Company phone number: (123) 222-2222

Company fax number: (123) 222-3333

Company Web site address: http://www.sometownschool.org

Company e-mail: sometownschool@sometownschool.org

Secondary e-mail: jardinem@sometownschool.org

Where I heard about job: Saw ad in the *Record*

Actions taken: Filled in application. Tailored resume and cover letter to job. Spoke to references to tell them I was applying for job and make sure I could still use them as references. Faxed application, resume, and cover letter. Mailed application, resume, and cover letter.

Actions needed to follow up: Review career portfolio; make extra copies of my resume; call if I don't hear back within three weeks.

Interview time, date, and location: Received call on 6/11 asking me to come in for interview; interview set for 2:00 p.m. on 6/17 with Michael Jardine.

Comments: Went to interview; they gave me a tour of school; very nice people working there; I would like the job; Mr. Jardine seemed impressed with some of my volunteer activities; he also seemed interested in my career portfolio; he said he was conducting interviews for the next week and would get back to me one way or another in a couple of weeks.

Extra actions: Write note thanking Mr. Jardine for interview.

Results: 6/30—Mr. Jardine called and asked me to come back for another interview to meet with some others in administration; 6/31—Mr. Jardine called and asked if I would be interested in the job!!! He asked me to come in next week to discuss salary and benefits!

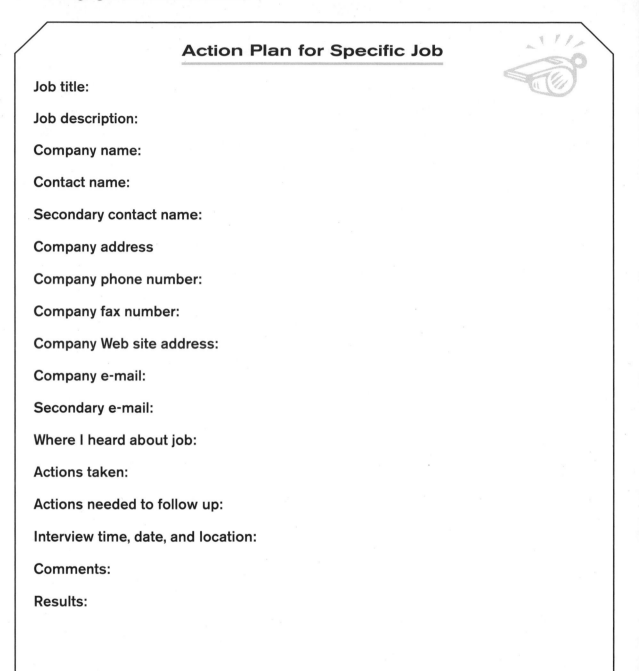

Action Plan for Specific Job

Job title:

Job description:

Company name:

Contact name:

Secondary contact name:

Company address

Company phone number:

Company fax number:

Company Web site address:

Company e-mail:

Secondary e-mail:

Where I heard about job:

Actions taken:

Actions needed to follow up:

Interview time, date, and location:

Comments:

Results:

your situation. If you are currently employed and looking for a new job, you may not be able to tackle as many actions as someone who is unemployed and has more time available every day. Keep in mind that some actions may take longer than others.

For example, putting together your career portfolio will take longer than making a phone call. So if you're working on your portfolio you might not accomplish more than one action in a day.

Try to make a commitment to yourself to take at least one positive action each day toward getting your dream career or becoming more successful in the career you currently have. Do more if you can. Whatever your situation, just make sure you take *some* action every single day.

Keeping a Daily Action Journal

In addition to an action plan, you'll find it helpful to keep an action journal recording all the career-related activities and actions you take on

> ### ⭐ The Inside Scoop
> Once you start writing in your daily action journal, you'll be even more motivated to fulfill your career goals.

a daily basis. Use the journal to write down all the things that you do on a daily basis to help you attain your career goals. You then have in one place a record of all the actions you have taken. Like your action plan, your action journal can help you track your progress.

How do you do this? Here's a sample to get you started. Names and phone numbers are fabricated for this sample.

Now What?

In this section, we've discussed being your own career manager, and we've talked about developing action plans and putting together a daily action journal. The next step is to discuss your personal career success book.

Daily Action Journal

Sunday, June 8

Read Sunday papers.
Checked education section of papers for interesting stories.
Read through classifieds. Found four openings I was interested in.
Surfed Internet looking for job openings in other areas.

Monday, June 9

Refined resume for specific jobs
Wrote cover letter for each job
Mailed resumes and cover letters.

(continues)

(continued)

Tuesday, June 10

Read daily newspapers and checked out classifieds.

Called George Windsor (212-212-2121), human resources director for Some City School District. I saw him doing an interview on news discussing shortage of summer school teachers. Cold call, not in. His secretary Louise said he would be in today, but would send me an application.

Surfed Internet looking for stories about teaching and education.

Wednesday, June 11

Read daily paper and scanned classified section.

Read education section of a couple of Sunday papers online

Got a "Thank you for coming in for an interview, but we've decided to hire someone else" letter. Called and thanked Ms. Jefferson for letting me know and asked if she could make any suggestions on how I could interview better or other places I could look for a job. She told me no one had ever called her and asked and suggested I revamp my resume to highlight my education and volunteer experience. She suggested I call a school in Orange County. She heard they were looking for a summer school teacher.

Thursday, June 12

Called Michelle Evans and told her how much I enjoyed her TV news interview on using art to improve communication skills. I asked if I could set up an appointment to come see her. I told her I just got my BA in education and was looking for a job teaching high school art, and I was really interested in volunteering with her project. It turns out she went to my alma mater. We set up a meeting for next Wednesday at 11 a.m. I sent a note thanking her for taking the time to speak to me and told her I looked forward to meeting her.

Friday, June 13

Worked on my career portfolio.

Received a call from Geoff Warren. He told me he was impressed with my resume and asked me to come in for an interview next Tuesday at 9:15 a.m. His number is 111-333-6666.

My Daily Action Journal

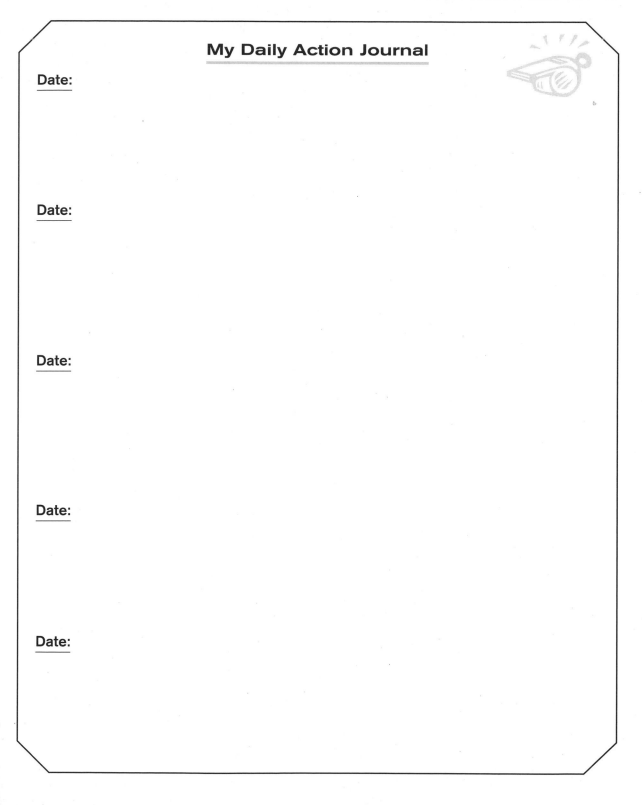

Date:

Date:

Date:

Date:

Date:

Your Personal Career Success Book

What is your personal career success book? It's a folder, scrapbook, notebook, binder, or group of notebooks where you keep all your career information. Eventually, you might have so much that you'll need to put everything in a file drawer or cabinet, and that's okay too. That means your career is progressing.

You will find your personal career success book useful no matter what segment of education you are pursuing.

What can go in your personal success career book? You can keep your action plans, your daily action journals, and all of the information you have and you need to get your career to the level you want to reach.

What else can go into your personal success career book? What about career related correspondence? It's always a good idea to keep copies of all the letters you send out for your career, as well as the ones that you receive which are career related. Don't forget copies of e-mail.

Why do you want to keep correspondence? First, it gives you a record of people you wrote to as well as people who wrote to you. You might also find ways to make use of letters people send you. For example, instead of getting a rejection letter, reading it, crumpling it up and throwing it in the trash, take the name of the person who signed it, wait a period of time then see if you can pitch another idea, another job possibility, anything which might further your career or get you closer to where you want to be. Call that person and ask if he or she can point you in another direction. Ask what you could have done better or differently. Take the advice constructively (whatever it is) and then use it for next time.

Will the person at the other end always help? Probably not, but they might, and all you need is one good idea or suggestion to get you where you want to go. It's definitely worth the call or the letter.

What else can go in your book? Keep copies of advertisements for jobs that you might want or be interested in now and even in the future. Keep copies of information on potential companies you might want to work for or that may offer employment opportunities.

"I don't need to write it down," you say, "I'll remember it when I need it."

Maybe you will and maybe you won't. Haven't you ever been in a situation where you do something and then say to yourself, "Oh, I forgot about that. If I had only remembered whatever it was, I wouldn't have done it like that." Or, "It slipped my mind." Writing things down means you're not leaving things to chance.

Keep lists in this book of potential support staff, or people who might be helpful in your career. Keep names and addresses of recruiters, headhunters, etc. You might not need an attorney now, but if you needed one quickly, who would you call? If you need an accountant, who would you use? How about a printer or banker? As you hear of professionals who others think are good, write down their names. That way you'll have information when you need it.

If everything is in one place, you won't have to search for things when you need them.

What else? You might keep lists of media possibilities, names, addresses, phone and fax numbers, and e-mail addresses. Let's say you're watching television and see an interesting interview about something in the area of education in which you're interested. It might be an interview with a teacher, a counselor, an administrator, or an author. At the time you think you're going to remember exactly what you saw, when you saw it, and who the reporter or producer was. Unfortunately, you will probably forget some of the details. You now have a place to jot down the information in a section of your book. When you need it, you know where to look!

Don't forget to clip out interesting interviews, articles, and feature stories. Instead of having them floating all over your house or office, file them in this book. Want to network a bit? Write the reporter a note saying you enjoyed his or her piece and mentioning why you found it so interesting. Everyone likes to be recognized, even people in the media. You can never tell when you might make a contact or even a friend.

It goes without saying you should also clip and make copies of all articles, stories, and features that appear in the print media about you. Having all this information together will make it easier later to put together your career portfolio.

What else is going into your personal career success book? Copies of letters of recommendation, notes that supervisors and colleagues have sent you, even letters from students thanking you for doing such a good job.

As your career progresses, you will have various resumes, background sheets, and other materials. Keep copies of them all in your book as well (even after you've replaced them with new ones). What about your networking and contact worksheets? They now have a place too.

We've discussed the importance of determining your *markets* and possible employers. This is where you can keep these lists as well.

Then, when you find new possibilities, just jot them down in your book. With your personal career success book, everything will be at your fingertips.

If you are like most people, you may attend seminars or workshops and get handouts or take notes. You now know where to keep them so you can refer back to them when needed. The same goes for conference and convention material. Keep it in your personal career success book.

You know how sometimes you just happen to see a company, business, or school where you would love to work? You just know you would fit right in. Until you have a chance to brainstorm and get your foot in the door there, jot down your ideas. You'll be able to come back to them later and perhaps find a way to bring that job to fruition.

You'll find success is easier to come by if you're more organized, and having everything you need in one place is key.

If you're now asking yourself, "Isn't there a lot of work involved in obtaining a career you want?" the answer is a definite yes.

"Can't I just leave everything to chance like most people and hope I get what I want?" you ask.

You can, but if your ultimate goal is to succeed in some aspect of education, the idea is to do everything possible to give yourself the best opportunity for success.

Planning for a successful career does take some work. In the end, however, it will be worth it, not only to you but to the students whose lives you have the opportunity to positively impact.

4

GET READY, GET SET, GO: PREPARATION

Opportunity Is Knocking:
Are You Ready?

Whether I'm giving a seminar on getting the career of your choice, a workshop on obtaining success in some other facet of life, or coaching someone on the phone, I always ask the same question: "If opportunity knocks, are you ready to open the door and let it in?"

While there are those who quickly say, "Yes," others say, "What do you mean? If opportunity knocks, I'll *get* prepared."

Unfortunately, that's not the way it always works. Sometimes you don't have a chance to prepare. Sometimes you need to be prepared at that very moment or you could lose out on an awesome opportunity.

Let's look at a couple of scenarios. First, imagine you are walking along the beach thinking about your career. "I wish I had a job as a high school principal," you say out loud, even though no one is there to hear you. "I wish I could find a really great job opening as the top administrator of a really large, prestigious high school," you continue, planning how success might come your way. As you're walking, the surf washes up and you see something shiny. You reach down to see what it is and pick up what appears to be a small brass lamp. All this time, you're still planning

your career as you're walking. "I wish I had an interview for that job right now," you say as you absentmindedly rub the side of the lamp.

You see a puff of smoke and a genie appears. "Thank you for releasing me," he says. "In return for that, I will grant you your three wishes."

Before you have a chance to ask, "What wishes?" you find yourself in an office sitting in front of a table where the superintendent of schools, along with a number of other people, are asking you questions and interviewing you for the job of your dreams. Evidently, the genie had been listening to you talking to yourself and picked up on your three wishes.

Here's the opportunity you've been wishing for! You're sitting at the interview you wished for and being interviewed by the superintendent of a large, prestigious school district. Are you ready? Or is this big break going to pass you by because you're not prepared?

Let's look at another scenario. In this scenario imagine you have a fairy godmother. She comes to you one day and says, "I can get you a one-on-one meeting with the head of the search committee looking for the next president of one of the most prestigious colleges in the country. The only catch is that you have to be ready to walk in his office door in half an hour." Would you be ready? Would you miss your big break because you weren't prepared? If your answer is, "Hmm, I might be ready . . . well, not really," then read on.

Want to think about another one? Let's imagine you are on your way to a weekend vacation in Las Vegas. You sit down in your seat on the plane and a man sits down next to you. You've seen him before, but where?

"I don't know why you look so familiar," you say to him.

All of a sudden you remember. The gentleman sitting next to you is one of the producers of *American Idol*. "I just saw you on the news,"

you say to him. "You're from *American Idol*. I love that show."

"Thank you," he says. "What do you do?"

"Actually I don't have a job right now," you tell him, "but I'm a teacher."

"Are you licensed?" he asks, "What age kids do you teach? I know we're looking for a new tutor for a couple of our younger contestants. You don't by any chance have a resume in that bag? We need someone ASAP."

Can you take advantage of the opportunity sitting right next to you? Or, would you let the opportunity pass you by because the only thing you were prepared to do was go on vacation?

⭐ ## The Inside Scoop

For some reason, which we never understood, my grandmother always kept a suitcase packed. "Why?" we always asked her.

"You can never tell when you have an opportunity to do something or go someplace," she replied. "If you're ready, you can go. If you're not prepared you might miss an opportunity."

Evidently she was right. While she didn't work in education, her story does prove a point. Here's her story.

My grandfather was a physician. After he died, my grandmother worked at a number of different jobs to keep herself busy and to earn a living. At one point she worked as a sales associate in a women's clothing store in a well-known resort hotel. The hotel always had the top stars of the day in theater, music, film, and television performing nightclub shows on holiday weekends. One weekend Judy Garland was doing a show at the hotel. According to the story we were told as children, Judy Garland wanted a few things from the clothing store and called the store to see if someone could bring up a few pieces for her to choose from.

The store was busy and the manager assigned my grandmother the job. She quickly chose some items and brought them up to the star's room. Judy was pleased with my grandmother's choices and after talking to her for a short time, evidently was also impressed with her demeanor and attitude.

While signing for the purchases, she said to my grandmother, "I need a nanny for my children. I think you would be the right one for the job. I'm leaving tomorrow morning. If you're interested, I need to know now." Without missing a beat, my grandmother took the job and by the next afternoon was on the road with Judy Garland serving as nanny to her children.

While clearly she didn't give two weeks' notice to her sales job, being at the right place at the right time certainly landed her an interesting job she seemed to love. I don't really remember how long she kept the position. What I do know, however, is that when an interesting opportunity presented itself, my grandmother was ready. Had she not been ready or hesitated, no doubt, someone else would have gotten the job.

The moral of the story is, when opportunity knocks you have to be ready to open the door.

Here's the deal on opportunity. It may knock. As a matter of fact it probably will knock. But if you don't open the door, opportunity won't stand there forever. If you don't answer the door, opportunity, even if it's *your* opportunity, will go visit someone else's door.

While you might not believe in genies, fairy godmothers, or even the concept that you might just be at the right place at the right time, you should believe this: In life and your career, you will run into situations where you need to be ready "now" or miss your chance. When opportunity knocks, you need to be ready to open the door and let it in.

How can you do that? Make a commitment to get ready now. It's time to prepare. Ready, set, let's go!

Look Out for Opportunities

Being aware of available opportunities is essential to taking advantage of them. While it's always nice when unexpected opportunities present themselves, you sometimes have to go out looking for them as well.

How many times have you turned on the television or radio and learned about an opportunity you wished you had known about so *you* could have taken advantage of it? How many times have you opened the newspaper and read that about an opportunity someone else experienced?

Would you rather open up the newspaper and read a feature story profiling a teacher developing an interesting program for children or be the teacher being profiled? Would you rather see a press release congratulating the new superintendent of schools or be the superintendent of schools?

Would you rather have a chance meeting with the head of a search committee for a job as president of a great college or hear from your friend that she ran into the individual?

Whether your goal is a career in teaching, administration, research, communications, the business segments of education any other area of the industry you want to be the one taking advantage of every available opportunity.

Here's the deal: If you don't know about opportunities, you might miss them. It's important to take some time to look for opportunities that might be of value to you.

Where can you find opportunities? You can find them all over. Read through newspapers, listen to the radio, look through trade journals, and watch television. Check out newsletters, schools, colleges, universities, trade associations, organizations, and Web sites.

Even if you're not a student, schools, universities, and colleges often offer seminars or have programs that might be of interest and are open to the public for a small fee. Contact associations and ask about opportunities. Network, network, and network some more, continually looking for further opportunities.

What kind of opportunities do you have? What types of opportunities are facing you? Is a well-known educator giving a presentation on alternative teaching methods? Is your local college giving a seminar on careers in education? Have you heard that the newspaper is looking for ideas for a new weekly education column?

Is there an upcoming fund-raiser at one of the local schools? Is a local civic organization looking for a speaker? Will a trade association conference be hosting a career fair? Is an acclaimed teacher speaking at a conference?

Have you heard of an opening as a department head at school in which you are working? Did you hear a news story on the radio discussing the opening of a new private school? Did you read in the newspaper that the new school is looking for more teachers in your field of expertise? Are schools in the area looking for summer school teachers?

Have you heard that one of the school's guidance counselors has decided to resign and move south? Does your local chamber of commerce hold networking events? Is there an interesting conference on education being held at the same time in the same city you are vacationing? These are all potential opportunities. Be on the lookout for them. They can be your keys to success.

Keep track of the opportunities you find and hear about in a notebook or if you prefer, use the Opportunities Worksheet provided. Here is a sample to get you started.

Here's an Opportunities Worksheet for you to fill in with your opportunities.

Opportunities Worksheet

University is giving presentation on teaching children with learning disabilities. June 14, 8:00 p.m. Call 222-2222 to get more info.

Conference of Literacy Educators coming to town. September 29. See if I can find a way to attend. Maybe see if I can do a story for local newspaper for better networking opportunities.

Newspaper had article on lack of summer school teachers. Call 339-2000 to get applications.

Chamber of Commerce is holding large networking event and recognizing the education community. September 16. Make reservation.

Daily News looking for people to interview to talk about why they chose teaching as a career.

Opportunities Worksheet

_____

_____

_____

_____

_____

_____

Self-Assessment and Taking Inventory

Let's now make sure you're ready for every opportunity. One of the best ways to prepare for something is by first determining what you want and then seeing what you need to get it. Remembering that you are your own career manager, this might be the time to do a self-assessment.

What's that? Basically your self-assessment involves taking an inventory of what you have and what you have to offer and then seeing how you can relate it to what you want to do. Self-assessment involves thinking about you and your career goals.

Self-assessment helps you define your strengths and your weaknesses. It helps you define your skills, interests, goals, and passions, giving you the ability to see them at a glance. Your self-assessment can help you develop and write your resume and make it easier to prepare for interviews.

Do you know what you want? Do you know what your strengths and weaknesses are? Can you identify the areas in which you are interested? Can you identify what's important to you in your career?

"But I already *know* what I want to do," you say. "This is a waste of my time. Do I *have* to do this?"

No one is going to make you do this. However, many people find that answering these questions now can help your career dreams come to fruition quicker. It may give you insight into something you had not yet thought of. It might help you fine-tune an idea for a career. It often helps give you the edge others might not have.

Doing a self-assessment is a good idea no matter what segment of education you are interested in pursuing. Before someone takes a chance on you they are going to want to know about you. If you have this done, you'll be prepared.

Strengths and Weaknesses

We all have certain strengths and weaknesses. Strengths are things you do well. They are advantages that others may not have. You can exploit them to help your career. Weaknesses are things that you can improve. They are things you don't do as well as you could.

What are your strengths and weaknesses? Can you identify them? Why are these questions important? Because once you know the answers, you know what you have to work on.

For example, if one of your weaknesses is you're shy and you don't like speaking in front of groups of people, you might take some public speaking classes or you might force yourself to network and go into situations which could help make you more comfortable around people. If you need better written-communication skills, you might take a couple of writing classes to make you a better writer.

⭐ Tip from the Top

If there is something that you need to do or that you determine can help you in your career, do it now! Don't procrastinate. In other words, don't put off until tomorrow what could have been done today (or at least this week). If you need more education, certification, additional skills, or anything else, don't put it off until "you have time." Get it now! If you need to work on your resume or your portfolio do it now and get it done. Procrastinating can seriously affect your career, because it means you didn't get something done that needed to be accomplished. Just the sheer thought of *having* to get something done takes time and energy. Instead of thinking about it, do it!

Are you a good salesperson who could be great? Think about taking some classes or workshops in selling. Are you a good presenter who could be spectacular? Think about taking a workshop or seminar in doing presentations? Do your computer skills need tweaking? Consider taking a quick class or workshop.

Do your interpersonal skills need some help? A class or seminar might be what you need. Do you need to learn how to organize your time better? Look for a time management seminar. Are you always stressed? Take a course in stress management. Do your negotiation skills need fine-tuning? You know what you need to do. Take a class.

Take some time now to define your strengths and weaknesses. Then jot them down in a notebook or use the Strengths and Weaknesses Worksheet provided. Be honest and realistic. Here are a couple of sample worksheets to help you get started. The first is for someone who wants a career as a high school art teacher. The second is for someone interested in a career in the administrative segment of education.

Now that you know some of your strengths and weaknesses it's time to focus on your personal inventory. Your combination of skills, talents, and personality traits are what helps determine your marketability.

Strengths and Weaknesses Worksheet— High School Art Teacher

My strengths:
I have a lot of energy.
I can get along with almost everyone.
I can follow instructions.
I'm a team player, yet can work on my own.
I am good at teaching others things in a simple to understand manner.
I'm creative and artistic.
I have a good memory.
I am great at motivating and inspiring others to do their best.

My weaknesses:
I'm shy.
I'm not good with numbers.
I don't test well.
I'm not organized.

What's important in my career?
I want to be a high school art teacher. I want to inspire creativity and artistic talents in young people. I also want to be a mentor to young people seeking a career in art. I want to continue with my own artwork as well and hope to have a private gallery showing.

Strengths and Weaknesses Worksheet—
Career in Education Administration

My strengths:
I am organized.
I get along with others.
I have strong interpersonal skills.
I have great communications skills.
I'm a team player.
I have a bachelor's degree in education.
I have a master's degree in education administration and am working on my Ph.D.
I was nominated and won state teacher five years ago.

My weaknesses:
I'm a perfectionist.
I am an overachiever.
I have a difficult time being on time for things.
I don't know how to use PowerPoint or Excel.

What's important in my career?
Now that I've worked as a teacher, I want my career to move into the administrative area of education. I would to help create rules and policies for a large high school as its principal. I want to work with the staff; helping them to improve their skills and helping them inspire students. I would love to help create a school that is looked at as a model of excellence in education. Eventually, I would like to move into a more advanced administrative position, perhaps as a superintendent of schools.

Tip from the Coach

A good way to deal with an interviewer asking you how you will deal with a specific weakness that *they* identify in you is by telling them that you are actively trying to change it into a strength. For example, if one of your weaknesses is you don't like speaking in public, you might say you are working on turning that into a strength by taking a public speaking class. Telling an interviewer you are working on your shortcomings helps him or her form a much better picture of you.

Tip from the Top

Accept the fact that at almost every interview you go on you will be asked about your strengths and weaknesses. Preparing a script ahead of time so you know what you are going to say and are comfortable saying it gives you the edge.

Strengths and Weaknesses Worksheet

My strengths:

_____

_____

_____

My weaknesses:

_____

_____

_____

What's important in my career?

_____

_____

_____

_____

_____

Tip from the Coach

If a human resource director, headhunter, recruiter, interviewer, or college admissions officer asks what your weaknesses are, try to indicate a weakness that might also be thought of as a strength. For example, you might say something like, "I'm a perfectionist. I like things to be done right." Try not to give anyone in those positions information on any of your *real* weaknesses. Remember that as friendly as these people might seem during interviews, their job is screening out candidates. You don't want to give an interviewer or anyone else a reason not to hire you.

What Are Your Skills?

Skills are acquired things that you have learned to do and you can do well. They are tools that you can use to help sell yourself. Keep in mind that there are a variety of relevant skills. There are job-related skills that you use at your present job. Transferable skills are skills that you used on one job and that you can transfer to another. Life skills are skills you use in everyday living such as problem solving, time management, decision making, and interpersonal skills. Hobby or leisure time skills are skills related to activities you do during your spare time for enjoyment. These might or might not be pertinent to your career. There are also technical skills connected to the use of machinery. Many of these types of skills overlap.

Most people don't realize just how many skills they have. They aren't aware of the specialized knowledge they possess. Are you one of them?

While it's sometimes difficult to put your skills down on paper, it's essential so you can see what they are and where you can use them in your career. Your skills, along with your talents and personality traits, make you unique. They can set you apart from others and help you not only land the career of your dreams, but succeed in it as well.

Once you've given some thought to your skills, it's time to start putting them down on paper. You can either use the worksheet provided or a page in a notebook.

Begin with the skills you know you have. What are you good at? What can you do? What have you done? Include everything you can think of, from basic skills on up, and then think of the things people have told you you're good at.

Don't get caught up thinking that "everyone can do that" and so a particular skill of yours is not special. *All* of your skills are special. Include them all in your list.

Review these skill examples to help get you started. Remember this is just a beginning.

- computer proficiency
- public speaking
- time management
- analytical skills
- organizational skills
- presentation skills
- counseling skills
- writing skills
- listening skills
- verbal communications
- management

Tip from the Top

Keep in mind that some skills also need *talent*. For example, writing is a skill. It can be learned. To be a great writer, however, you generally need talent. Cooking is a skill. To be a great chef, you need talent. Teaching is a skill. The best teachers, however, are also talented.

- selling
- problem solving
- language skills
- leadership
- math skills
- decision-making skills
- negotiating skills
- art skills
- money management
- word-processing skills
- computer repair
- teaching skills
- customer service
- cooking
- Web design
- singing
- songwriting
- acting
- playing an instrument
- interior decorating
- playing a sport

Tip from the Coach

Don't limit the skills you list to just those that relate to the area of education in which you are interested. Include all your skills. Even when a skill seems irrelevant, you can never tell when it might come in handy.

Skills Worksheet

Your Talents

You are born with your talents. They aren't acquired like skills, but they may be refined and perfected. Many people are reluctant to admit what their talents are, but if you don't identify and use them, you'll be wasting them.

What are your talents? You probably already know what some of them are. What are you not only good at but better at than most other people? What can you do with ease? What has been your passion for as long as you can remember? These will be your talents.

Are you a talented teacher, inspiring students to want to learn? Does your talent lie in being able to make even complicated things easy to learn?

Are you a talented negotiator? Can you bring two sides to an agreement when no one else can? Are you a prolific writer? Are you a great fund-raiser? Can you tell stories in such a manner that people listening want to hear more? Do you tell jokes in such a manner that those listening just can't stop themselves from laughing? Can you make people feel comfortable with a simple look?

Does your talent fall in the science area? How about math? What about art? Do you have that "eye" to be able to see just the right employee for a specific job? Can you look at someone and just *know* that with a little training and work they can be great?

Think about it for a bit and then jot your talents in your notebook or on the Talents Worksheet. Here are a couple of examples to get you started.

Sample 1

Talents Worksheet

I have good interpersonal skills. I get along with most people.

People feel comfortable telling me things.

I am multilingual and can speak English, Spanish, and French.

People feel they can relate to me.

I am funny and can break the ice with a joke to make people feel comfortable.

I have the ability to make people around me feel good about themselves.

Sample 2

Talents Worksheet

I am a talented writer and can bring stories to life with my words.

I am very creative.

I have a great sense of humor. I can make almost everyone I'm around feel better by making them laugh.

I have the ability to inspire people.

I have the ability to motivate people.

I am a great public speaker.

I am very persuasive.

Fill in your talents.

```
┌─────────────────────────────────────────────────────────┐
│                   Talents Worksheet                        │
│                                                            │
│  _____  │
│                                                            │
│  _____  │
│                                                            │
│  _____  │
│                                                            │
│  _____  │
│                                                            │
│  _____  │
└─────────────────────────────────────────────────────────┘
```

Your Personality Traits

We all have different personality traits. The combination of all these traits is what set us apart from others. There are certain personality traits that can help you move ahead no matter what aspect of education you want to pursue. Let's look at what some of them are.

- ability to get along well with others
- adaptable
- ambitious
- analytical
- assertive
- caring
- charismatic
- clever
- compassionate
- competitive
- conscientious
- creative
- dependable
- efficient
- energetic
- enterprising
- enthusiastic
- flexible
- friendly
- good listener
- hard worker
- helpful
- honest
- imaginative
- innovative
- inquisitive
- insightful
- life-long learner
- observant
- optimistic
- outgoing
- patient
- passionate
- personable
- persuasive
- positive
- practical
- problem solver
- reliable
- resourceful

◎ sense of humor

◎ self-starter

◎ self-confident

◎ sociable

◎ successful

◎ supportive

◎ team player

◎ understanding

What are your special personality traits? What helps make you unique? Think about it, and then jot them down in your notebook or on the Personality Traits Worksheet.

Personality Traits Worksheet

Your Special Accomplishments

Special accomplishments make you unique and often will give you the edge over others. What are your special accomplishments?

Have you won any awards? Were you awarded a scholarship? Were you asked to deliver a paper at a national conference? Have you won a writing competition? Did you do especially well in school?

Were you the president of your class? Were you the chairperson of a special event? Have you won a community service award? Were you nominated for an award, even if you didn't win?

Has an article about you appeared in a regional or national magazine or newspaper? Have you been a special guest on a radio or television show? Are you sought out as an expert on some subject in education? Are you sought out as an expert on subjects outside of education? Being an expert on anything will set you apart from others.

All these things are examples of some of the special accomplishments you may have experienced. Think about it for a while, and you'll be able to come up with your own list. Once you identify your accomplishments, jot them down in your notebook or on your Special Accomplishments Worksheet.

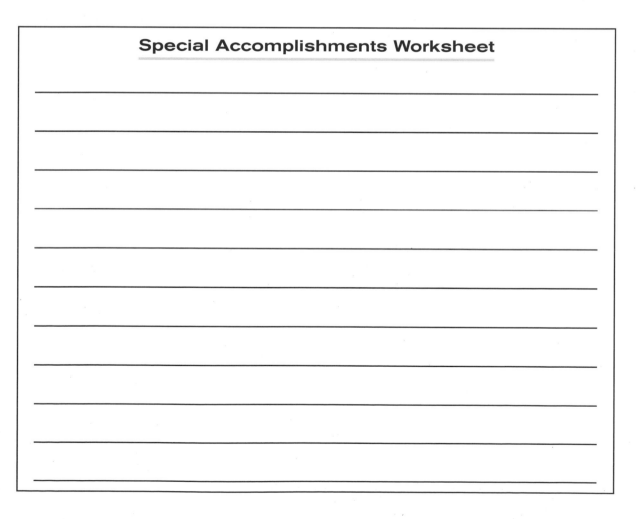

Special Accomplishments Worksheet

Your Education and Training

Education and training are important to the success of your career no matter what you want to do. For most jobs in the field of education, a college education is mandatory. Many careers also require a post secondary education.

In addition to your formal education, there may be other opportunities that will prove useful in your career. These may encompass classes, courses, seminars, workshops, programs, on-the-job training, and learning from your peers. Every opportunity you have to learn anything can be a valuable resource in your career, and your life.

What type of education and training do you already possess? What type of education and training do you need to get to the career of your dreams? What type of education and training will help you get where you want to go?

Would some extra classes help you reach your career goal? Is there a special seminar that will help give you the edge? How about a course in public speaking? What about a class in time management? How about a stress management seminar? What about a seminar in facilitating? How about an immersion class in a second language?

Do you need some classes to get certified in your field or to help move your career forward? Do you need additional education to keep your license?

Do you need to get your master's degree? What about your Ph.D? How about taking some

---

★ **Tip from the Coach**

Courses, seminars, and workshops are great ways to meet and network with industry insiders. Actively seek them out.

★ **The Inside Scoop**

At the beginning of your career, when you don't have a lot of professional experience, employers often will look at your resume to see what type of education and training you have gone through.

---

workshops or seminars? What about attending some conferences? The options are yours.

Now is the time to determine what education or training you have and what you need so that you can go after it.

Fill in the Education and Training Worksheet with your information so you know what you need to further your career and meet your goals.

Location, Location, Location: Where Do You Want to Be?

Location can be an important factor in your career. Where do you need to live if you want a great career in education? Is one location better than another? Here's the good news! Careers in education are available throughout the country.

There are a ton of options. Depending on what you want to do, you might work in a rural setting, the suburbs, or a large city. You might work on the East Coast, the West Coast, or the middle of the country. Sometimes you get to choose. Other times you have to go where the jobs are.

Will the biggest cities be the best? Not always. If you're just starting out you might find it easier to locate opportunities in smaller areas. That way you can get some experience, make some contacts, and hone your skills. Teaching in smaller, rural schools may also provide different experiences and challenges than teaching in larger, city schools.

Education and Training Worksheet

What education and training do I have?

_____

_____

What education or training do I need to reach my goals?

_____

_____

What classes, seminars, and workshops have I taken which are useful to my career aspirations?

_____

_____

_____

What classes, seminars, workshops, and courses can I take to help advance my career?

_____

_____

_____

Where is the right location for you? While you need to be in the location where there are openings, remember this: you want to be in an area where you will be comfortable. If you love the hustle and bustle of a city, you might not be comfortable setting up your life in a small, rural town. On the other hand, if you grew up in a small rural area and love that type of life, you might not *want* to live in a city. Some people are more flexible than others. Only you can decide where you want to be.

Location Worksheet

Type of area in which I currently reside:

_____

Location of job or career choice I want:

_____

Other possible locations:

_____

You might want to use the Location Worksheet to help you decide where you want to look for a job.

Reviewing Your Past

Let's now look at your past. What have you done which can help you succeed in your career in education?

Make a list of all the jobs you have had and the general functions you were responsible for when you held them. Then, make a list of the volunteer activities in which you have participated. Look at this information and see what functions or skills you can transfer to your career in education.

Remember that many skills are transferable. It doesn't necessarily matter if all your skills are directly related to education.

"Give me some examples," you say.

Were you a counselor at a camp? Were you a tutor? Did you lead a study group in college? Have you taught Sunday school? Were you a Girl Scout or Boy Scout leader? The skills used in these activities may help you in your career as a teacher.

Have you worked as the director of a summer camp? Were you a key holder in a retail store? Have you held jobs in corporate America? The skills used in any of these situations might help if you are seeking a career in education administration.

Did you work as a high school teacher? Were you an instructor in a college? These experiences might be useful in a career as a corporate trainer.

Have you held a job as a reporter for a local newspaper? That shows that you know how to develop and write an article or news story and can do it in a timely fashion. These skills can easily be transferred if you are interested in a career as an education reporter or journalist. They might also be transferred if you are interested in writing textbooks in a subject area in which you have expertise. They can also be transferred to skills needed to be a publicist or publications director at a school, college, or university.

Have you worked as a bookkeeper? What about a job in the bookkeeping department of a school or college? With some education and certification you might be able to fulfill your goals of working as a CPA for a school district.

Have you worked in retail sales? Have you sold advertising for a newspaper? How about selling commercials for television or radio stations? Have you worked as a real estate salesperson? Do you love selling? You could use your sales skills in a career as a sales representative for textbooks.

Were you on your college student activities board? This might help transfer to a career as a campus activities director. Have you written grants successfully? This might transfer to a career as a dean of workforce development.

Have you volunteered and helped a not-for-profit organization execute a special event? Were you the fund-raising chairperson for a local not-for-profit organization? Did you bring in thousands of dollars for the organization when you ran the membership drive? You might use those talents in the fund-raising department of a college. You might also transfer your skills to a position doing the fund-raising for an association related to some aspect of the education industry.

Remember, the idea is to use your existing education, training, talents, skills, and accomplishments to get your foot in the door. Once in you can find ways to move up the ladder so you can achieve the career of your dreams. When going over your list of past positions include both part-time jobs you had as well as full-time ones. Look at the entire picture, including not only your jobs but also your accomplishments, and see what they might tell about you.

"Like what?" you ask.

Did you graduate from high school in three years instead of four? That illustrates that you're driven and can accomplish your goals. Were you the chairperson for a not-for-profit charity event? That illustrates that you take initiative, work well with people, can delegate, and organize well. Do you sing in your church choir?

Have you volunteered to handle the choir's music? This shows you can sing and that you have the dedication to attend rehearsals. Handling the music illustrates your organizational skills.

Now that you have some ideas, think about what you've done and see how you can relate it to your dream career. Everything you have done in your life including your past jobs, volunteer and civic activities, and other endeavors can help create your future dream career in education.

Using Your Past to Create Your Future

When reviewing past jobs and volunteer activities, see how they can be used to help you get closer to the career you are seeking in education. Answer the following questions:

- What parts of each job accomplishment or volunteer activity did you love?
- What parts made you happy?
- What parts gave you joy?
- What parts of your previous jobs excited you?
- What skills did you learn while on those jobs?
- What skills can be transferred to your career in the segment of education you are interested in pursuing?
- What accomplishments can help your career in education?

Jot down your answers in your notebook or use the "Using Your Past To Create Your Future" worksheet provided.

The more ways you can find to use past accomplishments and experiences to move closer to success in your career in education, the better you will be. Look outside the box to find ways to transfer your skills and use jobs and activities as stepping-stones to get where you're going.

⭐ **Tip from the Top**

If you're just out of school, your accomplishments will probably be more focused on what you did while in school. As you get more established in your career, your accomplishments will be more focused on what you've done *during* your career.

Using Your Past to Create Your Future

Past Job/ Volunteer Activity/ Accomplishment	Parts of Job/ Volunteer Activity/ Accomplishment which I Enjoyed	Skills I Learned and Can Transfer to Career in Education

Your Passions and Goals

Once you know what you have, it's easier to determine what you need to get what you want. You've made a lot of progress by working on your self-assessment, but you have a few more things to do. At this point, you need to focus on exactly what you want to do.

In what area of education do you want to be involved? What are you interested in? Do you want to be an elementary school teacher? Do you want to specialize? Is your passion teaching art or music? Is it your dream to teach junior or high school students? What subject do you want to teach?

Do you want to be a guidance counselor? Would you like to be a health teacher? Would you like to be a physical education teacher? Do you want to be a reading specialist? Do you want to be a college or university instructor or professor? What subject area will be your specialty?

Are you more interested in the administrative segment of the industry? Do you want to be a department head? An elementary school principal? A high school principal? Do you want to be a school psychologist?

Are you dreaming of a career as the marketing director or public relations director of a college? What about a career as a fund-raiser for a university? Do you want to be a coach in a school with a prestigious sports department?

Do you want to work in the business end of the industry? Do you think you might like a career as a corporate trainer?

Do you want to teach English as a second language? Are you interested in teaching vocational or technical classes?

There are so many opportunities. It's all up to you.

You began working on determining exactly what you wanted to do earlier in the book. Continue to refine your list of things that you enjoy and want to do. Previously you defined your career goals. Now that you've assessed the situation, are they still the same?

What are your passions? What are your dreams? Think about these things when making your career choices. You owe it to yourself to have a career that you love, that you're passionate about, and that you deserve. Now, with a bit of effort, you're on your way!

5

JOB SEARCH STRATEGIES

If you've decided that your dream career is in some aspect of education, you're in luck. As a result of the growing emphasis on improving education in this country, the demand for people to work in this industry is increasing. There are thousands of jobs in the various segments of the industry as well as the peripherals. One of them can be yours!

We've covered some of the various opportunities in previous chapters. Some jobs are easier to obtain. Some may be more difficult. This section will cover some traditional and not so traditional job search strategies.

It's important to recognize that *getting* the job is just the beginning. What you want is a career.

Using a Job to Create a Career

Unfortunately you can't just go to the store and *get* a great career. Generally, it's something you have to work at and create. How do you create your dream career? Developing the ultimate career takes a lot of things, including sweat, stamina, and creativity. It takes luck and being in the right place at the right time. It takes talent, education, and training. It takes perseverance and passion. And it takes faith in yourself that if you work hard for what you want and don't give up, you will get it.

You have to take each job you get along the way and make it *work* for you. Think of every job as a rung on the career ladder, every assignment within that job as a stepping-stone. To complete the puzzle takes lots of pieces and lots of work, but it will be worth it in the end.

Every job you get along the way helps to sharpen your skills and adds another line to your resume. Every situation is an opportunity to network, learn, and most of all to get noticed.

If you know what your ultimate goal is, it is much easier to see how each job you do can get you a little closer. Every situation, no matter how small or insignificant you think it may be, gives you another experience, hones your skills, helps you to gain confidence, and gives you the opportunity to be seen and discovered. Every job can lead you to the career you've been dreaming about.

One of the things you should know is that while almost anyone can get a *job*, not every-

---

★ Tip from the Coach

It may take some time to get where you want to in your career. Try to make your journey as exciting as your destination.

---

one ends up with a career. As was discussed in a previous section of this book, the difference between a job and a career is that a job is a means to an end. It's something you do to get things done and to earn a living. Your career, on the other hand, is a series of related jobs you build using your skills, talents, and passions. It's a progressive path of achievement.

When you were a child, perhaps your parents dangled the proverbial carrot on a stick in front of you, tempting you to eat your dinner so you could have chocolate ice cream and cake for dessert. Whether dinner was food you liked, didn't particularly care for, or a combination, you probably ate it most of the time to get to what you wanted: dessert. In this case, your dessert will be ultimate success in your career in some segment of the education industry.

Use every experience, every job, and every opportunity for the ultimate goal of filling your life with excitement and passion while getting paid. Will there be things you don't enjoy doing and jobs you wish you didn't have along the way? Perhaps. But there will also be things you love doing and jobs you look back on and remember with joy.

Your Career: Where Are You Now?

Where are you in your career now? Are you still in school? Are you just starting out? Are you in another field and want to move into a career in education? Do you know what you want to do with the rest of your life?

Tip from the Coach
Don't get so caught up in getting to your goal that you don't enjoy your journey.

The Inside Scoop
I recently saw a movie called *The Ron Clark Story.* It was a true story of a young teacher who used innovative teaching methods to inspire students. Clark, a man who truly loved teaching, made his mark in education after teaching a group of children in Harlem who were classified as low achievers. Through inspiration, motivation, and unique teaching methods, Clark helped the children score higher than the gifted students in the district. He went on the receive Disney's Teacher of the Year Award in 2002. In 2007, Clark opened a privately funded school in Atlanta called the Ron Clark Academy. The school serves low-income students in that area.

Even though he founded the school, Clark decided to follow his passion, focusing on teaching instead of handling the day-to-day administrative details. It is quite evident to anyone seeing him speak that he truly created a career that he loves.

Whether your goal is to become a teacher, an administrator, or anything else in the education industry, go after your passion and create a career *you* love.

If you already know what you want to do, great! You're in good shape. You need only to prepare by getting the education, training, and experience necessary and you're ready to find the job or jobs that will lead you to your dream career.

Moving into Education: Career Changing

Are you currently working in another industry but really want to be in some segment of education? If so, you're not alone. Many people dreamed about a career in education from the time they were very young, but for a variety of reasons ended up in other industries. Is this you? If so, read on.

Perhaps at the time you needed a job. Possibly it looked too difficult to obtain a career in education. Maybe you couldn't afford the time or money to finish your education. Maybe you just didn't know how to go about it. Maybe you weren't ready. Maybe people around you told you that you were pipe dreaming. Maybe people told you that a career in education *was not* what you wanted to do. Maybe you were scared. Or maybe someone offered you a job in a different industry and you took it for security. There might be hundreds of reasons why you wanted a career in education, but you didn't pursue it at the time. The question is, do you want to be there now?

"Well," you say, "I do, but . . . ."

Before you go through your list of *buts* ask yourself these questions. Do you want to give up your dream? Do you want to live your life saying, "I wish I had," and never trying?

Wouldn't you rather find a way to do what you wanted than never really be happy with what you're doing? Wouldn't it be great to look at others who are doing what they want and know that *you* are one of them? Here's the good

---

⭐ Tip from the Coach

Are you living someone else's dream? You can't change your past, but you can change your future. If your dream is to work in an aspect of education, go for it. Things might not change overnight, but the first step you take toward your new career will get you closer to your dream. Every day you put it off is one more day you're wasting doing something you don't love. You deserve more. You deserve the best.

---

news. You can! You just have to make the decision to do it!

How can you move into a career in education from a different industry? How can you change your career path? Of course, it will depend on the segment of education in which you aspire to work, but it's not as hard as you think. What you need to do is take stock of what you have and what you don't have.

Then see how and where you can transfer your skills and accomplishments to find ways you can use them in the career of your choice.

"What if I want to be a teacher? What if I want to be a guidance counselor? Don't I need to do more than just transfer skills?" you ask.

Yes, you do. You can still transfer any applicable skills, but if your dream is to work as a teacher or guidance counselor and you are either just starting your career or want to move into one of those areas, you probably are going to have to get some additional education or training before going on your job search.

Do you have an MBA and want to work in administration? Transfer your education and skills, take some classes and you're on your way.

Don't want to be a teacher or professor? Don't want to work in educational administration? There are a ton of other opportunities.

Do you have strong writing skills? Consider seeking out a position with a college or university in the public relations or marketing department. Think about working at a college or university handling the publicity or public relations for their sports program. What about a job as an education reporter for a newspaper or periodical?

Are your skills in the number crunching area? What about seeking out a position in the accounting or bookkeeping department of a school system, college, or university?

Do you have office skills? Are you a good manager? Do you have good organizational skills? Consider a job as an administrative assistant in a school principal's office, a superintendent's office, or the office of a college president.

Do you have information technology (IT) skills? Are you a Webmaster? Do you have other computer skills? Transfer them to some segment of the education industry!

Are your skills in marketing? Are you working in marketing in another industry? Consider a position in the marketing department of a college, university, or for a collegiate sports team.

Are your skills in sales? Lucky you! The possibilities are endless. Every industry needs sales people. Whether you're selling equipment, books, educational materials, or anything else, there are always opportunities in sales. What about using your sales skills to recruit students for a college or university? What about using your sales skills to recruit student athletes?

"Wait a minute," you say. "What if I don't want to work in the area where my skills are? What if I want to do something totally different? What then?"

Here's the deal. Use your skills and your talents to get your foot in the door. Once in, you have a better opportunity to move into the area you want.

Can you do it? Yes! Thousands of people are successful in the industry. You can be too!

Should you quit your present job to go after your dream? And if so, when should you do it? Good questions. Generally, you are much more employable if you are employed. You don't have that desperate "I need a job" look. You don't have the worries about financially supporting yourself and your family if you have a job. You don't have to take the wrong job because you've

---

> ## ⭐ Words from the Wise
>
> If you are working at another job until you get the one you want, it's not a good idea to keep harping on the fact that you're only there until you get your big break or the job of your dreams. If your supervisor thinks you are planning on leaving, not only will you probably not get the choice assignments, but coworkers who are *stuck* in the job you are using as a stepping-stone often feel jealous.

---

been out of work so long that *anything* looks good.

It's best to work on starting your dream career while you have a job to support yourself. Ideally, you'll be able to leave one job directly for another much more to your liking.

Of course, in some situations, you might want to (or need to) devote most of your time to your career. For example, it might be difficult for some to go to school and hold down a full-time job. There are some people who do it, but it can be difficult. Only you can make the decision on how to go about your starting your career. Take some time to decide what would be best for you.

You must focus on exactly what you want to do, set your goals, prepare your action plan, and start taking actions now. You're going to have to begin moving toward your goals every day: a job that can lead to the career of your dreams.

Over the years I've often seen people take a job because the "money" was there, even though the job wasn't exactly what they wanted. Then, as time goes on, they are offered more money or promotions and find it difficult to "give it up," even to pursue their goals. Don't get so busy that you forget where you're going and what you want. If you have a dream don't forget your goals.

⭐ ### The Inside Scoop

In your journey to obtaining your perfect career in education, you might take some jobs that, while considered stepping-stones, are not where you ultimately want to end up career-wise. No matter what type of career you aspire to, it is essential that you remember your ultimate goal. Don't get so wrapped up in the job you have that you forget where you're going.

The question many ask is, "When do I quit the job that I have to go after the job that I want?" No one can answer this for you, but try to be realistic. You don't want to ever be in the position where you *can't* do what you want because you don't have any funds. Do you have a nest egg put away? In order to have the best shot at what you want to do, you need to be as financially stable as possible.

We've already discussed that you are usually more marketable if you are currently employed. This doesn't mean you shouldn't work toward your goals. Continue searching out ways to get where you're going.

"Working takes all my energy," you say. "I don't have time to do everything. If I'm working, I just don't have enough time to put into creating my dream career. I don't have time to do everything."

You're going to have to make time. It's amazing how you can expand your time when you need to. Remember your action plan? It's imperative that you carve time out of your day to perform some of your actions.

If you think you don't have the time, look at your day a little closer. What can you eliminate doing? Will getting up a half an hour early give you more time to work on your career? How

about cutting out an hour of TV during the day or staying off the computer for an hour? Even if you can only afford to take time in 15-minute increments, you usually can find an hour to put into your career.

Moving from One Segment of the Education Industry to Another

Are you working in one segment of the education industry and want to work in another? Are you, for example a teacher who wants to become a principal? Are you a principal who wants to become a superintendent? Are you a professor who wants a career in administration? Are you a teacher who wants to write textbooks? Are you a student activities director who wants to be a dean of students?

What do you do? Check out the requirements. Look into what education you need to reach your goals. Find a mentor. Ask questions. Find what you need to do to get the career of your dreams and then do it!

What should you *not* do? To begin with, don't give up before you get started. Don't get so caught up in how difficult something will be that you don't look for a way to do it. Most of all, don't discount your dreams.

Let's say you are a teacher who wants to become a principal. What do you do? You know you already have a bachelor's degree in education. You also are part way through your master's in education. What classes have you already taken that are applicable for a career as a school administrator? What other types of classes do you need to take? What kind of program can help you move into the job of your dreams? If you research what you need to do and take it step by step, you will be on your way to getting the job of your dreams.

Finding the Job You Want

Perseverance is essential to your success, no matter what you want to do, what area of the industry you want to enter, and what career level you want to achieve. Do you want to know why most people don't find their perfect job? It's because they gave up looking *before* they found it.

Difficult as it might be to realize at this point, remember that your job, your great career, is out there waiting for you. You just have to locate it. How do you find that all-elusive position you want? You look for it!

Basically, jobs are located in two areas: the open job market and the hidden job market. What's the difference? The open job market consists of jobs that are advertised and announced to the public. The hidden job market consists of jobs that are not advertised or announced to the public.

Where can you find the largest number of jobs? Are they in the hidden job market or the open job market? A lot depends exactly on what you want to do in the industry. Teaching jobs in public schools, for example, are generally advertised in the open market. You need to be aware, however, that there are a great many jobs that just aren't advertised. Why?

There are a few reasons. Some employers don't want to put an ad in the classified section of the newspaper because it might potentially mean that there could be hundreds of responses if not more.

"But isn't that what employers want?" you ask. "Someone to *fill* their job openings?"

Of course they want their job openings filled, but they don't want to have to go through hundreds of resumes and cover letters to get to that point. It is much easier to try to find qualified applicants in other ways and that is where the hidden job market comes in.

This doesn't mean, however, that you shouldn't look into the open market. Positions for public school teachers, for example, are usually advertised, but the smart thing to do to boost your job hunt is use every avenue to find your job. With that being said, let's discuss the open job market a bit and then we'll go on to talk about the hidden job market in more detail.

The Open Job Market

When you think of looking for a job, where do you start? If you're like most people, you head straight for the classifieds. While, as we just noted, this strategy may not always be the best bet, it's at least worth checking out, especially if you are looking for a teaching position. Let's go over some ways to increase your chances of success in locating job openings this way.

The Sunday newspapers usually have the largest collection of help wanted ads. Start by focusing on those. You can never tell when an employer will advertise job openings, though, so you might also want to browse through the classified section on a daily basis if possible.

Will you find a job you want advertised in your local hometown newspaper? That depends on what type of job you're seeking and where you live. If you live in a small town and you're looking for a position as the dean of students of a major university, probably not. If you're looking for a position as an elementary school teacher, your chances are better.

What do you do if you don't live in the area where you want to look for a job? How can you get the newspapers?

There are a number of solutions. Larger bookstores and libraries often carry Sunday newspapers from many metropolitan cities in the country. If you're interested in getting newspapers from specific areas, you can also usually order short-term subscriptions. One of the easiest ways to view the classified sections of newspapers from around the country is by going online to each specific newspaper's Web site. The home page will direct you to the classified or employment section. Start your search from there.

What do you look for once you get the newspapers? That depends on the specific job you're after, but generally look for key words. If you want a job as an elementary school teacher, for example, you would look for key words such as "Elementary School Teacher," "Teacher-Elementary School," or "Education." If you are looking for a job as a marketing director for a college or university, you might look for key words such as "Marketing Director," "Education," "University Marketing," or "Marketing."

Don't forget to look for specific company names as well, such as "Some Town School District," "LMR University," "Sandford Educational Textbook Company," and so on.

In some cases, all the jobs in education are in a specific section of the classifieds. In others, the jobs are scattered throughout the classified section.

Keep in mind that in many situations, large schools, colleges, universities, or companies also use boxed or display classified ads. These are large ads that may advertise more than one job and usually have a company name and/or logo.

There also may be employment agencies ads specializing in jobs in a specific area of education, which may advertise openings in the employment agency area of the classifieds.

The Trades, Industry Publications, Newsletters, and Web Resources

Where else are jobs advertised? The trades are often a good source. Trades are periodicals geared toward a specific industry. Every industry has trade magazines and newspapers, and the education industry is no exception.

Where do you find them? Contact the trade association geared toward the specific area of the industry in which you are interested. (Trade associations are listed in the appendix in the back of this book.)

How can you use the trades to your advantage? Read them faithfully. If you don't want to invest in a subscription, go to your local public or college library to see if they subscribe to trade magazines. Many of the trades also have online versions of their publication. Browse through the "Help Wanted" ads in the classified section of each issue to see if your dream job is there.

Newsletters related to various areas of the education industry might offer other possibilities for job openings. What about Internet Web sites such as Monster.com, Hotjobs.com, and other employment sites? Don't forget business Web sites. Schools, colleges, and universities, generally host Web sites. Many of these sites have specific sections listing career opportunities at their institution. It's worth checking out.

Are you already working in the education industry and seeking to move up the career ladder? Do you, for example, have a job in a college in the marketing department and want to move up a rung on the career ladder? Many schools, colleges, and universities post their employment listings in the human resources department or in employee newsletters. What if you don't have a job there already and are interested in finding out about internal postings? This is where networking comes into play. A contact at the school can keep you informed.

If you're still in college or you graduated from a school that had programs in the area in which you are interested, check with the college

★ **Words from the Wise**

If you are going to use an employment agency to help you find a job, remember to check *before* you sign any contracts to see who pays the fee—you or the company. There is nothing wrong with paying a fee. You simply want to be aware ahead of time of what the fee will be.

placement office. In some cases, companies, schools, and universities searching to fill specific positions may go to colleges and universities where they know there are specific programs.

Employment Agencies, Recruiters, and Headhunters

Let's take a few minutes to discuss employment agencies, recruiters, and headhunters. What are they? What's the difference? Should you use them?

Employment agencies may fall into a number of different categories. They may be temp agencies, personnel agencies, or a combination of the two. Temp agencies work with companies to provide employees for short-term or fill-in work. These agencies generally specialize in a number of career areas. Some agencies even provide workers for longer term projects.

How do they work? Basically, a company tells an agency what types of positions they are looking to fill and the temp agency recruits workers they feel are qualified for those positions. The business then pays the agency and the agency pays the employee.

When you work in this capacity, you are not working for the company, school, or university. You are an employee of the temp agency. Generally, in this type of situation, you do not pay a fee to be placed.

Personnel agencies, on the other hand, work in a different manner. These agencies try to match people who are looking for a job with companies that have openings. When you go to a personnel agency they will interview you, talk about your qualifications, and if the interviewer feels you are suitable, will send you to speak to companies that have openings for which you are qualified. You may then meet with a human resources director or someone else in the human resources department of the company with the opening. You may or may not get the job. There are no guarantees using a personnel agency.

If you do get the job, you will generally have to pay a portion of your first year's salary to the personnel agency that helped you get the job. In some cases, the employer will split the fee with you. Check ahead of time so you will have no surprises.

You should not be required to pay anything up front. You may be asked to sign a contract. Before you sign anything, read it thoroughly and understand everything. If you don't understand what something means, ask.

Recruiters, headhunters, and executive search firms are all similar. These firms generally have contracts with employers who are looking for employees with specific skills, talents, and experience. It is their job to find people to fill those positions.

The difference between recruiters, headhunters, and executive search firms and the employment or personnel agencies we discussed

★ **The Inside Scoop**

Employment agencies in most states are required to be registered with the department of labor and licensed. Check out employment agencies *before* you get involved.

previously is that you (as the job seeker) are not responsible for paying a fee, instead, the fee will be paid by the employer.

How do these companies find you? There are a number of ways. Sometimes they read a story in the paper about you or see a press release about an award you received. Sometimes someone they know recommends you.

In some cases they just cold call people who have jobs like those they are trying to fill and ask if they know anyone who might be looking for a similar job they might recommend. You might recommend someone, or you might even say you are interested yourself.

What if no one calls you? Are you out of luck? Not at all. It's perfectly acceptable to call recruiters and headhunters yourself.

What you need to do is find the firms that specialize in the industry you are looking for. So, for example, if you are a superintendent looking for a job in that field, you would look for executive recruiters that specialize in the administrative area of the education.

How do you find them? There are over 5,000 executive recruiting agencies in the United States. You can search out firms on the Internet or look in the Yellow Pages of phone books from large, metropolitan areas.

You might also check out trade magazines and periodicals. Many have advertisements for recruiters in their specific career area.

Why do companies look to recruiters to find their employees? Generally, it's easier. They have someone screening potential employees, looking for just the right one. As recruiters don't generally get paid unless they find the right employee, they have the perfect incentive.

Should you get involved with a recruiter? As recruiters bring job possibilities to you, there really isn't a downside. As a matter of fact, even if you have a job that you love, it's a good idea to keep a relationship with headhunters and recruiters. You can never tell when your next great job is around the corner.

Here are a few things that can help when you are working with a recruiter.

- Tailor your resume or CV to the specific sector of the industry in which the recruiter works. You want your qualifications to jump off the page.
- Make sure you tell your recruiter about any companies to which you do not want your resume sent. For example, you don't want your resume sent to your current employer, or you might not want your resume sent to a company where you just interviewed.
- Call the recruiter on a regular basis.

The Hidden Job Market

While we just discussed that a good number of jobs in education *are* advertised just by virtue of the manner in which schools, colleges, and universities work, lets talk a bit about the hidden job market. Many people think that their job search begins and ends with the classified ads. If they get the Sunday paper and their dream job isn't in there, they give up and wait until the next Sunday. I am betting that once you have made the decision to have a career in education, you're not going to let something small like not finding a job opening listed in the classifieds stop you. So what are you going to do?

While there may be job openings in which you are interested advertised in the classifieds, it's essential to realize that many jobs are not advertised at all. Why? In addition to not wanting to be bombarded and inundated by tons of resumes and phone calls, for example, some employers may not want someone in another school or company to know that they are looking for a new marketing director or a new publicity director until they hire one. As a matter of fact, they may not want the person who currently holds the job to know that he or she is about to be let go. Whatever the reason, once you're aware that all jobs aren't advertised you can go about finding them in a different manner.

Why do you want to find jobs in the hidden job market? The main reason is because you will have a better shot at getting the job. Why? To begin with, there is a lot less competition. Because positions aren't being actively advertised, there aren't hundreds of people sending in their resume trying to get the jobs. Not everyone knows how to find the hidden job market, nor do they want to take the extra time to find it, so you also have an edge over other potential job applicants. Many applicants in the hidden job market also often come recommended by someone who knew about the opening. This means that you are starting off with one foot in the door.

While there are entry-level jobs to be found in the hidden job market, there are also a good number of high-level jobs. This can be valuable when you're trying to move up the career ladder.

How does the hidden job market work? Basically, when a company needs to fill a position, instead of placing an ad, they quietly look for the perfect candidate. How do they find the candidates without advertising? Let's look at some ways this is accomplished and how you can take advantage of each situation.

◎ Employees may be promoted from within the company.

□ That is why it is so important once you get your foot in the door and get a job to keep yourself visible in a positive manner. You want supervisors to think about you when an opening occurs. For example, if you're working in the publicity department of a college and your goal is a career in marketing, drop subtle hints during conversations with supervisors in your department and the marketing department. You might, for example, say something like, "I love working in publicity. Learning how to properly publicize the school, events, and programs was one of my goals when I decided to work at the school. I also always wanted to learn about marketing." You're not saying you don't like your job. You're not saying you want to leave your job. What you're doing is planting a seed. If you have been doing an amazing job in your current position and anything opens up in marketing, you just might be suggested.

◎ An employee working in the company may recommend a candidate for the position.

□ This is another time that networking helps. Don't keep your dreams to yourself. Tell others what type of job you're looking for and what your qualifications are. You can never tell when a position might become available. Employers often ask their staff if they know anyone who would be good for this job. If you shared your qualifications and dreams, someone just might recommend you.

◎ Someone who knows about an opening may tell friends, relatives, or coworkers who then apply for the job.

□ In some cases, it's not another employee who knows about an opening, but it might be someone who has contact with the company. For example, a school psychologist at one school, might be at a conference and hear that another facility is looking for a new chief financial officer. He or she might tell a brother's neighbor to call up and apply for the job. He or she might also mention it to a colleague who mentions it to someone else.

◎ Sometimes it may be someone outside the company who hears about the job. The UPS delivery person for example, may be delivering packages to a school office when he or she overhears a conversation about the administrative assistant leaving. If you had networked with the UPS delivery person and mentioned you were looking for a job, he or she might stop by and tell you about the opportunity. Then, all you would have to do is contact the school.

◎ People may have filled in applications or sent resumes and cover letters to the company asking that they be kept on file. When an opening exists, the human resources department might review the resumes and call one of the applicants.

  ▫ Even if there are no jobs advertised, it is often worth your while to send a letter and your resume to the human resources department asking about openings. Be sure to ask that your resume be kept on file.

◎ Suitable candidates may place cold calls at just the right time.

  ▫ Difficult as it can be to place cold calls, it might pay off. Consider committing yourself to making a couple of cold calls every day. Do some research. Then, depending on

---

The Inside Scoop

When making a cold call, try to get the name of the person you're trying to reach ahead of time so you can ask for someone by name. How? Just call up and ask the receptionist.

---

the area of education in which you are interested in working, call the director of human resources in an attempt to set up an interview. Who can you call? Depending on what type of job you are looking for, you might call public or private schools, colleges, or universities. You might call trade associations involved in various aspects of education. How about companies selling textbooks? What about companies selling equipment to schools? What about education-oriented Web sites? The beauty of a cold call is that it can be made to anyone.

◎ People may have networked and caught the eye of those who need to fill the jobs.

  ▫ Finding positions in the hidden job market is a skill in itself. One of the best ways to do this is by networking. Through networking you can make contacts and your contacts are the people who will know about the jobs in the hidden market.

Networking in Education

Often, it's not just what you know, but who you know. Contacts are key in every industry and education is no exception. Networking is therefore going to be an important part of succeeding. It is so important that in some situations it can often make you or break you.

"How so?" you ask.

If you don't have a chance to showcase your skills and your talents to the right people, it's difficult to get the jobs you want, the promotions you want, and the career of your dreams.

Networking is important in every area of education, no matter what segment you aspire to work in. The fact of the matter is, without the power of networking it is often difficult to get your foot in the door. That doesn't mean you *can't* get your foot in the door, it just is harder.

Earlier chapters have touched on networking and because of its importance to your career success, we will continue discussing it throughout the book. What is essential to understand is that networking isn't just something you do at the beginning of your career. It's something you're going to have to continue doing for as long as you work.

How do you network? Basically, you put yourself into situations where you can meet people and introduce yourself. Later in the book we discuss more about networking basics and offer some networking exercises that you'll find useful. Basically, however, what you should be doing at this point is learning to get comfortable walking up to people, extending your hand, and introducing yourself.

Voice of Experience

You never want to be in the position where someone remembers that they met you and remembers that you would be perfect for a job, yet they have no idea how to get hold of you. Don't be stingy with your business cards. Give them out freely.

Tip from the Top

When networking at an event, don't just zero in on the people you think are the *important* industry insiders and ignore the rest. Try to meet as many people as you can. Always be pleasant and polite to everyone. You never can tell who knows who and who might be a great contact later.

"Hi, I'm Ron Lemon. Isn't this an interesting event? What a great opportunity this was to learn more about innovative teaching methods," you might say at a seminar.

The person you meet will then tell you his or her name and perhaps something about him or herself. You can then keep talking or say, "It was nice meeting you. Do you have a card?"

Make sure you have your business cards handy and when you are given a card, give yours as well.

Every situation can ultimately be an opportunity to network, but some are more effective than others. Look for seminars, workshops, and classes that professionals in the area of the education in which you are interested potentially might attend.

Why would an industry professional be at a workshop or seminar? There are many reasons. They might want to network just like you do, they might want to learn something new, or they might be teaching or facilitating the workshop.

Where else can you meet and network with professionals in education? What about at their place of work? Schools, colleges, universities, tutoring centers, education-oriented trade associations; the list goes on.

"But I can't just walk in someone's office I don't know and introduce myself," you say.

You're right. That probably won't work. You probably wouldn't walk unannounced into the office of a school superintendent and say, "Hi." You probably wouldn't walk into the office of the executive director of an education-oriented trade association, a college president, or a college dean. So what can you do?

If you don't know someone in the type of company you want to work, you're going to have to get creative in your networking. How can you network with employees of those companies? Here's a strategy you might want to try.

Find one or two organizations, companies, colleges, or facilities in which you might be interested in working and locate the physical address.

Choose a day when you have some time to spare. Generally, it needs to be on a weekday because those are the days most business takes place. Get dressed in appropriate clothing, and go to the location of the company, college, or facility you've chosen. Now stand outside the building and look around. Are there restaurants, coffee shops, diners, or bars nearby? There probably are. If it's a college or university, is there a cafeteria or lunchroom? Is it open to the public? Why does all this matter?

Because people working in these offices, the college or university, or whatever, have to eat lunch somewhere and get their coffee somewhere. After work on Friday they might want to stop into the bar on the corner for happy hour.

What does that mean to you? If you can determine where the company employees hang out, you can put yourself in situations in which to network with them.

Can you find out which restaurants, diners, and coffee shops the employees frequent? You often can, if you stand outside around lunchtime and watch to see who goes where.

Some office buildings have thousands of employees in different businesses. How do you know which are the employees from the company you have targeted? You might have to eavesdrop a little and listen for clues in things people say as they walk out the door. You might stop in the building and ask someone. Get on the elevator and ask the elevator operator. Ask the security guard standing in the lobby. You might even stop into a couple of the coffee shops, diners, or restaurants and ask the host or hostess.

"Hi, I was supposed to have a lunch meeting with someone from Union College and I'm embarrassed to say, I'm not sure which coffee shop the meeting was set for," you might say. "Do a lot of the employees from the college come in here?"

At this point, the hostess will either give you a blank look that means you probably are in the wrong place (or she really doesn't know) or tell you that you are indeed in the right location. She might even say, "Yes, we just did a takeout order for them a few minutes ago," or something to that effect.

Once you've found the correct location, wait until it's nice and busy and there is a slight line. People will usually talk to other people even if they don't know them when they are standing in lines. Start up conversations and hope that you're standing near the people from the organization you're looking for. What about sitting at the counter (if there is one)? It you get lucky, you might end up sitting next to someone from the organization you are targeting.

This whole process is often a lot easier if you are trying to network with people who work at a college or university and there is a cafeteria or lunchroom, because the odds are you will be running into people who work in the facility.

The tricky part in this entire procedure is being able to network in this type of situation. Some people are really good at it and some people find it very difficult. What you're dealing with when doing this is first finding the correct people and then starting a conversation that may let you turn the person into a networking contact. If you do it right, it can pay off big time. You might meet someone, for example, who works in the administrative office and strike up a conversation.

You never can tell what may happen from there. You might mention you were thinking about filling in an application because you were looking for a job at the university in the IT department. Your new contact might say, "I don't think there are any positions in that department, but the webmaster just put in her letter of resignation." You might get a referral, set up an interview, or even end up with a job.

Does this technique always work? Sometimes it does and sometimes it doesn't. The important thing to know is that it might help you get your foot in the door where you otherwise might not have.

If you find networking in this manner difficult, it might be easier for you to do at a bar during a "happy hour" because people tend to talk more in these situations. Remember, though, that while it's okay to drink socially, your main goal is to network and make contacts. You won't do yourself any favors becoming intoxicated and then acting outrageously or saying something inappropriate.

Where else might people who work in education congregate? What about joining the PTA at a local school and volunteering to work on some events? What about volunteering to help with one of their fund-raisers? Even if the school staff doesn't get involved in the actual planning or execution of events, they generally attend them.

What about finding out if any of the colleges or universities in the area are having galas, cultural activities, or other types of fund-raising events? They often need volunteers to help with these events as well.

It is more effective to your career to meet the executive director of an educational trade association or the president or the human resources director of a college when you're being introduced as a volunteer who helped pull an event together than knocking on his or her door and saying, "Hi, do you have a minute?"

How else can you get to the right people? Sometimes all it takes is making a phone call. Consider calling a trade association, for example, asking to speak to the communications director and telling him or her about your career aspirations. Ask if he or she would be willing to give you the names of a couple of industry people that you might call. Contact a college public relations director and ask who you might talk to if you were interested in a career as a college activities director. Contact an education reporter and ask if he or she can give you insight into career opportunities. You just might be surprised.

The Inside Scoop

It's great to network with those at the top, but a good and often more practical strategy is to try networking with their assistants and support team. The people at the top might not always remember you; those a step or two down the line usually will. Additionally, a recommendation from these people about you to their boss can do wonders for your career.

"Why would anyone want to help me?" you ask.

Most people like to help others. It makes them feel good. Don't expect everyone to be courteous or to go out of their way for you, but if you find one or two helpful people, you may wind up with some useful contacts.

To get you started thinking, here's a sample script of how such a conversation might go.

Education Trade Association Executive Director: Hello, this is Kyra Robertson.

You: Hi, this is Tony Johnson. I'm not sure if you're the right person to speak to about this, but would it be okay if I tell you what I'm looking for so you can point me in the right direction?

Education Trade Association Executive Director: Sure, go ahead.

You: Thanks. First of all, I'm not selling anything. I'm getting my bachelor's degree in communications in May. My goal is to have a career in some aspect of education. I don't want to be a teacher, but I want to work in a school, and I want to make a difference. I don't really know any of the *right* people to bounce this off of. I was wondering if you might have some ideas about who I could talk to or how I can meet with some people within the industry. I know there are opportunities. I just don't really know where they are. I was hoping you would be able to give me some suggestions.

Education Trade Association Executive Director: I wish I could help, but I'm not sure who I could suggest. Sorry.

You: Well, at this point, I'm just trying to get my foot in the door. Do you have any suggestions of people who might be able to give me a couple of names?

Education Trade Association Executive Director: You probably could contact anyone in membership. I'm not sure who specifically could help you though.

You: I would appreciate any help. Would it be a big imposition for me to come in one day when you're not too busy to just meet with you for a couple of minutes, just to get a couple of ideas? I would appreciate any help. I promise I won't take a lot of your time.

Education Trade Association Executive Director: I'm pretty busy for the next few weeks and I'm not sure how I could really help. We have our annual conference at the end of the month. I'm sorry. I'm really swamped. My assistant is on maternity leave and our conference coordinator was just in an accident so things are really piling up.

You: Well, thanks for your time. Can I leave my number?

Education Trade Association Executive Director: Not a problem. Did you say you were getting your degree in communications?

You: Yes, I'll have a degree in communications. I also have taken a number of educational administration courses. I just went to a really interesting seminar on community relations in education.

Education Trade Association Executive Director: I don't know if you would be interested, but I could get you a pass to our conference. In addition to the seminars, we have a number of networking sessions. Are you interested?

You: Thanks. That would be great.

Education Trade Association Executive Director: Why don't you fax your information over and I'll make sure you get a conference pack. The number is 111-222-3333. Be sure to stop by at the conference and introduce yourself.

You: Thank you. That's great. I look forward to meeting you.

See how easy it is? You just have to ask.

"But what if someone says no?" you ask. "What if they won't help?"

Well that might happen. The conversation may not go in the direction you want it to. Some people will say, "No." So what? If you don't ask, you'll never know.

"But what do I say if someone says no?"

Simply thank them nicely for their time and hang up. Don't belabor the point. Just say, "Thanks anyway. I appreciate your time."

It will be difficult the first couple of times you make a call like that, but as you begin to reach out to others it will get easier. Pretty soon, you won't even think about it.

Where else can you network? A lot of that depends on what segment of the industry you are trying to target. Look for opportunities.

"Bu how do I get through to the industry professionals?" you ask.

You're going to have to be creative. For example, let's say you read a press release in the paper about an upcoming event to benefit a school, college, university, or other educational institution or organization. What do you do? First, make sure you go.

"I can't afford to go to a big fund-raiser," you say.

Get creative. Volunteer to be a host or hostess. Offer to help serve. See if you can cover the event for the newspaper. Think outside of the box.

Events don't always have to be just oriented to education to be good networking opportunities. For example, you might want to go to join Kiwanis or Rotary and go to their meetings. You might want to join the chamber of commerce and go to their events. Why? Industry professionals attend these events. It's a good place to meet people on a more even playing field.

Remember that these are business function. Behave professionally and make sure to watch for any opportunities to network, which is the main reason that you're there. Here are some tips on what to do and what not to do:

◎ Do not bring anyone with you. Go alone. It will give you more opportunities to meet people.

◎ Do not smoke, even if other people are. You can never tell what makes someone remember you. You don't want it to be that you smell of tobacco.

◎ Don't wear strong perfume, cologne, or aftershave. Aside from the possibility of some people being allergic to it, you don't want this to be the reason people remember you.

◎ Do not use any illegal drugs, even if other people are.

Here are some things you *should do.*

◎ Do bring business cards to give out to everyone.

◎ Do bring a pen and small pad to take down the names and phone numbers of people who don't have cards.

> ### ★ Tip from the Coach
> Remember that networking is a two-way street. If you want people to help you, it's important to reciprocate. When you see something you can do for someone else's career, don't wait for them to ask for help. Step in, do it, and do it graciously.

◎ Do meet as many people as possible. If given the opportunity, briefly tell them what your goal is and ask if they have any suggestion about who you can contact.

Follow up on the contacts and information you gather at these meetings. Don't neglect this step or you will have wasted the opportunity. Call, write, or e-mail contacts you have made in a timely fashion. You want them to remember meeting you.

The Right Place at the Right Time

Have you ever looked down while you were walking and seen some money sitting on the ground? It could have been there for a while, but no one else happened to look down at that time. You just happened to be at the right place at the right time.

It can happen anytime. Sometimes you hear about an interesting job opening from an unlikely source. You might, for example, be standing in a long line at the bakery. The woman in back of you asks if you would mind very much if she went ahead of you because she is rushing out of town to visit her daughter. It seems she needs to pick up the bakery's famous chocolate cake because it is her daughter's favorite and she misses it since moving away to take a job as the headmistress at a prestigious private school.

You of course agree to let her get ahead of you. While standing in line chatting you mention that you just graduated from college in May and have a teaching degree.

"I don't suppose your daughter needs a history teacher at her school," you say, half kidding, to the woman. "I've been sending out resumes, but haven't found a job yet. I loved student teaching. My supervisor was my old history teacher, Mr. Maples."

"My daughter had Mr. Maples too," the woman says. "He was her favorite teacher."

"Here, take my card," you say, pulling one out of your pocket. "I enjoyed chatting with you. Have a good trip."

Tuesday morning your phone rings. It's the woman's daughter. Coincidentally she did need a history teacher at her school. She called your student teacher supervisor who said you were great! She wants you to come up for an interview, ASAP.

You go, and guess what? You got the job!

Think it can't happen? It can and it does. It's just a matter of being at the right place at the right time.

There is no question that being in the right place at the right time can help. The question is, however, what is the right place and the right time and how do you recognize it?

The simple answer is it's almost impossible to know what the right place and right time is. You can, however, stack the deck in your favor. How? While you never know what the right place or the right time to be someplace is, you can put yourself in situations where you can network. Networking with people outside of the industry can be just as effective and just as important as networking with industry professionals.

The larger your network, the more opportunities you will have to find the job you want. The more people who know what you have to offer and what you want to do the better. Who do you deal with every day? Who do these people know and deal with? Do any of these people in your network and your extended network know about your dream career in education?

If you are unemployed and don't have to worry about a current boss or supervisor hearing about your job aspirations then spread the news about your job search. Don't keep it a secret. The more people who know what you're looking for in a career, the more people who potentially can let you know when and where there is a job possibility.

If I haven't stressed it enough, if at all possible do not keep your career aspirations to yourself. Share them with the world.

Cold Calls

What exactly is a cold call? In relation to your career, a cold call is an unsolicited contact in person, by phone, letter, or e-mail with someone you don't know in hopes of obtaining some information, an interview, or a job. It is a proactive strategy.

Let's focus on the cold calls you make by phone. They are much like the call we just discussed with the education trade association executive director.

Many find this form of contact too intimidating to try. Why? Because not only are you calling and trying to sell yourself to someone who may be busy and doesn't want to be bothered, but you are also afraid of rejection. None of us like rejection. We fear that we will get on the phone, try to talk to someone, and they will not take our call, hang up on us, or say no to our requests.

The majority of telemarketing calls made to homes every day are cold calls. In those cases the people on the other end of the phone aren't trying to get a job or an interview. Instead, they are attempting to sell something such as a product or a service. When you get those calls, the first thing on your mind is usually how to get off the phone. The last thing you want to do is buy anything from someone on the other end. But the fact of the matter is, people do buy things from telemarketers if they want what they're selling.

With that in mind, your job in making cold calls is to make your call compelling enough that the person on the other end responds positively. Why would you even bother making a cold call to someone? It's simply another job search strategy and it's one that not everyone attempts, which gives you an edge over others.

How do you make a cold call? It's really quite simple. If you wanted to make a cold call to a potential employer, you just identify who you want to call, put together a script to make it easier for you, and then make your call. Keep track of the calls you make. You may think you'll remember who said what and who you didn't reach, but after a couple of calls it gets confusing. Check out the Cold Call Tracking Worksheet sample below for the type of information you should record. Then use the Cold Call Tracking Worksheet provided.

⭐ **Voice of Experience**

You will find it easier to make cold calls if you not only create a script, but practice it as well. In order to be successful in cold calling you need to sound professional, friendly, and confident.

Cold Call Tracking Worksheet

Company	Phone Number	Name of Contact	Date Called	Follow-up Activities	Results
Tri County BOCES	111-222-2222	Jane Aubrey	5/6	Send resume.	Asked for resume, will get back to me after reviewing my qualifications.
Any Town School District	111-111-1111	Brian Tuttle	5/9	Send resume.	Will keep resume on file, no current opening. Call back in a few months.
Genesee Private Academy	111-222-3333	John Michaels	5/9	E-mailed resume.	Will review resume and get back to me.
Some City School District	111-999-0000	Tyler Taylor	5/11	Call back in two weeks.	

Who do you call? That depends on who you're trying to reach. You might call private schools, public schools, colleges, universities, vocational or technical schools, headhunters, trade associations, educational equipment companies, or educational publishing companies. Every call you make is a potential opportunity that can pan out for you.

Here's an example.

You: Hi, Ms. Anderson. This is Burt Johnson. I'm not sure you're the right person to speak to, but I was hoping I could tell you what I was looking for and perhaps you could point me in the right direction. Are you in the middle of something now, or would it be better if I call back later?

Ms. Anderson: What can I do for you?

You: I was wondering if you knew of any opportunities doing corporate media training for executives.

Ms. Anderson: What do you want to do?

You: I'm interested in doing corporate media training. You know, preparing executives for media interviews, giving speeches, helping them know what to say and what not to say during a corporate crisis, things like that.

Ms. Anderson: We don't have any positions like that here.

You: I understand. I'm trying to get some leads on where to call. Do you have any suggestions? I have my bachelor's degree in communications and broadcast journalism and I'm working on getting my master's. I interned at WYOO in the news department and worked for the *Larry Smith Show* for six months, preparing guests.

Ms. Anderson: You worked at the *Larry Smith Show*? I wish they hadn't cancelled that. I loved it.

You: I wish they hadn't cancelled it too. It was a really fun job.

Ms. Anderson: You know, you might want to speak to our public relations di-rector. She is the president of one of the industry trade associations. She might be able to give you some leads on names.

You: That would be great.

Ms. Anderson: Her name is Donna Trip-per. You can reach her at extension 3084. Tell her I suggested you call her. As a mat-ter of fact, let me transfer you right now.

You: Thanks for your help. I appreciate it.

As you can see, it's not all that difficult once you get someone on the phone.

"But what if they say no?" you ask.

Cold Call Tracking Worksheet

Company	Phone Number	Name of Contact	Date Called	Follow-up Activities	Results

So they say no. Don't take it personally. Just go on to your next call and use your previous call as practice.

Where do you find people to call? Browse company Web sites for names. Read trade journals. Read the newspaper. Look for magazine articles and feature stories. Watch television and listen to the radio. Go through the Yellow Pages. You can get names from almost anyplace. Call up. Take a chance. It may pay off.

Depending on where you're calling and the size of the company, in many cases when you start your conversation during a cold call, the person you're speaking to will direct you to the human resources (HR) department. If this is the case, ask who you should speak to in HR. Try to get a name. Then, thank the person who gave you the information and call the HR department, asking for the name of the person you were given. Being referred by someone else in the company will often get you through. Try something like this:

> **You:** Good afternoon, would Donna Tripper be in?
>
> **Secretary:** Who's calling?
>
> **You:** Burt Johnson. Ms. Anderson suggested I call.

Believe it or not, the more calls you make, the more you will increase your chances of success in getting potential interviews.

If you're really uncomfortable making the calls, or you can't get through to the people you're trying to reach by phone, consider writing letters. It takes more time than a phone call, but it is another proactive method for you to potentially get through to someone.

Creating Your Own Career

Do you want one more really good reason to find the hidden job market? If you're creative and savvy enough, you might even be able to *create* a position for yourself even if you are only on the first or second rung of the career ladder. What does that mean? Here an example.

Let's go back to Burt Johnson. The company he called didn't have a corporate trainer position. If he *sells* the idea, he might just be able to *create* a position for himself doing what he wants to do.

Need another example? Let's say you're working as a secretary in the counseling department of a college. You notice that a large number of first year students come in around their birthday, depressed that they are not with their family on their special day. You get an idea. Wouldn't it be great to have a party-in-a-box care package complete with a birthday cake, candles, a card, and a CD from home recorded via phone with the student's family singing happy birthday? It could be marketed to student's families via e-mail and direct mail. You work out the project details and, excitedly share your idea with your supervisor. He thinks it's a great idea, too, and brings it to his supervisor. Before you know it, the bookstore, food service, and a number of other departments are involved. While there was no position planned, people see value in your idea and in you. They ask you if you would be interested in becoming the coordinator of the project. Voila! You've created your own position and you've moved up the ladder.

"What if I don't yet have a job. Is it still possible to create a position?"

If you are creative, have some initiative, and are aggressive enough to push your idea you can. What you have to do is come up with something that you could do for a company, school, or college that you want to work for. It should be something that isn't being done now or that you could do better.

Do you have any ideas? Put fear aside and think outside of the box. Get creative. Come up with an idea, develop it fully, put it on paper so you can see any problems, and fine-tune it. Then, call up the company that you want to work with, lay out the idea, and sell them on it. You've just created your own job!

6

TOOLS FOR SUCCESS

The right tools can make it easier to do almost any job. Imagine, for example, trying to paint your house without the right brushes, quality paint, and a good ladder. It could happen, but it would probably be more difficult to do a really good job. Imagine trying to bake a cake without measuring spoons, measuring cups, pans, and a good working oven. You might be able to do it, but your chances of success are diminished.

Obtaining jobs and creating a wonderful career is a project in itself. Tools can make it easier. Every trade has its own set of tools that help the tradesman (or woman) achieve success. Without these tools, their job would be more difficult, if not impossible, to accomplish.

Whatever area of education you are pursuing, there are certain tools that can help you achieve success faster. These may include things like your resume, CV (curriculum vitae), business and networking cards, brochures, career portfolio, and professional reference sheets, among others. This chapter will help get you started putting together these tools.

Your Resume as a Selling Tool

Whether utilizing publicity, ads in newspapers or magazines, television or radio commercials, billboards, banners on the Web or a variety of additional marketing vehicles, there is virtually no successful company that does not advertise or market their products or services in some manner.

Why do they do this? The main reasons is to make sure others are aware of their product or service so they can then find ways to entice potential customers to buy or use that product or service.

What does this have to do with you and your career? When trying to succeed in any career, it is a good idea to look at yourself as a *product*.

What that means in a broad sense is that you will be marketing yourself so people know you exist, so they begin to differentiate you from others, and so they see you in a better light.

How can you entice potential employers to hire you? How can you help people in the industry to know you exist?

The answer is simple. Start by making your resume a selling tool! Make it your own personal

---

Tip from the Coach

Your resume will be useful at every level of your career. It is not a do-it-once, get-a-job, and never-need-it-again document.

---

printed marketing piece. Everyone sends out resumes. The trick is making yours so powerful, that it will grab the attention of potential employers.

Resumes are important no matter what area of the education field you are pursuing. Does your resume do a great job of selling your credentials? Does it showcase your skills, personality traits, and special talents? Is your resume the one that is going to impress the employers or human resources directors who can call you in for that all important interview and ultimately land you the job you are after? Is it going to land you the job you've been dreaming about?

If an employer doesn't know you, their first impression of you might very well be your resume. This makes your resume a crucial part of getting an interview that might ultimately lead to your dream job.

A strong resume illustrates that you have the experience and qualifications to fill a potential employer's needs. How can you do this? To begin with, learn to tailor your resume to the job you're pursuing. One of the biggest mistakes people make in job hunting is to create just one resume and then use it every single time they apply for a position no matter what the job.

If this is what you've been doing, it's time to break the habit. Begin by crafting your main resume. Then edit it to fit the needs of each specific job opening or opportunity for which you are applying.

⭐ Tip from the Top

When replying to a job advertisement, use words from the advertisement in both your resume and your cover letter. It makes you look like more of a *fit* with the company's expectations.

⭐ Words from the Wise

If you're using different versions of resumes, make sure you know which one you send to which company. Keep a copy of the resume you use for a specific job with a copy of the cover letter you send. Do it *every* time. Otherwise when sending out numerous resumes and letters it's very easy to get confused.

"But," you say, "I want to work as a teacher. Can't I use the same resume for every teaching job?"

Here's the answer in a nutshell. You can use the same resume only *if* you are going for the exact same type of job. For example, you might use the same resume if you are applying for two jobs teaching high school in similar types of schools.

However, if you are applying for one job as a high school English teacher in a small private school and another job teaching English in a large, public, city school you might want to tailor your resume to each job a bit, highlighting any skills and experiences which would be relevant to each position.

Similarly, if you are applying for one job as the director of marketing for a community college and another job as director of marketing for a public school system you would probably want to tailor each resume for each specific position.

Before computers became commonplace, preparing a different resume for every job was far more difficult. In many cases, people would prepare one resume and have it professionally printed by a resume service or printer. That was it. If you wanted to change your resume, you had to go back to the printer and have it done again, incurring a major expense.

Today, however, most of us have access to computers, making it far easier to change resumes at will. Do you want to change your career objective? What about the order of the components on your resume? Do you want to add something? Do you want to delete something? You are in control. You can create the perfect resume every time with the click of a mouse.

Always keep a copy of your resume on your computer and make sure you note the date it was done and its main focus. For example, you might save your resumes as kindergarten teacher resume, reading specialist resume, third grade teacher resume, private school teacher resume and so on. If you don't have your own computer, keep your resume on a CD or a flash drive so you always have access to it without having to type it all over again.

How can you make your resume a better marketing tool? Present it in a clear, concise manner, highlighting your best assets. Organize things in an order that makes it easy for someone just glancing at your resume to see the points that sell you the best and makes them want to take a second look.

The decision about the sequence of items in your resume should be based on what is most impressive in relation to the position you are pursuing. Do you have a lot of work experience? Put that information first. Are your accomplishments extraordinary? If so, highlight those first. Do you have little experience, but you just graduated cum laude with a degree in education or education administration? Then perhaps your education should be where your resume should start.

Sometimes it helps when creating your resume to imagine that you just received it in the mail yourself. What would make you glance at it and say "Wow"? Would you continue reading or would you glance at it and hope that there was a more interesting resume coming in?

One of the most important things to remember is that there really is no *right* or *wrong* type of resume. The right one for you will end up being the one that ultimately gets you the position you want. There are so many ways to prepare your resume that it is often difficult to choose one. My advice is to craft a couple different ones, put them away overnight and then look at them the next day. Which one looks better to you? That probably will be the style you want to use.

Here are some tips that might help:

◎ Tailor each resume for every position.
◎ Make sure you check for incorrect word usage. No matter what position you're pursuing, most employers prefer to have someone who has a command of the English language. Check to make sure you haven't inadvertently used the word

★ Tip from the Top

Even if you have your own computer, keep updated copies of your resume on a CD or a flash drive. You can never tell when your computer hard drive will die just at the time someone tells you about a great opportunity or you see an advertisement for the perfect job. If your resume is on a CD or other media, you simply need to just put it in another computer, tailor your resume for that particular job, and send it off. You can also toss a CD or a USB flash drive in your briefcase or bag to keep with you if you are away from home and want to add something to your resume quickly. Adding a handwritten line when you change your phone number or address or even whiting out the wrong information just is not acceptable.

their for *there*, *to* for *too* or *two*, *effect* for *affect*, *you're* for *your*, *it's* for *its*, and so on.

◎ Don't rely solely on your computer's spelling and grammar checker. Carefully go over your work yourself as well.

◎ Every time you edit your resume or make a change, check carefully for errors. It is very easy to miss a double word, a misspelled word, or a wrong tense. Have a friend or family member look over your resume. It is often difficult to see mistakes in your own work.

◎ Tempting as it is to use different colored inks when preparing your resume, don't. Use only black ink.

◎ Use a good quality paper at least 40-pound weight for printing your resumes. Paper with texture often *feels* different, so it stands out. While you can use white, beige, or cream colored papers, soft light colors such as light blue, salmon pink, gray, or light green will help your resume standout from the hundreds of white and beige ones.

◎ Make sure your resume layout looks attractive. You can have the greatest content in the world, but if your resume just doesn't look right, people may not actually read it.

◎ You know the saying, "You can't judge a book by its cover"? Well, you really can't, but if you don't know anything about the book or its contents you just might not pick it up *unless* the cover looks interesting.

◎ When sending your resume and cover letter, instead of using a standard number-10 business envelope and

---

⭐ **Words from the Wise**
No matter what color paper you use for your resume and cover letters, make sure they photocopy well. Some colored papers photocopy dark or look messy. Even if you aren't photocopying your resume, a potential employer might.

---

folding your resume, use a large manila envelope. That way you won't have to fold your resume and your information will get there looking clean, crisp, and flat.

◎ Don't use odd fonts or typefaces. Why? In many large companies, resumes are scanned by machine. Certain fonts don't scan well. What should you use? Helvetica, Times, Arial, and Courier work well.

◎ Similarly, many fonts don't translate well when e-mailing. What looks great on the resume on your computer may end up looking like gibberish at the recipients end . . . and you probably will never know. Once again, use Helvetica, Times, Arial, or Courier.

◎ When preparing your resume, make your name larger and bolder than the rest of the text. For example, if your resume is done in 12-point type, use 14-, 16-, or 18-point type for your name. Your name will stand out from those on other resumes.

◎ Remember to use white space effectively. Margins should be at least one inch on each side as well as on the top and bottom of each page. White space also helps draw the reader's attention to information.

Redefining Your Resume

You probably already have a resume in some form. How has it been working? Is it getting you the interviews you want? If it is, great. If not, you might want to consider redefining it.

You want your resume to stand out. You want it to illustrate that you are successful in your past accomplishments. You want potential employers to look at your resume and say to themselves, "That's who I want working here!"

How do you do that? Make your resume compelling. Demonstrate through your resume that *you* believe in yourself because if *you* don't believe in *you,* no one else will. Show that you have the ability to solve problems and bring fresh ideas to the table.

First decide how you want to present yourself. What type of resume is best for you? There are a couple of basic types of resumes. The chronological resume lists your jobs and accomplishments, beginning with the most current and going backward. Functional resumes, which may also be referred to as skills-based resumes, emphasize your accomplishments and abilities. One of the good things about this type of resume is that it allows you to lay it out in a manner that spotlights your key areas, whether they are your qualifications, skills, or employment history.

What's the best type of resume for you? That depends on a number of factors including where and what level you are in your career. If you are just entering the job market and you haven't held down a lot of jobs, but you have relevant experience through internships and/or volunteer activities, you might use the functional type of resume. If, on the other hand, you have held a number of jobs in the field and climbed the ladder with each new job, you might want to use the chronological type of resume. You can also sometimes combine

> ## Voice of Experience
> Your resume is your place to toot your own horn. If you don't, no one will know what you have accomplished.

elements from both types. This is called a combination resume. As I noted earlier, there is no one right way. You have to look at the whole picture and make a decision.

Use common sense. Make sure your best assets are prominent on your resume. Do you have a lot of experience? Are your accomplishments above the bar? Did you graduate cum laude? Do you have a master's degree? Do you have a Ph.D.? Determine what would grab a potential employer's eye and find a way to focus first on that.

What Should Your Resume Contain?

What should you include in your resume? Some components are required and some are optional. Let's look at some of them.

What do you definitely need? You absolutely need your name, address, phone number, and e-mail address if you have one. You also should have your education and any training as well as your professional or work experience. You want to include your work accomplishments and responsibilities so potential employers know what you have done and what you can bring to the table. What else? You should include certifications, licenses, professional affiliations and memberships, honors, awards, and any additional professional accomplishments.

What else might you want to put in your resume? You may want to include your career objective, a summary of skills, and a career summary.

> ### ⭐ Tip from the Top
> Many people sabotage themselves by giving more information than is required on their resume. When preparing your resume, always stop to think, "Will this help or hinder my career?"

What should you *not* put in your resume? Your age, marital status, any health problems, current or past salaries, and whether or not you have children. What else should you not include? Any weakness you have or think you have.

Career Summary

Let's take a moment to discuss your career summary. While a career summary isn't a required component, it often is helpful when an employer gets huge numbers of resumes and gives each a short glance. A career summary is a short professional biography, no longer than 12 lines, which tells your professional story. You can do it in a number of ways. Here's an example:

> Seasoned elementary school educator with passion for developing and utilizing innovative teaching methods. Ability to teach, motivate and inspire students to go beyond their expectations. Proven accomplishments include raising classroom testing scores over 30 percent. Tri-County 2007 Teacher of the Year. Member of Some City School District Committee for Improving Curriculum. Multilingual. Excellent communication skills with ability to interact with students, parents, faculty, and administrators.

A potential employer looking at this might think, "This Carolyn Topper has increased classroom testing scores, was teacher of the year, and looks very motivated. The ability to speak more than one language is always a plus. Her cover letter states she is moving to the area to be closer to her family, so she might have ties to the community. Why don't I give her a chance to tell me more and bring her in for an interview?"

"What if I'm just out of college and have no experience?" you ask. "What would my career summary look like?"

In situations like this you have to look toward experience and jobs you held prior to graduating. How about this:

> Recent graduate of State University with major in elementary art education. (4.0 GPA.) Member of college campus activities board, assisting in the development of campus art programs. Chairperson of college's first annual arts and crafts show. Assisted in the development of after school art program during student teaching practicum. Ability to creatively motivate and inspire students to develop their artistic talents.

If you prefer, you can use a bulleted list to do your career summary.

- Recent graduate of State University with a major in elementary arts education. GPA of 4.0.
- Student teacher, Some Town Elementary School.
- Member of college campus activities board, assisting in the development of college art programs.
- Chairperson of college's first annual arts and crafts show with an estimated attendance of 4,500 people and over 100 artists and craftspeople.
- Assisted in the development and administration of after-school art program during student teaching practicum.

Career Objective

Do you need a career objective in your resume? It isn't always necessary, but in certain cases it helps. For example, if you are just starting out in your career, having a career objective or a specific goal illustrates that you have some direction; that you know where you want to go in your career.

When replying to an advertisement for a job opening, make sure your career objective on your resume is as close to the job you are applying for as possible. For example, if you are applying for a job as a high school music teacher you might make your career objective, "To work in a high school setting as a music teacher where I can fully utilize my skills to motivate and inspire students and cultivate an appreciation for music."

If, on the other hand, you are sending your resume to a school or company "cold" or not for a specific job opening, don't limit yourself unnecessarily by stating a specific career objective. If you use a career objective in this type of situation, make sure it is general.

In many instances, you might send copies of your resume with a cover letter to companies you want to work for that aren't actively looking to fill a job. Your hope is to garner an interview. If your resume indicates, for example, that your sole goal is to work as the public relations director for a collegiate sports department, you might be overlooked for a position in the marketing or public relations department of the entire college. Your career goal in this situation instead might be, "A career in a college or university setting which will utilize use my creativity and communication skills and my degree in marketing and public relations." Remember, you want the person reviewing your resume to think of all the possible places you might fit in the organization.

Education

Where should you put education on your resume? That depends. If you recently have graduated from college, put it toward the top. If you graduated a number of years ago, put your education toward the end of your resume. Do you need to put the year you graduated? Recent graduates might want to. Other than that, just indicate the college or university you graduated from, your major, and degree.

"What if I went to college, but didn't graduate? What should I put on my resume?" you might ask.

While most careers in education generally require at least a bachelor's degree if not a master's or Ph.D., on occasion, there may be some sort of position where, while a degree is preferred, it will not be required.

If you went to college, but didn't graduate, simply write that you attended or took coursework toward a degree. Will anyone question you on it? That's hard to say. Someone might. If questioned, simply say something like, "I attended college and then, unfortunately, found it necessary to go to work full time. I plan on getting my degree as soon as possible. I only have nine credits left to go, so it will be an easy goal to complete."

Similarly if a job requires a master's degree or Ph.D. and you haven't completed the educational requirements, simply put down that you are taking the coursework toward your degree.

In addition to your college education, don't forget to include any relevant noncredit courses, seminars, and workshops you have attended. While you probably wouldn't want to add in classes like flower arranging (unless this had to do with your job in someway), you might include educational courses that are not industry oriented, but might help you in your career, such as public speaking, writing, grant writing, communications, or team work.

Professional and Work Experience

List your work experience in this section of your resume. What jobs have you had? Where did you work? What did you do? What were your accomplishments?

How far back do you go? That once again depends where you are in your career. Don't go back to your job as a babysitter when you were 15, but you need to show your work history.

In addition to your full-time jobs in or out of education, include any part-time work that relates to the area of education you are pursuing, as well as any job that illustrates skills, accomplishments, or achievements.

Skills, Personality, and Traits

There's an old advertising adage that says something to the effect of, "Don't sell the steak, sell the sizzle." When selling yourself through your resume, do the same thing. Do not only state your skills and personality traits—make them sizzle! Do this by using descriptive language and key phrases.

Need some help? Here are a few words and phrases to get you started.

- ◎ Creative
- ◎ Dedicated
- ◎ Hard working
- ◎ Highly motivated
- ◎ Energetic
- ◎ Self-starter
- ◎ Fully knowledgeable
- ◎ Strong work ethic
- ◎ Team player
- ◎ Problem solver

Accomplishments and Achievements

What have you accomplished in your career in or out of education? Have you improved test scores? Have you increased college enrollment?

Have you developed a new, innovative method of teaching?

Have you written a weekly education column? Won an industry award? Have you done the publicity for a college? Have you written a large grant? Have you written an acclaimed article on some aspect of education?

Have you implemented an innovative program? Have you supervised other faculty members?

Have you started a tutoring business? Have you taught people who speak another language how to speak English? Have you taught adults how to read?

Your achievements inform potential employers not only about what you have done, but also about what you might do for them.

Sit down and think about it for a while. What are you most proud of in your career? What have you done that has made a difference or had a positive impact on the company or school for which you worked? If you are new to the workforce, what did you do in school? What about in a volunteer capacity?

Just as you made your skills and personality traits sizzle with words, you want to do the same thing with your accomplishments and achievements. Put yourself in the position of a human resources director or the owner of a company for a moment. You get two resumes. Under the accomplishments section one says, "Worked

Tip from the Coach

When writing about your accomplishments, use action words to illustrate your experience. Words like *achieved*, *accomplished*, *demonstrated*, *inspired*, *motivated*, *supervised*, and so on.

as grade 9–12 choral music teacher." The other says, "Worked as choral music teacher for grades 9–12. In addition to classroom teaching, had total responsibility of school choir, garnering first place in state competitions over last two years. Also oversaw a variety of other extracurricular school projects, including annual high school musical and an array of musical competitions and talent shows involving over 80 percent of the student body and faculty." Which resume would catch your eye?

You can help your accomplishments and achievements sizzle by adding action verbs to your accomplishments. Use words like *achieved, administered, applied, accomplished, assisted, strengthened*, and others.

Honors and Awards

When drafting your resume include any honors you have received whether or not they have anything to do with any part of the education industry. These honors help set you apart from other candidates. Did one of your newspaper articles win a journalism award? Did you run for your local library board of directors and win the seat? Were you honored with the Volunteer of the Year award at a local hospital? How about the Community Service Award from your local civic group. While these accomplishments might have nothing to do with the education industry, they do show that you are a hard worker and good at what you do.

Community Service and Volunteer Activities

If you perform community service or volunteer activities on a regular basis, include it on your resume. Community service and volunteer activities you perform illustrate to potential employers that you "do a little extra." Additionally, you can never predict when the person review-

ing your resume might be a member of the organization with which you volunteer. An unexpected connection like that can help you stand out in a positive way. In addition, illustrating that you are involved in the not-for-profit world may be a plus to potential employers.

Hobbies and Interests

What are your hobbies and interests? Do you collect old baseball cards? Do you have a collection of vintage baseball bats? Do you collect cookbooks? Do you collect NASCAR memorabilia? Are you a hiker? Do you volunteer with a literacy program? Are you a CASA volunteer? Are you involved in pet rescue? While many career counselors feel that hobbies or personal interests have no place on a professional resume, I disagree. Why?

Here's a secret. You can never tell what will cause the person or persons reviewing the resumes to make a connection. Perhaps he or she has the same hobby as you. Perhaps he or she is a volunteer with a literacy program in which you participate. Anything that causes you to standout in a positive manner or that causes a connection with your potential interviewer will help your resume garner attention, helping you to land an interview.

References

The goal for your resume is to have it help you *obtain* an interview. If you list your references on your resume, be aware that someone may check them to help them decide if they should interview

---

⭐ **Words from a Pro**

If you are instructed to send references with your resume, attach them on a separate sheet with your cover letter.

you. You don't really want people giving their opinions about you *until* you have the chance to sell yourself. With this in mind, it usually isn't a good idea to list your references on your resume.

If you are uncomfortable with this, include a line on your resume stating, "References are available upon request."

Your Resume Writing Style

How important is writing style in your resume? Very important. Aside from conveying your message, your writing style helps to illustrate that you have written communication skills.

When preparing your resume, write clearly and concisely and do not use the pronoun "I" to describe your accomplishments. Instead of writing "I developed innovative teaching methods for my class. I raised testing scores in my

---

Tip from the Coach

Don't stress if you can't get your resume on one or two pages. While most career specialists insist a resume should only be one or two pages at most, I strongly disagree. You don't want to overwhelm a potential employer with a 10-page book, but if your resume needs to be three or four pages to get your pertinent information in, that's okay. Keep in mind, though, that lengthy resumes or CVs (curriculum vitae) are generally used by high-level professionals who have many years of experience and work history to fill the additional pages. If your resume is longer than normal, you should use a brief career summary at the beginning so a hiring manager can quickly see what your major accomplishments are. If they then want to take their time to look through the rest of the resume, your information will be there.

The Inside Scoop

Instead of just making your resume an outline of your accomplishments, make it a powerful marketing tool.

---

class 30 percent," try "Developed key innovative teaching methods resulting in a 30 percent increase in one year in class testing scores." Note the inclusion of a time period. It's good to be specific about your achievements.

Instead of "I want to be a corporate trainer at CLT Enterprises," try "Using my talent and skills to secure a position as corporate media trainer at one of the premier public relations agencies in the world."

Creating Industry-Specific Resumes

How can you create resumes specific to the area of education you are pursuing? Once you've created your basic resume, tailor each resume for the specific position or area you are pursuing, and find ways to relate your existing skills to that resume.

Use all your experiences, talents, and skills to help you obtain the career you want. Transfer skills and experience when you can.

One thing you should *never* do is lie on your resume. Don't lie about your education. Don't lie about experience. Don't lie about places you've worked. Don't lie about what you've done. If you haven't picked up on it yet, *do not lie*. Once someone knows you have lied, that is what they will remember about you and they may pass on that information to others.

"Oh, no one is going to find out," you might say.

Don't bet on it. Someone might find out by chance, deduce the truth based on knowledge within the industry, or hear the facts from a coworker or industry colleague. Someone, just by chance, may be surfing the net and see your name. When the truth comes out, it can end up blowing up in your face.

"By that time, I'll be doing such a good job, no one will fire me," you say.

That's the best-case scenario and there's a chance that could happen, but think about this: Once someone lies to you, do you ever trust that person again? Probably not; and no one will trust you or anything you say. That will hurt your chances of climbing the career ladder. The worst-case scenario is that you will be fired, left without references, lose some of your contacts, and make it much more difficult to find your next job.

If you don't have the experience you wish you had, try to impress the human resources director, hiring manager, or recruiter with other parts of your resume and your cover letter. If you have the experience and you are trying to advance your career, this is the time to redefine your resume. Add action verbs. Add your accomplishments. Make your new resume shine. Create a marketing piece that will make someone say, "We need to interview this person. Look at everything he has done."

When creating your resume for a career in education, you want it to reflect your knowledge

---

Tip from the Coach

One of the mistakes that many people make when preparing their resume is that they keep adding accomplishments without deleting any of the earlier or less important ones. While it's very tempting to do this, it's not always the best idea.

---

of the field. Be sure your resume shows evidence of skills, experience, productivity, and your personal commitment to quality in education.

Your CV: Curriculum Vitae

What exactly is a CV? CV is short for curriculum vitae. What's the difference between a CV and a resume? That depends who you ask. Some people use the words interchangeably. Some say a resume is a one- or two-page summary of your employment history, experience, and education, while a CV is a longer, more comprehensive and detailed synopsis of your qualifications, education, and experience. So what's the answer?

Generally, it's somewhere in between. Your resume *is* a summary of your employment history and education, which highlights your skills, talents, and education. Your CV would be a longer, detailed synopsis of these things plus teaching and research experience you might have, articles or papers you have published, research projects you have done, and presentations you have made. The CV gives you the opportunity to list every paper, project, presentation, and so on.

How do you know which type of document to use? Generally, it depends on the type of job for which you are applying. You will often use your CV instead of a resume if you are applying

---

Words to the Wise

As people often use the words CV and resume interchangeably, don't assume that just because someone asks you for your CV, that they actually want that particular document. They might really want your resume.

for a job in research, administration, and careers in higher education.

What About References?

References are another of your selling tools. Basically, references are the individuals who will vouch for your skills, ethics, and work history when a potential employer calls. A good reference can set you apart from the crowd and give you the edge over other applicants. A bad one can seriously hinder your career goals.

It's always a good idea to bring the names, addresses, and phone numbers of the people you are using for references with you when you apply for a job or when you are going on an interview. If you're asked to list them on an employment application, you'll be prepared.

Who should you use for references? To begin with, you'll need professional references. These are people you've worked with or who know you on a professional level. They might be current or former supervisors or bosses, your student teaching supervisor, the director of a not-for-profit organization you've worked with, internship program coordinators, former professors, and so on.

Do your references have to be from within the educational world? If you have references in the industry, it can't hurt. What you are looking for, however, are people who you can count on to help sell you to potential employers. Those will be your best references.

Always ask people if they are willing to be a reference before you use them. Only use people you are absolutely, positively sure will say good things about you. Additionally, when searching out your references, try to find people who are articulate and professional.

Who would be a bad reference? A boss who fired you, a supervisor you didn't get along with, or anyone you had any kind of problem with,

> ### ★ Tip from the Coach
> In some cases, employers might ask for personal references as well as professional references. These are people such as family, friends, or neighbors who know you well. Be sure to have a list of three to five personal references as well as their contact information readily available in case you need it.

whatsoever. Do not use these people for references, even if they tell you that they'll give you a good one. They might keep their word, but they might not, and you won't know until it's too late.

"What if I didn't get along with my supervisor?" you ask. "Isn't a potential employer going to call her anyway?"

You are right. Your potential employer probably *will* call your former supervisor. The trick is getting a list of three to five *good* references. That way, no matter what anyone else says, you will still look good.

You might be asked to list references on an employment application, but it's a good idea to

> ### ★ The Inside Scoop
> If you give your references an idea of exactly what type of job you're pursuing, what skills are important in that position, or even what you want them to say, you stand a better chance of them leading the conversation in the direction you want it to go. You might tell a reference, for example, that you're applying for a position as the assistant director of alumni relations at a college and that the job description calls for someone very organized with an ability to multitask. In most cases when your reference gets a call, he or she will remember what you said and stress your important selling points.

prepare a printed sheet of your professional references that you can leave with the interviewer. Basically, this sheet will contain your list of three to five references, including their names, positions, and contact information. As with your resume, make sure it is printed on high-quality paper.

Here's an example to get you started.

Professional Reference Sheet for Jean Sullivan

Mr. Gene Smith
Principal
Tri-Town High School
120 Route 9W
Anytown, NY 11111
(111) 222-2222
smithgene@tritownhs.edu

Ms. Jennifer Speer
Student Teacher Supervisor
Tri-Town High School
120 Route 9W
Anytown, NY 11111
(111) 222-1111
speerjenn@tritownhs.edu

Professor Clifford Knolls
State University
State Town, NY 12222
(222) 444-5555
cliffknolls@stateu.edu

Ms. Lea Strong
Sunset General Hospital Auxiliary
   President
Sunset General Hospital
222 Sunset Road
Anytown, NY 11111
(111) 333-3333

Personal References

In addition to professional references, you might also be asked to provide personal references. These are friends, family members, or others who know you. You probably won't need to print out a reference sheet for your personal references, but make sure you have all their contact information in case you need it quickly.

As with professional references, make sure the people you are using know you are listing them as references. Give them a call when you're going on an interview to let them know someone might be contacting them. Ask them to let you know if they get a call.

Letters of Recommendation

As you go through your career, it's a good idea to get letters of recommendation from people who have been impressed with your work. Along with references, these help give potential employers a better sense of your worth. How do you get a letter of recommendation? You usually simply have to ask. For example, let's say you are close to completing an internship.

Say to your supervisor, "I've enjoyed my time here. Would it be possible to get a letter of recommendation from you for my files?"

Most people will be glad to provide this. In some cases, people might even ask you to write it yourself for them to sign. Don't forego these opportunities, even if you feel embarrassed about blowing your own horn. The easiest way to do it is by trying to imagine you aren't writing about yourself. In that way you can be honest and write a great letter. Give it to the person and say, "Here's the letter we discussed. Let me know if you want anything changed or you aren't comfortable with any piece of it." Nine times out of 10, the person will just sign the letter as is.

Who should you ask for letters of recommendation? In many cases, the people you ask will be the same ones you ask to be your reference. If you are still in school or close to graduating, you might ask professors with whom you have developed a good relationship. Don't forget internship coordinators or supervisors, your student teaching supervisor, former and current employers, executive directors of not-for-profit, civic, or charity organizations you have volunteered with, and so on.

In some situations the people you ask may just write generic letters of recommendation stating that you were a pleasure to work with, or were good at your job. If the person writing the letter knows the type of position you're pursuing, he or she might gear the letter to specific skills, traits, and talents needed.

Your letters of recommendation will become another powerful marketing tool in your quest to career success in education. What do you do with them? Begin by photocopying each letter you get on good quality, white paper, making sure you get clean copies. Once that's done you can make them part of your career portfolio, send them with your resume when applying for position, or bring them with you to interviews.

Creating Captivating Cover Letters

Unless instructed otherwise by a potential employer or in an advertisement, always send your resume with a cover letter. Why? Mainly because if your resume grabs the eye of someone in the position to interview you, he or she often looks at the cover letter to evaluate your written communications skills as well as to get a sense of your personal side. If your letter is a good one, it might just get you the phone call you've been waiting for. On the other hand, a poorly

written letter might just keep you from getting that call.

What can make your letter stand out? Try to make sure your letter is directed to the name of the person to whom you are sending it instead of "Hiring Manager," "Director of Human Resources," "To Whom It May Concern," or "Sir or Madam."

"But the name of the person isn't in the ad," you say. "How do I know what it is?"

You might not always be able to get the correct name, but at least do some research. You might, for example, call the school or company advertising the opening and ask the name of the person to whom responses should be directed.

If you are sending your resume to a company cold, it's even more important to send it to a specific person. It gives you a better shot at someone not only reviewing it, but also taking action on it.

It's okay to call the company and say to the receptionist or secretary, "Hi, I was wondering if you could give me some information? I'm trying to send my resume to someone at your company and I'm not sure who to send it to. Could you please give me the name of the human resources director [or who ever you are trying to target]?"

If he or she won't give it to you for some reason, say thank you and hang up. While schools and colleges generally will freely give out this type of information, there may be some companies which, for various reasons, will not give out names easily.

How do you get around this? Wait until lunchtime or around 5:15 p.m. when the person you spoke to might be at lunch or done with their workday, call back, and say something to the effect of, "Hi, I was wondering if you could please give me the spelling of your HR director's name?"

If the person on the other end of the phone line asks you to be more specific about the name simply say, "Let's see, I think it was Brownson or something like that. It sounded like Brown something."

Don't worry about sounding stupid on the phone. The person at the other end doesn't know you. This system usually works. Believe it not, most companies have someone working there whose name sounds like Brown or Smith.

The person on the phone may say to you, "No, we don't have a Brownson. What department are you looking for? It was HR wasn't it?"

When you say yes, he or she will probably say, "Oh, that's not Brownson, it's John Campbell. Is that who you're looking for?"

Then all you have to say is, "You know what, you're right. Sorry, I was looking at the wrong notes. So that's C-A-M-P-B-E-L-L?"

Voila. You have the name. Is it a lot of effort? Well, it's a little effort, but if it gets you the name of someone you need and ultimately helps get you an interview, isn't it worth it?

By the way, this technique not only works getting names you need, but other information as well. You might have to be persistent and it might take you a few tries, but it generally always gets you the information you need.

You also can sometimes get names from the Internet. Perhaps the company Web site lists the names of their key people. Key names for large companies may also often be located on Hoovers.com, an online database of information about businesses. While this site is a paid service, many of the key names you may need are available free.

Do what you can to get the names you need. It can make a big difference when you direct your letters to someone specific within the company.

No matter what segment of education in which you are trying to locate a job, those who are in the position to hire you may be receiving a large number of resumes, letters, and phone calls. What can help your letters stand out? Make them grab the attention of the reader. How? Make sure your cover letters are creative.

Take some time and think about it. What would make *you* keep reading? Of course, there will be situations where you might be better off sending the traditional "In response to your ad" letter. But what about trying out a couple of other ideas?

Take a look at the sample cover letter. Would this letter grab your attention? Would it make you keep reading? Chances are it would. After grabbing the reader's attention, it quickly offers some of the applicant's skills, talents, and achievements. Would you bring in Mark Hilton for an interview? I think most employers would.

MARK HILTON
111 South Street
Different Town, NY 22222
Phone: 111-444-5555
markhilton@moreinernet.com

Ms. Susan Toney
Human Resources Manager
Compton University
Some City, NY 11111

Dear Ms. Toney:
CONGRATULATIONS!
I'm pleased to inform you that you have just received the resume that can end your search for Compton University's new marketing director. In order to claim your "prize," please review my resume and call as soon as possible to arrange an interview. I can guarantee you'll be pleased you did!

As the assistant director of marketing at Blue County Community College, I helped coordinate the marketing activities for a year before being promoted to the position of full-fledged director of marketing. During my two-year tenure in this position, I developed and implemented local and regional advertising campaigns as well as a number of innovative promotional programs designed to enhance awareness of the college and drive student enrollment. With the help of these programs, enrollment increased 38 percent.

In this position I additionally developed a number of strategic partnerships, working with other large corporate businesses and developing sponsorship opportunities, saving monies for the college on events while generating large amounts of media attention for both entities.

While I love what I do now, my dream and passion has been a career in marketing at a large, prestigious university. I have recently completed a number of professional certifications in both general marketing and educational marketing.

I welcome the challenge and opportunity to work with the Compton University and believe my experience, skills, talents, and passion would be an asset to your organization.

I look forward to hearing from you.

Sincerely yours,
Mark Hilton

Now check out some other creative cover letters.

THOMAS BELL
332 F Avenue
Different Town, NY 33333
Phone: 666-999-9999
thomasbell@moreinernet.com

Mr. Glen Ross, Hiring Manager
Valley School District
102 Third Avenue
Another Town, NY 22222

Dear Mr. Ross:
    DO YOU WANT TO RAISE TEST SCORES IN YOUR SCHOOL?
    While I can't guarantee higher test scores in every classroom, I can promise you I will do my best to raise test scores in my class by motivating students and developing innovative, relevant methods of teaching every student in my classroom if you give me a chance.

I'm an enthusiastic, passionate, and dedicated individual who has just fulfilled part of my dream of becoming a great teacher by graduating from New State University with a bachelor's degree in elementary education. I cannot wait to fulfill the rest of my dream by getting a teaching job, having my own classroom, and inspiring young people to love to learn.

I cannot wait to utilize everything I have learned in college, during student teaching, and during my volunteer activities. Most of all, I cannot wait to inspire, motivate, and excite children to want to learn, and to help them find exciting ways to do so.

While in college I volunteered in a program teaching the children of migrant workers who needed extra help with math and reading basics. The children were tested in both reading and math before their involvement in the program. At the end of the semester, the children in my group had increased test scores by 30 percent.

I believe my love of teaching, together with my passions, skills, and talents, would be an asset to your students and your school.

I have enclosed my resume for your review and would very much appreciate the opportunity to meet with you to discuss the openings for elementary teachers in your school, which you advertised in the *Times* on Sunday.

Thank you for your consideration. I look forward to hearing from you.

Sincerely yours,
Thomas Bell

GERALD HUBBER
929 South Avenue
Different Town, NY 33333
Phone: 111-999-9999
ghubber@moreinternet.com

Ms. Rachel Block
Human Resources Director
State University
811 Avenue A
Anytown, NY 11111

Dear Ms. Block:

IS YOUR COLLEGE IN NEED OF FUNDS?

Thousands of dollars can be yours with just one call . . . to me!!!

I was excited to learn about the opening for the Director of Fund-Raising and Development at Champlain University. How lucky for me that just as I moved back into the area, the perfect job became available.

I recently graduated from Kingston University with a double major in business administration and marketing. Before you pass by my resume for lack of experience, I urge you to read on. I'm sure you will agree that what I lack in professional experience, I more than make up for in my volunteer activities.

While still in college, I volunteered to work on fund-raising for a large not-for-profit theater in the area. I began by assisting in the coordination of a number of fund-raising events. I soon was helping develop and implement additional fund-raising events and activities for the theater, helping to raise over $800,000. After researching and writing a number of grants, I was also able to secure three large grants totaling close to $1 million, which the theater desperately needed.

While working on that project, I was approached by a board member from the local hospital, who asked if I would be willing to volunteer to help them with their annual giving campaign.

I jumped at the opportunity and learned all about cultivating donors and prospective donors. I was very excited to help with the hospital's efforts and even more pleased when they raised over $10 million dollars. (Of course, it wasn't just my volunteer efforts bringing in that amount, but my solicitations of donors helped increase the number and amount of major gift donors.

Although I was offered a paid position with the hospital upon graduation, I have ties in this community and I really wanted to move back to the area.

I love the excitement of being on a campus and have a true passion for not only raising funds, but for cultivating donors.

I'm an enthusiastic, creative, motivated team player who can also work effectively on my own. I am focused and goal oriented. If you give me the chance, I'll be Champlain University's number-one cheerleader.

I have enclosed my resume, copies of news stories on some of the fund-raising programs I was involved with, as well as a brief outline of a number of ideas I developed for fund-raising and development for other organizations.

I would appreciate the opportunity to meet with you to discuss this exciting opportunity.

Thanks for your consideration. I look forward to hearing from you.

Sincerely yours,
Gerald Hubber

More Selling Tools—Business and Networking Cards

The best way to succeed at almost anything is to do everything possible to stack the deck in your favor. Most people use a resume to sell themselves. As we just discussed, done right, your resume can be a great selling tool. It can get you in the door for an interview. But putting all your eggs in one basket is never a good idea. What else can you do to help sell yourself? What other tools can you use?

Business cards are small but powerful tools that can positively impact your career if used correctly. We've discussed the importance of

---

⭐ **Tip from the Coach**

Business cards are networking cards. You give them to people you meet so they not only remember you and what you do, but how to contact you if necessary. These are important no matter what aspect of the education industry you aspire to succeed.

business cards throughout the book. Let's look at them more closely.

Whatever level you're at in your career, whatever area of the industry you're interested in pursuing, business cards can help you get further. If you don't have a job yet, business cards are essential. At this point, they may also be known as networking cards because that is what they are going to help you do. If you already have a job, business cards can help you climb the ladder to success. Get your business cards made up, and get them made up now! They will be very useful in your career.

Why are cards so important? For a lot of reasons, but mainly because they help people not only remember you, but also find you. Networking is so essential to your success in the industry that once you go through all the trouble of doing it, if someone doesn't remember who you are or how they can contact you, it's almost useless.

How many times have you met someone during the day or at a party and then gone your separate ways. A couple days later, something will come up where you wish you could remember the person's name or you remember their name, but have no idea how to get hold of them.

The Inside Scoop

Don't try to save money by making business cards on your computer. They never really end up looking professional and you don't really end up saving any money.

How badly would you feel if you found out that you met someone, told him or her that you were looking for a job, they ran into someone else who was looking for someone with your skills and talents, and they didn't know how to get hold of you? Business cards could have helped solve that problem.

When was the last time you ran into someone successful who didn't have business cards? They boost your prestige and make you feel more successful. If you feel more successful, you'll be more successful.

So, what's your next step? Start by determining what you want your business cards to look like. There are a variety of styles to choose from. You might want to go to a print shop or an office supply store such as Staples or Office Max to look at samples, or you can create your own style.

Samples of Business and Networking Cards

Harry Moulton

Career Goal: Position in College Career Counseling
Master's Degree in Counseling from State University

P.O. Box 1600   Phone: 111-222-1111
Anytown, NY 11111   Cell: 888-999-0000
E-mail:hmoulton@someinternet.com

Samples of Business and Networking Cards, continued

Charles Anthony
Corporate Trainer

P.O. Box 909   Phone: 111-888-8888
Anytown, NY 11111   Cell: 888-111-1111
E-mail: canthony@someinternet.com

---

420 Maple Avenue
Anytown, NY 11111

LAURIE RODGERS
Middle School/High School Teacher
Certified in Physical Education and Health

Phone: 111-333-3333
Cell: 888-999-0000
E-mail: lrodgers@someinternet.com

---

492 Circle Street   Phone: 222-111-1111
Anytown, NY 11111   Cell: 111-999-0000
E-mail: jamesevans@allinternet.com

James Evans
Graduate of State University – Elementary Education Major

Student Teaching – Round Lake Elementary School, 3rd Grade

Summer Job – Assistant Director-Anytown Village Day Camp

Samples of Business and Networking Cards, continued

Linda Dupree

Curriculum Director
Rocky Mount High School

34 School Street   Phone: 333-999-9999
Rocky Mount, NY 11111
E-mail: ldupree@rockymountschool.edu

JENNY CAPLOW

Reading Specialist
Anytown Elementary

P.O. Box 1400   Phone: 111-444-5555
Anytown, NY 11111
E-mail: jcaplown@anytownelementary.edu

Order at least 1,000 cards. What are you going to do with that many cards? You're going to give them to everyone. While everyone might not keep your resume, most people in all aspects of business keep cards.

Simple cards are the least expensive. The more design, graphics, or features you add, the more the cost goes up.

What should your cards say? At the minimum include your name, address (or P.O. box), and phone number (both home and cell if you have one). It's a good idea to add in your job or your career goal or objective. You might even briefly describe your talents, skills, or traits.

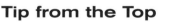 **Tip from the Top**

If you are currently employed, your employer will often provide you with business cards.

Words from the Wise

If you don't feel comfortable putting your physical home address on your business card, get a post office box.

Tip from the Coach

Look at other people's business cards in all industries to try to find a style you like. Then fit your information into that style.

Your business card is your selling piece so think about what you want to sell. Check out some of the samples to get ideas.

Remember that cards are small and that limits the number of words that can fit so the card looks attractive and can be read easily. If you want more room, you might use a double-sided card (front and back) or a double-sized card that is folded over, in effect giving you four times as much space. I've seen both used successfully. The double-sized card can be very effective for a mini-resume.

You have a lot of decisions on how you want your business cards to look. What kind of card stock do you want? Do you want your card smooth or textured, flat or shiny? What about color? Do you want white, beige, or a colored

card? Do you want flat print or raised print? What fonts or typefaces do you want to use? Do you want graphics? How do you want the information laid out? Do you want it straight or on an angle? The decisions are yours. It just depends on what you like and what you think will sell you the best.

Brochures Can Tell Your Story

While you're always going to need a resume, consider developing your own brochure, too. A brochure can tell your story and help you sell yourself. Sometimes, something out of the ordinary can help grab the attention of someone important.

What's a brochure? Basically it is a selling piece that gives information about a product, place, event, or person, among other things. In this situation, the brochure is going to be about you. While your resume tells your full story, your brochure is going to illustrate your key points.

Why do you need one? A brochure can make you stand out from other job seekers.

What should a brochure contain? While it depends to a great extent on what segment of the industry you are pursuing, there are some basic things you should include.

Of course, you need your name and contact information. Then add in your selling points. Maybe those are your skills. Perhaps they are your talents or accomplishments. What about something unique or special that you do? Defi-

The Inside Scoop

At every career-oriented seminar I give, when we get to the section on business cards, someone always raises his or her hand and says something to the effect of, "I don't have a job yet. What kind of cards do I make up? What would they say? Unemployed? Unemployed, but wants to work? Unemployed, but wants to be a teacher?"

So before you think it or say it, the answer is, no. You definitely don't put the word unemployed on your card. You will put your name, contact information, and career goals on your business card, and then use them to become employed in your career of choice.

nitely try to illustrate what *you* can do for a school, university, or company, and what benefits they will obtain by hiring you. A brief bio is often helpful to illustrate your credentials and credibility. What about including three or four quotes from some of your letters of recommendation. For example:

- ◎ "One of the best interns we ever had participate in our internship program." Scott Lewis, Green Community College
- ◎ "A real team player who motivates the team." Joe Green, Tri-County Vocational School
- ◎ "One of our favorite student teachers." Kimberly Jones, student teacher supervisor, Anytown Elementary School

Keep your wording simple. Make it clear, concise, and interesting.

What should your brochure look like? The possibilities are endless. Brochures can be simple or elaborate. Your brochure can be designed in different sizes, papers, folds, inks, and colors. You can use photographs, drawings, illustrations, or other graphics.

If you have graphic design ability and talent, lay out your brochure yourself. If you don't, ask a friend or family member who is talented in that area to help you. There are also software programs that help you design brochures. With these programs you simply type your information in and print it out. Some people with access to a laser color copier and/or printer create their own professional looking pieces.

The beauty of doing it yourself is that after you've sent out a number of brochures, you can improve and redesign them if they aren't doing anything for you and send out another batch. Be very sure, however, that your brochure looks professional or it will defeat the purpose.

If you want to design your brochure, but want it printed professionally, consider bringing your camera-ready brochure to a professional print shop. Camera-ready means your document is ready to be printed, and any consumer print shop should be able to help guide you through the steps needed to prepare your work for them. In addition to print shops, you might also consider office supply stores like Staples and Office Max that do printing.

If you don't feel comfortable designing your own brochure, you can ask a printer in your area if there is an artist on staff. Professional design and printing of a brochure can get expensive. Is it worth it? Only you can decide, but if it helps get your career started or makes the one you have more successful, probably the answer is yes.

Can brochures be effective? I certainly think so. Not only do I know a great number of people who have used them successfully in a variety of industries, I personally used one when I was breaking into the music business and have continued using them ever since. Here's my story.

At the time, I was sending out a lot of resumes and making a lot of calls in an attempt to obtain interviews. I had learned a lot about marketing and noticed that many companies used brochures. My father, who was a marketing professional, suggested that a brochure might just be

---

★ Tip from the Coach

You don't need 1,000 brochures. Start off with 100 or so and see how they work for you. If you're not seeing results, you may need to rework your brochure to make it a valuable marketing tool. Remember that in order for brochures to be effective, you have to send them out, so be sure you start working on a list of companies or people you want to target.

what I needed. By that time I had realized that if I wanted to *sell* myself I might need to market myself a little more aggressively than I was doing, so I decided to try the brochure idea.

We designed a brochure that was printed on an 11-by-17-inch paper folded in half, giving me four pages to tell my story. We artistically mounted a headshot on the front page and printed it in hot pink ink. The inside was crafted with carefully selected words indicating my accomplishments, skills, talents, and the areas in which I could help a company who hired me. The brochures were professionally printed and I sent them to various record labels, music instrument manufacturers, music publishers, music industry publicity companies, artist managers, and so on. I started getting calls from some of the people who received the brochure, obtained a number of interviews, and a even landed a couple of job offers. None of them, however, interested me.

Five years after I sent out my first brochure, I received a call from a major record company, which told me that at the time they first received my brochure they didn't need anyone with my skills or talents, but they thought the brochure was so unique that they kept it on file. Voila. Although five years had passed, they needed an individual with my skills. Someone remembered my brochure, pulled it out, and called me. By that time I was already on the road with another group and couldn't take the job, but it was nice to be called.

★ Words from the Wise

It is very easy to miss errors. Before you have your brochure printed, proofread it and then proofread it again. Then ask a friend or family member to proofread it as well.

★ Tip from the Coach

You are going to use your brochure in addition to your resume, not in place of it.

What was really interesting, however, is that companies and people I originally sent that first brochure to years ago still remember it. They can describe it to a tee and many of them still have it in their files.

When creating your brochure, make sure it represents the image you want to portray. Try to make it as unique and eye catching as possible. You can never tell how long someone is going to keep it.

Your Career Portfolio: Have Experience, Will Travel

People in creative careers have always used portfolios to illustrate what they have done and can accomplish. You can do the same.

What exactly is a career portfolio? Basically, it's a portfolio, binder, or book that contains your career information and illustrates your best work. In addition to the traditional printed components of a portfolio, many people in education are also using multimedia components, including video, PowerPoint, and Web pages. Your portfolio is a visual representation of what you have done and often illustrates what your potential might be.

Why do you need one? Because your career portfolio can help you get the positions you want, and that is what this is all about.

Consider this question. What would you believe more, something someone told you or something you saw with your own eyes? If you're like most people, you would believe something you saw. And that's what a good career portfolio can do for you. It can provide actual illustrations of what you've done and what you can do.

For example, you might tell a potential employer that you can write press releases. Can you really? If you have samples in your portfolio, you can pull out a couple and show your work.

You might tell a potential employer that you increased student enrollment. If you have a copy of the newspaper story discussing the increase in enrollment, he or she can see the increase in black and white.

What would be more impressive to you? Reading in someone's resume that they won the teacher of the year award, or actually seeing a copy of the award certificate? Reading that someone had developed an interesting program at a school, or seeing a copy of the article and picture about it in the newspaper?

Have you written press releases about your accomplishments that led to articles in the newspaper? Have others done articles or feature stories about you which appeared in the media?

Copies of all these documents can be part of your career portfolio. Often, if you have buzz around you, potential employers feel you will be a asset to the school, college, or company.

Don't think that your portfolio will only be useful when you are first trying to land a job. If you continue adding in new accomplish-

> ### Tip from the Top
> When compiling your portfolio be careful not to use any confidential work or documents from a company, even if you were the one who wrote the report or the letter. A potential employer might be concerned about how you will deal with their confidential issues if you aren't keeping other confidences.

ments, skills, and samples of projects you've worked on, your portfolio will be useful in helping your advancement throughout your career. Of course, as time goes on, omit some of your earlier documents and replace them with more current ones.

Having an organized system to present your achievements and successes is also helpful when going through employment reviews, or asking for a promotion or a raise. It also is very effective in illustrating what you've done if you're trying to move up the ladder at a different company.

Over the years I consistently get calls from people who have been to our seminars or called for advice who continue to use their career portfolios successfully in their careers in every industry. Work on developing your career portfolio, and this simple tool can help you achieve success as well.

Your portfolio is portable. You can bring it with you when you go on interviews and show it to potential employers. You can make copies of things in your portfolio to give to potential employers, or you can have everything at hand when you want to answer an ad or send out cold letters.

How do you build a detailed portfolio illustrating your skills, talents, experiences, and accomplishments? What goes into it? You want your portfolio to document your work-related talents and accomplishments. These are the assets that you will be *selling* to your potential employers.

> ### Tip from the Top
> Make good quality copies of key items in your portfolio to leave with interviewers or potential employers, agents, etc. Visit an office supply store to find some professional looking presentation folders to hold all the support documents you bring to an interview.

Sample of Profile for Career Portfolio

PROFILE
Meredith Baker

Education:

- State University—Master's Degree
  - Educational Administration
- State University—Bachelor's Degree
  - Major: Elementary Education

Additional Training:

- Seminar: Understanding the Needs of Children from Broken Homes
- Seminar: Teaching Methods for Making Math Fun
- Seminar: Using Journaling To Teach Writing Skills
- Seminar: Educational Administration: An Overview
- Workshop: Creating Books With Children
- Workshop: Bringing Theater Skills into the Classroom
- Workshop: Computer Skills for Kids
- Workshop: Teaching
- Workshop: Grant Writing
- Workshop: Web page design

Goals:

- Teaching elementary school; developing innovative curriculum for elementary schools.

Qualifications:

- Passionate teacher
- Hard working, dedicated, focused, motivated, and energetic
- Creative thinker
- Dedicated to finding ways to make every student excited to learn
- Computer skills
- Ability to develop and build Web sites
- Verbal and written communication skills
- Trilingual (English, Spanish, French)

Let's look at some of the things you might want to include in your portfolio.

◎ Your profile
◎ Resume
◎ Bio
◎ Reference sheets
◎ Skills and abilities
◎ Degrees, licenses, and certifications
◎ Experience sheet
◎ Summary of accomplishments
◎ Professional associations
◎ Professional development activities (conferences, seminars, and workshops attended as well as any other professional development activities)
◎ Awards and honors
◎ Volunteer activities and community service
◎ Supporting documents
◎ Samples of work
◎ Your philosophy of education
◎ Newspaper, magazine, and other articles or feature stories about you
◎ Articles you have written and published
◎ Reports you've done
◎ Letters of recommendation
◎ Letters or notes people have written to tell you that you've done a good job.
◎ Special letters or notes from students or parents indicating how you have helped or made a positive difference to them or their children.
◎ Work samples (examples of lesson plans, photos of classroom activities, video of classroom activities, etc.)
◎ Classroom management style (if you are pursuing a teaching career)

> **Words from a Pro**
>
> If you're dealing with an unknown printer or company, ask to see samples of their work ahead of time. Then be sure to get a proof, which you can check for errors and approve before your portfolios are printed.

◎ Management theory and style (if you are pursuing a career in educational administration and business)
◎ Photos of you accepting an award or at an event you worked on
◎ Photos of events you were involved in
◎ News stories or feature articles generated by your execution or supervision of a project. (For example, if your class raises money for a local family whose house burned down, or three of your students won top prizes in a citywide science fair.)
◎ Volunteer activities

Remember, this list is just to get you started. Some of the components listed may be related to you and some may not. You can use anything in your portfolio that will help illustrate your skills, talents, and accomplishments.

In order to make it easier to locate information in your portfolio, you might want to develop a table of contents and then use dividers.

Here's a sample of a profile that a teacher might use in her portfolio. Use it to give you an idea on getting started on yours.

Whatever segment of the education industry you are pursuing, use every tool you can to make sure you get the edge over others who want the same success you do.

7

GETTING YOUR FOOT IN THE DOOR

Whether I'm giving a career seminar or doing a career consultation, people looking for advice on getting that perfect job consistently tell me that if they only could get their foot in the door they would be on their way. In a way they're right.

One of the keys to a great career is getting your foot in the proverbial door. If you can just get that door open, even if it's just a crack, you can slip your foot in and then you're on the road to success. Why? Because once you get your foot in, you have a chance to sell yourself, sell your talent, and sell your products or services.

It seems easy, but the problem is, sometimes the hardest part is getting your foot in the door. Whether you simply walk in off the street to see someone or call to make an appointment, you often are faced with the same situation. You need to get past the receptionist, the secretary, or whoever the "gatekeeper" happens to be between you and the person with whom you want to speak.

Here's what you need to know. Whenever there is a job opening, someone will get the job and unfortunately someone won't. Rejection is often part of the process in getting a job. However, to feel rejected when you didn't even get the chance to really be rejected because you can't get through to someone is quite another thing.

It's not personal, but the secretary, receptionist, assistant, and even the person you're trying to reach, often think of you and most other unsolicited callers as unwanted intruders who waste their time. It doesn't really matter whether you're trying to sell something or get a job, unless the people you are trying to reach can see what you can do for them, it's going to be hard to get through.

In reality you are trying to sell something. You're trying to sell *you, your skills,* and *your talents.* You're trying to get a job. What you need to do, however, is try not to let these gatekeepers know exactly what you want.

I am in no way telling you to lie or even stretch the truth. What I'm telling you to do is find a way to change their perception of you and what you want. Get creative.

Some areas of education are easier to enter, while other segments of the industry are more competitive. And while there generally always is a gatekeeper, sometimes it's easier to get past him or her.

You might not think you have to worry about getting past a gatekeeper if you are pursuing a career in one of the segments of the industry that is in great demand, but you can never tell. You might, for example, want to interview in a school in which it may be more difficult to get a job. You might want to go after a department head position. You might want to work as a corporate trainer at a large corporation or go after a position as a tutor on the road with a young recording group or artist. You might want to create your own position in a college or a corporation or even a school. There are so many possibilities in which there *could* be a gatekeeper in your way. So it is always good to be prepared.

In many situations you might be answering an advertisement or visiting the human resources offices of a school, college, university, or corporation to fill in an application. If, for example, you are applying for an advertised job as a teacher in a public school you might not have to *worry* about getting past the gatekeeper, but that doesn't mean he or she isn't there.

No matter which segment of the industry you are pursuing, there will be times when you need to get past a gatekeeper so you can get your foot in the door. Before you rush in and find the door locked, let's look at some possible keys to help you get in.

Will you need every key? Probably not, but once you learn what some of the keys are you'll have them if you need them.

Getting Through to People on the Phone

Let's start with the phone. If your goal is to talk to a specific person or make an appointment, it's important to know that many high-level business people don't answer their own phone. Instead, they rely on secretaries, receptionists, or assistants to handle this task. And that's not even counting the dreaded voice mail.

You can always try the straightforward approach. Just call and ask to speak to the person

you are looking for. If that works, you have your foot in the door. If not, it's time to get creative.

Let's look at a couple of scenarios and how they might play out. In this scenario Joy Block is trying to land an interview in an attempt to create a position as an education reporter.

Scenario 1

Receptionist: Good afternoon, WRADO.

You: Hello, this is Joy Block. Can I please speak to Ron Evans?

Receptionist: Does he know what this is in reference to?

You: No, I'm looking for a job as an education reporter and would like to see if I could set up an interview.

Receptionist: I'm sorry. Mr. Evans isn't looking to fill any positions at this time. Thank you for calling.

You: Thanks. Good-bye.

With that said, you're done. Is there something you could have said differently which might lead to a better ending? Let's look at another scenario.

Scenario 2

Sometimes mentioning a job to the gatekeeper is not a good idea Let's say you are trying to create your own position or you are going after a position so coveted that those already working in the company may not be open about helping those on the outside. What can you do?

Creativity is the name of the game.

Secretary: Good afternoon, WRADO.

You: Is Mr. Evans in please?

Secretary: Who's calling?

You: Joy Block.

Secretary: May I ask what this is in reference to?

You: Yes, I was trying to set up an informational interview. Would Mr. Evans be the person who handles this or would it be someone else?

[Asking the question in this manner means that you stand a chance at the gatekeeper giving you a specific name that you can call if Mr. Evans is the wrong person.]

Secretary: Informational interview for what purpose?

You: I was interested in exploring the interest people who listen to radio have in education-oriented issues I thought as the program director, Mr. Evans might be someone who might have some knowledge in that area. Would he be the right person?

[Make sure you are pleasant. This helps the person answering the phone want to help you.]

Secretary: You probably would be better off speaking to our station owner, Martha Risson. Would you like me to switch you?

[What you are really doing is helping her get you off the phone, even if it means she is dumping you on someone else.]

You: Yes, that would be great. What was your name?

[Try to make sure you get the name. In this manner, when you get transferred, the person answering at the other end will be more apt to help you.]

Secretary: Mandy Lerner.

You: Thanks for your help. I really appreciate it.

Secretary: I'll switch you now.

Elizabeth Lasko: Martha Risson's office. This is Elizabeth. May I help you?

You: Hi, Elizabeth, Mandy Lerner suggested that Ms. Risson might be the right person for me to speak to. I'm interested in exploring the interest people who listen to radio have in education-oriented issues. Ms. Lerner said Ms. Risson might know something about that area.

Elizabeth: What type of project are you working on? Is this a school project or something?

You: No, I'm out of school. As a matter of fact I have my master's in education and a teaching license.

[Notice that you are not really answering her question at all. At this point, Ms. Lasko probably will either say, sorry, Ms. Risson is very busy, or she will keep pumping you for information.]

Elizabeth: Ms. Risson is out of the office this week. She should be back next Monday.

You: I know she is busy. Do you think she would have 10 minutes for me if I stop in sometime next week, or would it be better to call her? I'm really interested in hearing her thoughts on education.

Elizabeth: I know she is very interested in education herself. She's on the college board of directors you know. She is pretty busy next week, but she might be able to spare a few minutes on Wednesday. Would that work for you?

[Do not say, "Let me check my calendar." If at all possible, take the time you are given for the meeting, no matter what else you have to juggle around.]

Elizabeth: I'm going to double check with Ms. Risson when she calls up later. If you don't hear from me, why don't you come over around 9:30 a.m. Wednesday. Do you have our address?

You: It is 429 Main Street, isn't it?

Elizabeth: That's where we are located. You might want to also speak to Bob Reid from the *Daily Times*. He is on the college board with Ms. Risson. He might be able to give you some information on education and the print media. He's pretty busy too. I hear he's looking for an education reporter.

You: I bet that would be a great job.

Elizabeth: His number is 444-9999. His secretary's name is Lisa. Tell her I told you to call.

You: Thanks so much for your help. I'm going to call as soon as I hang up. You've been really helpful. I'll see you next week.

Once you get into the meeting, you might or might not be able to talk Ms. Risson into the idea of creating a position for an education reporter. That will be up to you. You have, however, networked your way into another meeting at the newspaper, where you have heard someone is looking for an education reporter, a position you have not seen advertised.

I can hear you saying, "That kind of thing doesn't really happen."

To that I reply, it can and it does. I've seen it happen numerous times. In order for it to happen, however, you have to find ways to get past the gatekeeper.

Here's another scenario.

Scenario 3

Receptionist: Good afternoon, ABC Corporation.

You: Hi, I'm working on a project involving corporate trainers. Do you know who in your company I might speak to that might know something about that area?

[Here is where it can get a little tricky. If you are very lucky, he or she will just put you through to someone in publicity, public relations, or human resources. If you're not so lucky, he or she will ask you questions.]

Receptionist: What type of project?

You need to be ready with a plausible answer. What you say will, of course, depend on your situation. If you are in college, you can always say you are working on a project for school. If not, you can say you are doing research on career opportunities in corporate training (or whatever area of the industry you are pursuing.) If you have writing skills, you might contact a local newspaper or magazine to see if they are interested in an article on careers in corporate training, (or whatever segment of the industry you are targeting.) If you can't find someone to write for, you can always write a story on "spec." This means that if you write a story, you can send it to an editor on speculation. They might take it, and they might not. Don't think about money at this point. Your goal here is to get the "right people" to speak to you and to get an appointment.

This method of getting to know people is supposed to give you credibility, not make you non-credible. The idea will only be effective if you *really* are planning on writing an article or a story and then carry through.

One of the interesting things about writing an article (whether on spec or on assignment) is that you can ask people questions and they will usually talk to you. They won't be looking at you as they might if you were looking for a job.

Voice of Experience
Make sure you get the correct spelling of the name of everyone who helps you. Send a short note, thanking them for their help. This is not only good manners—it also helps people remember who you are in a positive way.

What you've done in these situations is changed people's perception about why you are talking to them. One of the most important bonuses of interviewing people about a career in various industries is that you are making invaluable contacts.

While it might be tempting, remember to use this opportunity to ask questions and network. Do not try to sell yourself. After you write the article, you might call up one of the people you interviewed, perhaps the human resources director, and say something like, "You made a career in corporate training so interesting, I'd like to explore a career like that. Would it be possible to come in for an interview or to fill in an application?"

What can you do if none of these scenarios work? The receptionist may not be very eager to help. He or she may have instructions to "not let anyone through." It may be his or her job to block unsolicited callers and visitors from the boss. What can you do?

Here are a few ideas that might help. See if you can come up with some others yourself.

- ◎ Try placing your call before regular business hours. Many executives and others you might want to talk to come in early, before the secretary or receptionist is scheduled to work.
- ◎ Try placing your calls after traditional business hours when the secretary probably has left for the day. The executives and others you want to reach generally don't push a time clock and often work late. More importantly, even if people use voice mail, they may pick up the phone themselves after hours, in case their family is calling.
- ◎ Lunch hours are also a good time to attempt to get through to people. This is a little tricky. The executive may use voice mail during the lunch hour period, or he or she may go out for lunch. On the other hand, you might get lucky.
- ◎ Sometimes others in the office fill in for a receptionist or secretary and aren't sure what the procedure is or who everyone is. While you might not get through on the first shot, you might use this type of opportunity to get information. For example, you might ask for the person you want to speak to and when the substitute tells you he or she isn't in and asks if you want to leave a message, say something like, "I'm moving around a lot today. I'll try to call later. Is Mr. Brown ever in the office after 6:00 p.m.?" If the answer is, yes, ask if you can have his direct extension in case the switchboard is closed.

Remember the three Ps to help you get through. You want to be:

- ◎ Pleasant
- ◎ Persistent
- ◎ Positive

Words from the Wise
Friday afternoon is the worst time to call someone when you want something. The second worst time is early Monday morning.

Always be pleasant. Aside from it being general good manners to be nice to others, being pleasant to gatekeepers is essential. Gatekeepers talk to their bosses and can let them know if you were annoying or obnoxious. When someone tells you his or her boss "never takes unsolicited calls or accepts unsolicited resumes," tell them you understand. Then ask what they suggest. Acknowledge objections, but try to come up with a solution.

Be persistent. Just because you don't get through on the first try doesn't mean you shouldn't try again. Don't be annoying, don't be pushy, but don't give up. People like to help positive people. Don't moan and groan to the secretary about how difficult your life is. He or she will only want to get you off the phone.

Persistence and the Guilt Factor

Don't forget the guilt factor. If you consistently place calls to "Mr. Keane" and each time his secretary tells you he is busy, unavailable, or will call you back and he doesn't, what should you do? Should you give up? Well, that's up to you. Be aware that persistence often pays off. In many cases, after a number of calls, you and the secretary will have built up a "relationship" of sorts. As long as you have been pleasant, he or she may feel "guilty" that you are such a nice person and his or her boss isn't calling you back.

★ Voice of Experience

While persistence can work, don't be annoying. Calling more than once a day or in most cases, even more than once a week (unless you are given specific instructions by the secretary, receptionist, or person's assistant to do so) will put you on the annoying list.

In these cases, the secretary may give you a tip on how to get through, tell you to send something in writing, or ask the boss to speak to you.

Voice mail is another obstacle you might have to deal with. This automated system is often more difficult to bypass than a human gatekeeper. Many people don't even bother answering their phone, instead letting their voice mail pick up the calls and then checking their messages when convenient.

Decide ahead of time what you're going to do if you get someone's voice mail. Try calling once to see what the person's message is. It might, for example, let you know that the person you're calling is out of town until Monday. What this will tell you is that if you are calling someone on a cold call, you should probably not call until Wednesday because they probably will be busy when they get back in town.

If the message says something to the effect of, "I'm out of town, if you need to speak to me today, please call my cell phone," and then provides a phone number, don't call the cell phone. You don't *need* to speak to him or her; you *want* to. There is a big difference between *needs* and *wants*. You are cold calling a person who doesn't know you to ask for something. It is not generally a good idea to bother them outside the office.

If you call a few times and keep getting the voice mail, you're going to have to make your move. Leave a message something like this: "Hi, this is Tony Harris. My phone number is (111) 444-4444. I'd appreciate it if you could give me a call at your convenience. I'll look forward to hearing from you. Have a great day."

If you don't hear back within a few days, try again: "Hi, Mr. Brenner. This is Tony Harris. (111) 444-4444. I called a few days ago. I know you're busy and was just trying you again. I look

> ### ★ Words from the Wise
> Be aware that even if you block your number, certain companies pay to "see" your number. Generally these are companies using toll-free numbers such as 1-800 phone numbers, but in certain cases companies with toll-free numbers may also unblock your number.

forward to hearing from you. Thanks. Have a great day."

You might not hear from Mr. Brenner himself, but one of his assistants might call you. What do you do if you don't get a call back? Call again. How many times should you call? That's hard to say. Persistence may pay off. Remember that the person on the other end may start feeling guilty that he or she is not calling you back and place that call.

Be prepared. When you get a call back, have your ducks in a row and be ready and able to sell yourself. Practice ahead of time if need be and leave notes near your phone.

I suggest when making any of these calls that you block your phone number so that no one knows who is calling. To permanently block your phone number from showing on the receiver's caller ID, call your local phone company. Most don't charge for this service. You can also block your phone number on a temporary basis by dialing *67 before making your call. Remember that as soon as you hang up, this service will be disabled, so you will need to do this for each call.

Getting Them to Call You

While persistence and patience in calling and trying to get past the receptionist is usually necessary, you may need something else, too. You want something to set you apart so the busy ex-

ecutives not only will want to see you, but will also remember you. You want them to give you a chance to sell yourself.

What can you do? Creativity to the rescue! The amount of creativity will depend, to a great extent, on the specific company or organization to which you are trying to get through.

Your goal is to get the attention of the important person who can give you a chance to sell yourself. Once you have his or her attention, it's up to you to convince them that they should work with you.

Let's look at some ideas that I have either personally used or others have told me worked in their quest to get an individual's attention so they could get a foot in the door. Use these ideas as a beginning, but then try to develop some more of your own. You are limited only by your own creativity and your ability to think outside of the box.

My Personal Number-One Technique For Getting Someone To Call You

I am going to share my number one technique for getting someone to call you. I have used this technique successfully over the years to get people to call me in an array of situations and in a variety of industries at various levels in my career. I first came up with it after I graduated from college when I was entering the workforce and wanted to get a job in the music industry.

At the time there was no book to give me ideas. There was no career coach. There was no one who really wanted to help, and I desperately needed help to get a job.

I had tried all the traditional methods. I tried calling people, but most of the time I couldn't get past the gatekeeper. When I did, no one called me back. I tried sending out resumes. As I had just graduated from college, I had no "real" experience. I didn't know anyone and didn't even know anyone who knew anyone. I needed a break. Here's what I did.

When I was younger my parents used to take raw eggs, blow out the contents, and then decorate the shells. Everyone always commented on how nice the decorated eggs were and how different they were. One day, for some reason, the eggs popped into my mind, and I came up with my method to get people to call me back. Here's how it works.

Get a box of eggs. Extra-large or jumbo work well. While either white or brown eggs can be used, because of the coloration differences in brown eggs start with white ones. Wash the raw eggs carefully with warm water. Then dry the shells well.

Hold one egg in your hand and using a large needle or pin punch a small hole in the top of the egg. The top is the narrower end. Then, carefully punch a slightly larger hole in the other end of the egg. You might need to take the needle or pin and move it around in the hole to make it larger. Keep any pieces of shell that break off.

Now, take a straw and place it on the top hole of the egg. Holding the egg over a bowl, blow into the straw, blowing the contents of the egg out. This may take a couple of tries. Because of concerns with salmonella, do not put your mouth directly on the egg.

Keep in mind that the bigger you have made the hole, the easier it will be to blow the contents out of the egg. However, you want the egg to look as "whole" as possible when you're done. The bigger the hole, the harder this is to accomplish.

After blowing the contents out of the egg, carefully rinse out the shell, letting warm water run through it. Get the egg as clean as possible. Shake the excess water out of the egg and leave it to dry thoroughly. Depending on the temperature and humidity when you are preparing the eggs, it might take a couple of days.

Do at least three eggs at one time in case one breaks or cracks at the next step. You might want to do more. After you get the hang of this, you're going to want to keep a few extra prepared eggs around for when you want to get someone's attention fast and don't have time to prepare new ones.

Next, go to your computer and type the words, "Getting the attention of a busy person is not easy. Now that I have yours, could you please take a moment to review my resume." You can customize the message to suit your purposes by including the name of the recipient if you have it, or specifying your background sheet, CV or what ever you want the recipient to look at and consider. Then type your name and phone number.

Use a small font to keep the message to a line or two. Neatly cut out the strip of paper with your message. Roll the strip around a toothpick. Carefully, insert the toothpick with the strip of paper into the larger of the holes in the egg. Wiggle the toothpick around and slowly take the toothpick out of the egg. The strip of paper should now be in the shell.

Visit your local craft store and pick up a package of those small moveable eyes, miniature plastic or felt feet, and white glue or a glue gun. Glue the miniature feet to the bottom of the egg, covering the hole. Make sure you use the glue sparingly so none goes on your message. Now, glue on two of the moving eyes making the egg look like a face.

Go back to your computer and type the following words. "CRACK OPEN THIS EGG FOR AN IMPORTMANT MESSAGE." Print out the line and cut it into a strip. You might want to use bright-colored paper. Glue the strip to the bottom of the feet on the egg.

Now you're ready. Take the egg and place it in a small box that you have padded with cotton, bubble wrap, or foam. These eggs are very fragile, and you don't want the egg to break in transit!

Wrap the egg-filled box in attractive wrapping paper and then bubble wrap to assure it won't move around. Put your resume (or CV, background sheet, etc.) and a short cover letter into an envelope. Put it on the bottom of a sturdy mailing box. Place the egg box over it.

Make sure you use clean boxes and pack the egg as carefully as possible. Address the box. Make sure you include your name and return address. Then either mail, UPS, FedEx, Airborne, or hand deliver it to the office of the person you are trying to reach. Even if that person has a secretary opening his or her mail, the chances are good that the "gift" will be opened personally. In the event that a secretary opens the package, he or she will probably bring the egg into the boss to crack.

So now the recipient has the egg in front of them. He or she will probably break it open, see the message, and glance at your resume. Here's the good news. By the time the person breaks open the egg, he or she won't even notice the hole on the bottom and usually has no idea how you got the message in there. Generally, people who have seen this think it is so neat that they want to know how you did it, so they call you to ask. (Believe it or not, everyone has someone else they wish they could get to call them back.)

Once you have the person on the phone, your job is to get an interview. You want to get into his or her office for a meeting. When you get that call, tell the recipient you would be glad to show him or her how you made the egg; but it's kind of complicated explaining it over the phone. Offer to show him or her how it is done and ask when you could come in.

Voila, you have an appointment. Now all you have to do is sell yourself.

Is your resume sitting in a pile of countless others? Do you want your resume to stick out among the hundreds that come in? Do you want an interview but can't get one? Are you having difficulties getting people to call you back?

While I love the egg idea and have used it to obtain appointments, call backs, and to get noticed throughout my career, there are other ideas that work too. You might want to try a couple of these.

Have you ever considered using these simple items to help you succeed? If you haven't, perhaps now is the time.

◎ Fortune Cookies
◎ Chocolate Chip Cookies
◎ Candy Bars
◎ Mugs
◎ Pizzas
◎ Roses

Fortune Cookies

Almost no one can resist, cracking open a fortune cookie to see what the "message" says. This can be good news for your career.

Some fortune cookie companies make cookies similar to the ones you get in Chinese restaurants but with personalized messages inside. What could you say? That depends on what you are looking for. How about something like, "Human Resources Director who interviews Michael Cashman will have good luck for the rest of the day. Michael's lucky number: 111-222-3333."

Whatever message you choose, remember that you generally need to make all the messages the same or it gets very expensive to have the cookies made. You also need to either print cards on your computer or have cards printed professionally that read something to the effect of "Getting the attention of a busy person is never easy. Now that I have yours, could you please take a moment to review my resume?" Or, "Getting the attention of a busy person is not easy. Now that I have yours, I was hoping you could take a few moments to give me a call." (Or set up an appointment or anything else you want. Make sure your name and phone number are on the card.)

Put a couple of cookies with the card and your resume or other material in a clean, attractive mailing box and address it neatly. Make sure you address the box to someone specific. For example, don't address it to Superintendent, MHS Central School System. Instead, address it to Mr. Allen Black, Superintendent, MHS Central School System. Don't send it to Personnel Services, Some County Community College. Instead, send it to Brooke Anderson, Personnel Director, Some County Community College.

"I've heard of sending fortune cookies," you say. "What else can I do?"

Here's a twist. Send the same package of cookies, the card, and whatever else you sent (your resume, CV, background sheet, etc.) every day for two weeks. Every day, after the first day, also include a note that says, "Cookies For [Name of person] For Day 2," "Cookies For [Name of Person] For Day 3," and so on. At the end of the two-week period, stop. By now your recipient will probably have called you. If not, he or she will at least be expecting the cookies. If you don't hear from your recipient, feel free to call the office, identify yourself as the fortune cookie king or queen, and ask for an appointment.

This idea can be expensive, but if it gets you in the door and you can sell yourself or your idea, it will more than pay for itself.

Another great idea, which can really grab the attention of a busy executive or anybody else for that matter, is finding a company that makes gigantic fortune cookies with personalized messages. These cookies are often covered in chocolate, sprinkles, and all kinds of goodies and almost command people to see who sent it. Send these cookies with the same types of messages and supporting material as the others. The only difference is, if you choose to send the gigantic cookies, you probably only need to send one. If you don't get a call within the first week, feel free to call the recipient yourself.

Chocolate Chip Cookies

Chocolate chip cookies are a favorite of most people. Why not use that to your advantage? Go to the cookie kiosk at your local mall and or-

---

The Inside Scoop

To avoid potential problems with people who have allergies, do not send any food with nuts as an ingredient. Nothing can ruin your chances of getting a job faster than causing an allergic reaction in the person you're trying to impress.

Words from the Wise

Make sure cookies are individually wrapped and factory sealed. Otherwise, some people may just toss them.

> ### ⭐ Voice of Experience
>
> Do not try to save money by making the cookies yourself. In today's world, many people won't eat food if they don't know where it came from or that it was not prepared by a commercial eatery.

der a gigantic, pizza-sized cookie personalized with a few words asking for what you would like done. For example:

◎ "Please Review My Resume . . . Stephen Smith"

◎ "Please Call Me For An Interview . . . . Pat Young"

Keep your message short. You want the recipient to read it, not get overwhelmed. Generally, the cookies come boxed. Tape a copy of your resume, or whatever you are sending to the inside of the box.

Write a short cover letter to your recipient stating that you hope he or she enjoys the cookie while reviewing your resume, while giving you a call, or whatever you want. Put this in an envelope with another copy of your resume. On the outside of the box, neatly tape a card with the message we discussed previously: "Getting the attention of a busy person is never easy. Now that I have yours, would you please take a moment to review my resume." Or ask the recipient to give you a call, or whatever you are hoping he or she will do. Make sure your name and phone number are on the card.

If the cookie company has a mail or delivery service, use it, even if it is more expensive than mailing it yourself. It will be more effective. If there is no mail or delivery service, mail or deliver the cookie yourself. You should get a call from the recipient within a few days.

Candy Bars

There have been a number of studies that tout chocolate as a food that makes people happy or at least puts them in a good mood. Keeping this in mind, you might want to use chocolate to grab someone's attention and move that person to call you. Most people love chocolate and are happy to see it magically appear in their office. There are a number of different ways you can use chocolate to help your career.

◎ Buy a large, high-quality chocolate bar. Carefully fold your resume or a letter stating what you would like accomplished and slip it into the wrapping of the chocolate bar.

◎ Buy a large, high-quality chocolate bar. Wrap the chocolate bar with your resume or the letter stating what you would like accomplished.

◎ There are companies that create personalized wrappings for chocolate bars. Use one to deliver your message.

◎ Create a wrapping on your computer. If you do this, make sure you leave the original wrapping intact and cover it.

Whatever method you choose, put the candy bar in an attractive box, and attach the card with the message, "Getting the attention of a busy person is never easy. Now that I have yours, could you please take a moment to review my resume?" (Or whatever action you are asking your recipient to take.) Add a cover letter and send it off.

Mugs

When was the last time you threw out a mug? Probably not for a while. How about using this idea to catch the attention of a potential employer? Depending on your career aspiration, have mugs printed with replicas of your business or networking card, key points of your resume, CV, or background sheet along with your name and phone number.

Add in a small packet of gourmet or flavored coffee or hot chocolate and perhaps an individually wrapped biscotti or cookie and, of course, the card with the message stating, "Getting the attention of a busy person is never easy. Now that I have yours, could you please take a moment to review my resume?" (Or whatever else you are requesting.) Put the mug, a short cover letter and your resume, background sheet, or other material in a box and mail or deliver to your recipient. Remember to always put your return address on the box.

Pizza

Want to make sure your resume or background sheet gets attention? Have it delivered to your recipient with a fresh, hot pizza. This technique can be tricky, but effective. It does have some challenges however.

Here they are. In order to guarantee the pizza gets there with your information, you really need to be in the same geographic location as the company or organization you're trying to reach. You will need to personally make sure that your information is placed in a high-quality ziplock bag or, better yet, is laminated and then taped to the inside cover of the pizza box. You also not only have to know the name of the person the pizza is to be delivered to, but that he or she will be there the day you send it and doesn't have a lunch date. It's difficult to call an office where no one knows you and ask what time the recipient goes to lunch. So you are taking the risk that you will be sending a pizza to someone who isn't there. One way to get around this is by sending it in the late afternoon instead. That way your recipient can have a mid-afternoon "pizza break." And even if your recipient isn't

there, his or her employees will probably enjoy the pizza and tell their supervisor about it the next day.

If you do this, make sure that you have the pizzeria delivering the pizza tape the card with the message about getting a busy person's attention on the front of the box, so even if the receptionist gets the pizza, he or she will know who it came from.

If you don't get a thank-you call that day, call the recipient the next morning. You probably will speak to the secretary or receptionist first. Just tell whoever you speak to that you were the one who sent the pizza the day before in hopes of getting the attention of the recipient so you might possibly set up a job interview.

Roses

A very effective, but pricey way to get your recipient's attention is to have a dozen roses delivered to his or her office. No matter how many things you have tried with no response, there are very few people who will not place a thank-you call when they receive a dozen roses.

Talk to the florist ahead of time to make sure that the roses you will be sending are fragrant. Send the roses to your recipient with a card that simply says something to the effect of, "While you're enjoying the roses, please take a moment to review my resume, sent under separate cover." Sign it "Sincerely hoping for an interview," and include your name and phone number.

It is imperative to send your information so it arrives on the same day or at the latest the next day, so the roses you sent are still fresh in the recipient's mind.

It's Who You Know

While, of course, there are some areas of education that are easier to enter, there generally is always some amount of competition to get most jobs. There are also individuals who are talented or skilled, yet never get past the front door. Knowing someone who can get you in the door most certainly will help.

Before you say, "Me? I don't know anyone," stop and think. Are you sure? Don't you know someone, anyone, even on a peripheral basis who might be able to give you a recommendation, make a call, or would be willing lend his or her name?

What about your mother's aunt's husband's friend's neighbor's boss? Sure it might be a stretch. But think hard. Who can you think of who might know someone who might be able to help? This is not the time to be shy.

Call your aunt. Explain what you're trying to do with your career. Then ask if she would be willing to talk to her husband's friend about talking to their neighbor about using his name to make an appointment with the neighbor's boss.

"But I don't need any help," you say, "I can do it on my own."

You might be able to and you might not, but why wouldn't you give yourself every edge possible? You're going to have to prove yourself once you get in the door. No one can do that for you.

What if you don't have a relative who has a contact down the line? What about one of your teachers? What about your son's teacher? What about one of your sister's teachers? Does he or she know someone at the school or college where you want to apply? What about a friend who is already working at the school? How about someone on the school board or someone on the college's board of directors? What about someone who is on the college's foundation? What about the tutor you used to help you get through your biology class?

What about your hair stylist? Your UPS delivery person? Your mailman or mail lady? Your clergyman or woman? What about one of your physicians? Your pharmacist? The possibilities are endless if you just look.

The trick here is to think outside of the box. If you can find someone who knows someone who is willing to help you get your foot in the door, then all you will have to do is sell yourself.

If someone does agree to lend his or her name, make a call, or help you in any manner, it's important to write thank-you notes immediately. These notes should be written whether or not you actually get an interview or set up a meeting.

⭐ The Inside Scoop

A woman called a few years ago seeking some advice. She had worked for a year as a fifth grade teacher and received good reviews. She loved her job, but was getting married and her future husband lived on the other side of the country. I advised her to call the state where she was going to be living and check out what she needed to do to become licensed there. Then, after she did what was needed and had all her ducks in a row, to set up a meeting with the principal at the school where she was currently working and ask if he had any connections at any schools in the state where she was moving.

"Why would he want to help me?" she asked. "I'm leaving his school."

"Because you were a good teacher and you got good reviews," I said. "You can't lose anything by trying."

The woman met with her principal, who was happy to make a call. Before long she was called for an interview. During the interview, she was told that the main reason she was called was because of the good reference her principal gave her.

If you do go on an interview, it's also a good idea to either call or write another note letting your contact know what happened.

Meeting the Right People

You think and think and you can't come up with anyone you know with a connection to anyone at all in the area of education in which you are trying to succeed. What can you do? Sometimes you have to find your own contacts. You need to meet the right people. How can you do this? The best way to meet the right people in education is to be around people working in or around education. There are several possible ways you might do this.

To begin with, consider joining industry organizations and associations. Many of these organizations offer career guidance and support. They also may offer seminars, workshops, and other types of educational symposiums. Best of all, many have periodic meetings and annual conventions and conferences. All of these are treasure troves of possibilities to meet people in the industry. Some of them may be industry experts or insiders. Others may be just like you: people trying to get in and succeed. The important thing to remember is, take advantage of every opportunity.

Workshops and seminars are great because not only can you make important contacts, but you can learn something valuable about the industry as well. Most of these events have question-and-answer periods built into the program. Take advantage of these. Stand up and ask a good question. Make yourself visible. Some seminars and workshops have breakout sessions to encourage people to get to know one another. Use these to your advantage as well.

During breaks, don't run to the corner to check your voice mail. Walk around and talk to

---

⭐ Tip from the Top

When you go to industry events it is important to have a positive attitude and to avoid any negative conversations with anyone about anything at the seminar or in the industry. You can never tell who is related to who or what idea someone originated. You want to be remembered as the one who is bright and positive, not a negative sad sack.

---

people. Don't be afraid to walk up to someone you don't know and start talking. Remember to bring your business or networking cards and network, network, network!

After the session has ended, walk up, shake the moderator's hand and tell him or her how much you enjoyed the session, how much you learned, and how useful it will be in your career. This gives you the opportunity to ask for his or her business card, so that you have the correct spelling of the person's name, as well has his or her address, and phone number. This is very valuable information. When you get home, send a short note stating that you were at the session the person moderated, spoke to him or her afterwards, and just wanted to mention again how much you enjoyed it.

You might also ask, depending on their position, if it would be possible to set up an informational interview at their convenience or if they could suggest who you might call to set up an appointment. If you don't hear back within a week, feel free to call the person, identify yourself, and ask again. These interviews might just turn into an interview for a job or even a job itself.

Another good way to meet people in the industry is to attend industry or organization

Words from a Pro

Don't just blend in with everyone else at a seminar or workshop. Make yourself visible and memorable in a positive way. Ask questions and participate when possible. During breaks, don't rush to make calls on your cell phone. Instead, try to meet more people and make more contacts.

Tip from the Coach

Many industry organization conference managers have begun having mini career fairs at these events to help industry people who have been downsized as well as for companies looking to fill jobs. Check out Web sites of association conferences ahead of time.

annual conventions. These events offer many opportunities you might not normally have to network and meet industry insiders.

There is usually a charge to attend these conventions. Fee structures may vary. Sometimes there is one price for general admission to all events and entry to the trade show floor. Other times, there may be one price for entry just to the trade show floor and another price if you also want to take part in seminars and other events.

The cost of attending these conventions may be expensive. In addition to the fee to get in, if you don't live near the convention location, you might have to pay for airfare or other transportation as well as accommodations, meals, and incidentals. Is it worth it? If you can afford it, absolutely! If you want to meet people in a specific area of education, these gatherings are the place to do it.

How do you find these events? Look in the appendix of this book for industry associations in your area of interest. Find the phone number and call and ask when and where the annual

convention will be held. Better yet, go to the organization's Web site. Most groups put information about their conventions online.

If you are making the investment to go to a convention or a conference, take full advantage of every opportunity. As we've discussed throughout this book, network, network, network, and network some more! Some events to take part in or attend at conventions and conferences might include:

◎ opening events
◎ keynote presentations
◎ educational seminars and workshops
◎ certification programs
◎ breakout sessions
◎ breakfast, lunch, and/or dinner events
◎ cocktail parties
◎ trade show exhibit areas
◎ career fairs

There is an art to attending conventions and using the experience to your best benefit. Remember that the people you meet are potential employers and new business contacts.

This is your chance to make a good first impression. Dress appropriately and neatly.

Do not get inebriated at these events. If you want to have a drink or a glass of wine, that's probably okay, but don't overdrink. You want potential employers or people you want to do

The Inside Scoop

Many industry trade organizations offer special convention admission prices for students. Make sure you ask ahead of time.

business with to know you're a good risk, not someone who drinks at every opportunity.

It is essential to bring business cards with you and give them out to everyone you can. You can never tell when someone will hear about a position, remember meeting you and getting your business card, and give you a call.

Collect business cards as well. Then when you get home from the convention or trade show, you will have contact names to call or write regarding business or job possibilities.

Walk the trade show floor. Stop and talk to people at booths. They are usually more than willing to talk. This is a time to network and try to make contacts. Ask questions and listen to what people are saying.

If you have good writing skills, a good way of meeting people within the industry is to write articles or interview people for local, regional, or national periodicals or newspapers. We discussed the idea earlier when talking about using your writing skills to help you obtain interviews. It can be just as effective in these situations.

How does this work? A great deal of it depends on your situation, where you live and the area of the industry you are targeting.

Basically, what you have to do is develop an angle or hook for a story on the segment of education in which you are interested in meeting people. For example, does the superintendent of schools go on biking vacations in or out of the country? Perhaps his or her adventures might make a good story. Is one of the school's teachers appearing on

a game show? Does one of the college professors not only collect art, but write about it in a major art magazine? Has the college president been asked to speak at a major education conference? Has someone who graduated from the local high school become the principal of the same school she graduated from 30 years earlier? These are angles or hooks you might use to entice a local or regional periodical let you do an article.

Your next step is to contact someone who might be interested in the story. If you're still in school, become involved with the school newspaper. If you're not, call up your local newspaper or a regional magazine and see if they might be interested in the article or feature story you want to write.

You probably will have to give them some samples of your writing and your background sheet or resume. You might also have to write on "spec" or speculation. What this means is that when you do the story they may or may not use it. If they do, they will pay you. If not, they won't.

Your goal here (unless you want to be an education reporter) is not to make money (although that is nice). Your goal is to be in situations where you have the opportunity to meet industry insiders. If you're successful, not only will you be meeting these people, you'll be meeting them on a different level than if you were looking for a job. You'll be networking on a different level as well.

Networking Basics

It's not always what you know but who you know. With that in mind, I'm going to once again bring up the importance of networking. You can never tell who knows someone in some area of the industry, so it is essential to share your career dreams and aspirations with those around you. Someone you mention your dreams or goals to

The Inside Scoop

Recruiters and headhunters often attend conferences and conventions in hopes of finding potential employees for their clients.

might just say, "My cousin is the assistant superintendent of schools upstate." Or, "Really. I just heard that the Middleburgh School is looking for a guidance counselor." Or, "I just saw an advertisement in the classifieds for a job like that."

Think it can't happen? Think again. It's happened to me, it's happened to others, and it can happen to you!

A registered nurse I know worked at a public health agency. One day while participating in a community health fair she began talking to someone in the booth next to hers who turned out to be the assistant superintendent of schools. She mentioned in passing that what she liked most about her current job was teaching young people about disease prevention, health issues, and healthy eating. They spoke for a while and the woman mentioned that the funding for her job was ending and she would have some free time. She told him that she would love to volunteer to give a couple of classes in healthy cooking at the school if the school was interested. The assistant superintendent thought it was a good idea and before long the woman had given a number of classes as part of an after school program at the high school. The classes were so well received that they asked the woman if she would consider giving similar classes at the middle school, which she did. As she was still looking for a new job, she also decided to sign up to be put on the substitute list at the school.

Coincidentally, during this time period, the high school home economics teacher resigned abruptly. The school was in desperate need of a replacement for the last month of school. The woman was called in to substitute and then given the job to finish out the year.

When the school began interviewing to fill the position, the woman applied. While she didn't have a teaching degree or teaching li-

cense, she eventually beat out the competition with the understanding that she would take some classes and get her state teaching license. Over the years, she consistently impressed her supervisors and became a favorite teacher in the school. The woman now has tenure and has been happily teaching for the last 10 years.

People always ask, "But do those things really happen?" and the answer is an unequivocal *yes*. These are not isolated incidents. Things like this happen all the time. Networking and sharing your dreams can and do work for others and it can work for you. But in order for it to happen, you have to be proactive.

Knowing how important networking can be to your career, let's talk about some networking basics.

The first thing you need to do is determine exactly who you know and who is part of your network. Then you need to get out and find more people to add to the list.

When working on your networking list, add the type of contact you consider each person. Primary contacts are people you know: your family members, teachers, friends, and neighbors. Secondary contacts are individuals who are referred to you by others. These would include, for instance, a friend of a friend, your aunt's neighbor, your attorney's sister, and so on.

You might also want to note whether you consider each person as a close, medium, or distant relationship. *Close* for example, would be family, friends, employers, and current teachers. *Medium* would be people you talk to and see frequently, such as your dentist, attorney, or your UPS, FedEx, or mail delivery person. *Distant* would include people you talk to and see infrequently or those you have just met or have met just once or twice.

Look at the Networking Worksheet on page 153 for an example.

Networking Worksheet

Name	Relationship/ Position	Type of Contact (Primary or Secondary)	Closeness of Contact (Close, Medium, or Distant)
Heather Johnston	Former Guidance Counselor	Primary	Medium
Will Alley	Bank Teller	Primary	Distant
Bob	UPS Delivery Person	Primary	Medium
Thomas Williams	Newspaper Reporter	Secondary	Distant
Tina	Sister-in-law	Primary	Close
Dr. Brenton	Dentist	Primary	Medium
Robert Allen	Attorney	Primary	Medium
Ashley Fontana	Education Reporter	Secondary	Distant
Dr. Harrison	College Advisor	Primary	Medium
Ann Morrison	President of the School Board	Secondary	Medium

It would be great to have a network full of people in the segment of education in which you hope to have your career. However, that may not be the case. That does not mean, though, that other people can't be helpful. Your network may include a variety of people from all walks of life. These may include

- family members
- friends
- friends of friends
- coworkers and colleagues
- teachers or professors
- your doctor and dentist
- your pharmacist
- your mail carrier
- your hairstylist
- your personal trainer
- your priest, pastor, or rabbi
- members of your religious congregation
- UPS, FedEx, Airborne, or other delivery person
- your auto mechanic
- your attorney
- the waitress at the local diner
- the server at the local coffee shop
- bank tellers from your local bank
- your neighbors
- friends of your relatives
- your college advisor
- business associates of your relatives
- people you work with on volunteer not-for-profit boards and civic groups
- coworkers at your current job

Now look at your list. Do you see how large your network really is? Virtually everyone you come in contact with during the day can be-

Networking Worksheet

Name	Relationship/ Position	Type of Contact (Primary or Secondary)	Closeness of Contact (Close, Medium, or Distant)

come part of your network. Just keep adding people to your list.

Expanding Your Network

How can you expand your network? There are a number of ways. Networking events are an excellent way to meet people. Industry networking events are, of course, the best, but don't count out non-industry events too. For example, your local chamber of commerce may have specific networking programs designed to help business people in the community meet and network.

How do you know if the people who are at the event have any possibility of being related to the area of education in which you're interested? You don't. But as we've discussed, you don't know who people know. People you meet may know others who *are* in the part of the industry you want to pursue.

Civic and other not-for-profit groups also have a variety of events that are great for networking. Whether you go to a regular meeting or you attend a charity auction, cocktail party, or large gala to benefit a nonprofit, you will generally find business people in the community you might not know. As an added bonus, many larger not-for-profit events also have media coverage, meaning that you have the opportunity to add media people to your network.

A good way to meet people involved in education is to attend events sponsored by educational institutions. Teachers, principals, and administrators, for example, generally attend events sponsored by PTAs. The same people also are on hand for school plays and talent shows.

College and university cultural and entertainment events are other good places to network with administrators, board members, and professors. Additionally, most colleges and universities have foundations which host fund-raising events that are generally full of higher-ups from the college.

How do you meet all these people? You might just walk around and network. Or you might want to volunteer to help with a fund-raiser or event so people start to know you and what you can do.

Those who take advantage of every opportunity to meet new people will have the largest networks. The idea in building a network is to go out of your comfort zone. If you just stay with people you know and are comfortable with, you won't have the opportunity to get to know others. You want to continually meet new people; after all you never know who knows whom.

Networking Savvy

You are now learning how to build your network. However, the largest network in the world will be useless unless you know how to take full advantage of it. So let's talk a little about how you're going to use the network you are building.

Previously we discussed the difference between skills and talents. Networking is a skill. You don't have to be born with it. You can acquire, practice, and improve the skill to network. What that means is, if you practice networking you can get better at it, and it can payoff big in your career!

Get out. Go to new places. Meet new people. The trick here is, when you're in a situation where there are new people, don't be afraid to walk up to them, shake their hand, and talk to them. People can't read your mind, so it's imperative to tell them about your career goals, dreams, and aspirations.

When you meet new people, listen to them. Focus on what they're saying. Ask questions. Be interested in what *they* are telling you. You can never tell when the next person you talk to will be the one who will be able to help you open the door *or* vice versa.

If you're shy, even the thought of networking may be very difficult for you. However, it is essential to make yourself do it anyway. Successful networking can payoff big in your career. In some situations it can mean the difference between getting a great job and not getting a job at all. It can also mean the difference between success and failure in your career. And that is worth the effort!

Just meeting people isn't enough. When you meet someone that you add to your network the idea is to try to further develop the relationship. Just having a story to tell about who you know or who you met is not enough. Arrange a follow up meeting, send a note, write a letter, or make a phone call. The more you take advantage of every opportunity, the closer you will be to getting what you want.

A good way to network is to volunteer. We just discussed attending not-for-profit events and civic meetings to expand your network, but how about volunteering to work with a not-for-profit or civic group? A moment ago we discussed volunteering with an event for a college foundation. There are a ton of opportunities just waiting for you.

I can imagine you saying, "When? I'm so busy now, I don't have enough time to do anything."

Make the time. It will be worth it. Why?

People will see you on a different level. They won't see you as someone looking for a job or trying to succeed at some level. Generally, people talk about their volunteer work to friends, family, business associates, and other colleagues. What this means is that when someone is speaking to someone else they might mention in passing that one of the people they are working with on an event or project is trying to get a job as a school administrator, trying to locate a position in marketing at a college or university, trying to land a position as an education reporter, or teacher, or almost anything else.

Anyone these people mention you or your situation to is a potential secondary networking contact. Those people, in turn, may mention it to someone else. Eventually, someone involved in the area of education you are pursuing might hear about you.

Another reason to volunteer is so people will see that you have a good work ethic. Treat volunteer projects as you would work projects. Do what you say you are going to do and do it in a timely manner. Do your best at all times. Showcase your skills and your talents and do everything you do with a positive attitude and a smile.

Volunteering also gives you the opportunity to demonstrate skills and talents people might not otherwise know you have. Can you do publicity? Can your write? How about organizing things? Do you get along well with others? Do you have leadership skills? What better way to illustrate your skills than by using them to put together an event, publicize it, or coordinate other volunteers?

★ The Inside Scoop

Volunteer to do projects that no one else wants to do and you will immediately become more visible.

★ Tip from the Coach

While volunteering is good for networking, don't get involved with too many organizations. Depending on your schedule, one, two, or even three is probably fine. Anything more than that, and you're on the road to burnout.

Best of all, you can use these volunteer activities on your resume. While volunteer experiences don't take the place of work experience, they certainly can fill out a resume short of it.

Don't just go to meetings. Participate fully in the organization. That way you'll not only be helping others, you will be adding to your network.

Where can you volunteer? Pretty much any not-for-profit, community group, school, or civic organization is a possibility. The one thing you should remember, however, is that you should only volunteer for organizations in whose cause you believe.

In order to make the most of every networking opportunity it's essential for people to remember you. Keep a supply of your business cards with you all the time. Don't be stingy with them. Give them out freely to everyone. That way your name and number will be close at hand if needed. Make sure you ask for cards in return. If people don't have them, be sure to ask for their contact information.

Try to keep in contact with people in your network on a regular basis. Of course, you can't call everyone every day, but try to set up a schedule of sorts to do some positive networking every day. For example, you might decide to call one person every day on your networking list. Depending on the situation, you can say you are calling to touch base, say hello, keep in contact, or see how they are doing. Ask how they have been, or talk about something you might have in common, or something they might think is interesting. You might also decide that once a week you will try to call someone and set up a lunch or coffee date.

Be on the lookout for stories, articles, or other tidbits of information that might be of interest to people in your network. Clip them out and send them along with a short note saying you saw the story and thought the person might be interested. If you hear of something someone in your network might be interested in, call him or her. The idea is to continue cultivating relationships by keeping in contact with people in your network and staying visible.

Keep track of the contacts in your network. You can use the sample sheet provided, a card file using index cards, a database, or a contact software program on your computer. Include as much information as you have about each person. People like when you remember them and their interests. It makes you standout.

Use your networking contact list. For example, a few days before someone's birthday send him or her a card. If you know someone collects old guitars, for example, and you see an article on old guitars, clip it out and send it. Don't be a pest, but keep in contact. People in sales have been using this technique for years. It works for them and it will help you in your career as well.

Tip from the Coach

Have you ever received a birthday card from someone who wasn't a close friend or relative? Someone who you just happened to mention to that your birthday was coming up in a few days? Remember how it put a smile on your face when you opened that card and read who it was from? Remember thinking how nice the person was who sent you the card? Remember thinking about what you could do nice for them? You might not have known them well, but you probably won't forget them now. If you do the same type of thing for others you will stand out as well.

You might want to use some of the items here and then add more information as it comes up. You don't have to ask people for all this information the first time you meet them. Just add it when you get it.

Networking and Nerve

Successful networking will give you credibility and a rapport with people in and out of the industry. But networking sometimes takes nerve, especially if you're not naturally outgoing. You have to push yourself to get out and meet people, talk to them, tell them what you are interested in doing, and then stay in contact. On occasion, you may have to ask people if they will help you, ask for recommendations, ask for

---

Words from a Pro

Keep a scrapbook of articles, photos, programs, and other supporting material from volunteer events you have worked and participated in. It will be useful when putting together your career portfolio.

Tip from the Top

After you have worked on a volunteer project, ask the executive director or board president if he or she would mind writing you a letter of recommendation for your file.

Networking Contact Information Sheet

Name
_____

Business Address
_____

Business Phone
_____

Home Address
_____

Home Phone
_____

E-mail Address
_____

Web Address
_____

Birthday
_____

Anniversary
_____

Where and When Met
_____

Spouse or Significant Other's Name
_____

Children's Name(s)
_____

Dog Breed and Name
_____

Cat Breed and Name
_____

Hobbies
_____

Interests
_____

Things Collected
_____

Honors
_____

Awards
_____

Interesting Facts

references, and so on. Don't let the fear of doing what you need to do stop you from doing it. Just remember that the end result of all this effort will be not only entrée into a career you want, but a shot at success.

As long as you're pleasant and not rude, there is nothing wrong with asking for help. Just remember that while people can help you get your foot in the door, you are going to have to sell yourself once you open it.

Networking is a two way street. While it might be hard for you to imagine at this moment that someone might want you to help them in some segment of their career. Reciprocate and reciprocate graciously. As a matter of fact, if you see or know someone you might be able to help, even in a small way, don't wait for that person to ask, offer your help.

Finding a Mentor or Advocate

Mentors and advocates can help guide and boost your career. A mentor or advocate in education can also often provide valuable contacts, which

> ### Words from the Wise
> It is not uncommon to run into someone who doesn't want to help you. This may be for any number of reasons, ranging from they really don't know how they can help, they don't have the time in their schedule, or they think that if they help you in your career it puts their position at risk. If you do ask someone to be your mentor and he or she says no, just let it go. Look for someone else. The opposite of the having a great mentor in your life is having someone who is sabotaging your career.

as we now know are essential to your success. The best mentors and advocates are supportive individuals who help move your career to the next level. While having a mentor in the education industry would be the ideal, that doesn't mean others from outside the industry might not be helpful.

Can't figure out why anyone would help you? Many people like to help others. It makes them feel good and makes them feel important. How do you find a mentor? Look for someone who is successful and ask. Sounds simple? It is simple. The difficult part is finding just the right person or persons.

> ### Tip from the Coach
> If someone asks you to be his or her mentor or asks for your help, and you can do it, say yes. As a matter of fact, if you see someone you might be able to help, do just that. You might think that you don't even have your own career on track or you don't have time. You might be tempted to say no. Think again. You are expecting someone to help you. Do the same for someone else. There is no better feeling than helping someone else. And while you shouldn't help someone for the sole purpose of helping yourself, remember that you can often open doors for yourself, while opening them for someone else.

> ### Tip from the Coach
> Can a mentor really help? Absolutely! While having a mentor is important in every industry, in education having a good mentor can really push your career upward quickly. I've personally seen a mentor help a teacher's aide become a full-fledged teacher, another help a teacher become a principal, and yet another help an assistant superintendent become a superintendent.

Sometimes you don't even have to ask. In many cases a person may see your potential and offer advice and assistance. It is not uncommon for a mentor to be a supervisor or former supervisor. He or she might, for example, hear of a better job or be on a search committee and recommend you. As your career goes on, the individual may follow you and your career, helping you along the way.

Time is a valuable commodity, especially to busy people. Be gracious when someone helps you or even tries to help. Make sure you say thank you to anyone and everyone who shares his or her time, expertise, or advice. And don't forget to ask if there is any way you can return the favor.

8

THE INTERVIEW

Getting the Interview

You can have the greatest credentials in the world, wonderful references, and a stellar resume, but if you don't know how to interview well, it's often difficult to land the job, especially if you're seeking a job in any aspect of education.

Whether your dream is to work in teaching, the administration or support segment of education, the business sector, or anywhere in between, the first step is always getting the job.

One of the keys to getting most jobs is generally the interview. Landing a job in most segments of education is no different. Let's take some time to discuss how to get that all-important meeting.

The interview is your chance to shine. During an interview you can show what can't be illustrated on paper. This is the time your personality, charisma, and talents can be showcased. This is where someone can see your demeanor, your energy level, your passion, and your attitude. Obtaining an interview and excelling in that very important meeting can help get you the job you want.

If you do it right, the interview can help make you irresistible. It is your chance to persuade the interviewer to hire you. It is your main shot at showing why *you* would be better for the job than anyone else, why hiring *you* would benefit the school, college, organization, or company, and why *not* hiring *you* would be a major mistake.

There are many ways to land job interviews. Some of these include

◎ responding to advertisements
◎ recommendations from friends, relatives, or colleagues
◎ making cold calls
◎ writing letters
◎ working with executive search firms, recruiters, or headhunters
◎ working with employment agencies
◎ attending job and career fairs
◎ finding jobs that have not been advertised (the hidden job market)

Responding to an advertisement is probably the most common approach people take to obtain a job interview. Where can you look for ads for jobs in education? Depending on the exact type of job you're looking for here are some possibilities:

◎ newspapers
◎ trade journals
◎ association Web sites

161

⭐ The Inside Scoop

No matter where you live, you can usually view the classified ads for most of the major newspapers throughout the country online. Go to the specific newspaper's main Web site and look for "classifieds," "jobs," or "employment."

◎ school, company, and organization Web sites

- ⊡ public schools
- ⊡ private schools
- ⊡ vocational or technical schools
- ⊡ colleges and universities
- ⊡ tutoring companies
- ⊡ educational equipment companies
- ⊡ educational textbook publishers
- ⊡ marketing firms and public relations agencies specializing in the education industry
- ⊡ corporations seeking corporate trainers
- ⊡ seminars companies seeking corporate trainers
- ⊡ career-oriented Web sites
- ⊡ education-oriented Web sites

Let's say you open up the newspaper or a trade magazine or see an advertisement on the Web that looks like one of these:

Green County Community College seeking to fill the following positions: Director of Marketing; Publicity Assistant; Director of Student Activities; Administrative Assistant to President. For consideration for these positions either fax resume to (111) 000-0000 or mail to P.O. Box 2222, Some Town, NY 11111.

Some Town Central School District seeking to fill the following full-time positions: High School Social Studies Teacher; English Teacher; Science Teacher; General Math Teacher; Spanish Teacher. State Certification required. For consideration forward resume and supporting documents to Some Town Central School District, Recruitment Services, P. O. Box 888, Some Town, NY 11111.

Once you see the ad you get excited. You have been looking for a job just like one of the positions in the advertisement. You can't wait to send your resume.

Want a reality check? There may be hundreds of other people who can't wait either. Here's the good news. With a little planning, you can increase your chances of getting an interview from the classified or display ad, and as we've just discussed, this is your key to the job.

Your resume and cover letter need to stand out. Your resume needs to generate an interview. Most importantly, in a broad sense, you want your resume to define you as the one-in-a-million candidate an employer can't live without, instead of one of the million others that are applying for a job.

In essence, it's essential that your resume and cover letter distinguish you from every other applicant going for the job. Why? Because if yours doesn't, someone else's will and he or she will be the one who gets the job.

Let's look at the journey a resume might take after you send it out in response to a classified ad. Where does it go? Who reads it? That depends. In smaller organizations your resume and cover letter may go directly to the person who will be hiring you. It may also go to that person's receptionist, secretary, administrative assistant, or an office manager.

In larger organizations your resume and cover letter may go to a hiring manager or human resources director. This would probably occur if you were answering an ad for a position at college, university, school district, etc.

If you are replying to an advertisement placed by an employment agency, your response will generally go to the person at the employment agency responsible for that client and job.

In any of these situations, however, your resume may take other paths. Depending on the specific job and organization, your response may go through executive recruiters, screening services, clerks, secretaries, or even receptionists. Whoever the original screener of resumes turns out to be, he or she will have the initial job of reviewing the information to make sure that it fits the profile of what is needed. But—and I repeat, but—that doesn't mean that if you don't have the exact requirements you should not reply to a job.

The trick is to tailor your resume as closely as possible to the specific job and write a great cover letter. For example, let's say the job re-

quirements for a position at a state college in the marketing department might look something like this:

DIRECTOR OF MARKETING—STATE UNIVERSITY. Creative, enthusiastic, team player with proven track record. Must have strong organization skills and excellent verbal and writing skills. Minimum requirements include bachelor's degree and four years experience in education oriented marketing, Media and community contacts helpful.

Now let's say that while you are creative and enthusiastic and have excellent verbal and writing skills, you don't have four years experience working in education-oriented marketing. Instead, you have two years of experience handling marketing for a health care facility. Prior to your current job, you were a journalist for a local newspaper. You have media contacts, but they're not in the community in which you're applying for a job nor are your community contacts. Should you not apply for the job? If you want it, I say go for it.

Here is what you need to know. When you are working on your resume and your cover letter in response to an ad, remember that skills are transferable. Skills for specific areas might need to be fine tuned, but teaching skills are teaching skills; administrative skills are administrative skills; sales skills are sales skills, writing skills are writing skills, and publicity and public relations skills are publicity and public relations skills. Stress what you have done successfully, not what you haven't done. Use your cover letter to help showcase these accomplishments.

No matter whom your resume and cover letter go to, your goal is to increase your chances of it ending up in the pile that ultimately gets called for an interview. Whoever the screener

Tip from the Top

Here is what you need to know: The requirements set forth in a job advertisement are the ideal requirements that the company would like; not necessarily what they are going to end up with. Yes, it would be great if they could find a candidate with every single requirement, but in reality, it doesn't always work like that. In many cases, while there may be a candidate who has all the qualifications, someone who is missing one or two stands out and ultimately is the one who lands the job.

of the resumes is, he or she will probably pass over any resumes that don't look neat and well thought out, or any with obvious errors.

What can you do? First, go over your resume. Make sure it is perfect. Make sure it is perfectly tailored to the job you are going after. Make sure it is neat, looks clean and not wrinkled, crumpled, or stained. If you are going to mail it, make sure it's printed on good quality paper.

Human resources and personnel departments often receive hundreds of responses to ads. While most people use white paper, consider using off-white or even a different color such as light blue or light mauve. You want your resume to look sophisticated and classy, but still stand out. Of course, the color of the paper will not change what is in your resume, but it will at least help your resume get noticed in the first place.

If the advertisement directs you in a specific method of responding to the ad, then use that method. For example, if the ad instructs applicants to fax their resumes, then fax it. If it says e-mail your resume, then use e-mail and pay attention to whether the ad specifies sending the file as an attachment or in the body of your e-mail. The company may have a procedure for screening job applicants.

If given the option of methods of responding, which should you use? Each method has its pros and cons.

◎ E-mail
  ▫ On the pro side, e-mail is one of the quickest methods of responding to ads. Many companies use the e-mail method.
  ▫ On the con side, you are really never assured someone gets what you sent and even if they do, you're not sure that it won't be inadvertently deleted. Another concern is making sure that the resume you sent reaches the recipient

> **Tip from the Top**
> Many school districts now require teachers to apply using online applications. Make sure you follow the directions provided on how to submit your application and any supporting materials and be sure to keep a copy of everything.

in the form in which you sent it. If you are using a common word processing program and the same platform (Mac or PC) as the recipient, you probably won't have a problem. If you are using a Mac and the recipient is using a PC or you are using different word processing programs, you might have a problem.

◎ Fax
  ▫ On the pro side, faxing can get your resume where it's going almost instantaneously.
  ▫ On the con side, if the recipient is using an old fashioned fax, the paper quality might not be great. The good news is that most companies now use plain paper faxes.

◎ Mailing or Shipping (USPS, FedEx, Airborne, or UPS)
  ▫ On the pro side, you can send your resume on good quality paper so you know what it is going to look like when it arrives. You can also send any

> **Tip from the Top**
> If faxing any documents, remember to use the "fine" or "best" option on your fax machine. While this may take a bit longer to send, the recipients will get a better copy.

supporting materials that might help you get the coveted interview. You can send it with an option to have someone sign for it when it arrives so you definitely know if and when it arrived.

- On the con side, it may take time to arrive by mail. One of the ways to get past this problem is to send it overnight or two-day express. It will cost more, but you will have control over when your package arrives.

When is the best time to send your response to an ad in order to have the best chance at getting an interview? If you send your resume right away, it might arrive with a pile of hundreds of others, yet, if you wait too long, the company might have already "found" the right candidate and stopped seriously looking at new resumes.

Many people procrastinate, so if you can send in your response immediately, such as the day the ad is published or the very next morning, it will probably be one of the first ones in. At that time the screener will be reading through just a few responses. If yours stands out, it stands a good chance of being put into the "initial interview pile."

If you can't respond immediately, then wait two or three days so your resume doesn't arrive with the big pile of other responses. Once again, your goal is to increase your chances of your resume not being passed over.

When you are trying to land an interview through a recommendation from friends or colleagues, cold calls, letters, executive search firms, recruiters, headhunters, employment agencies, people you met at job fairs, through other networking events, or any aspect of the hidden job market, the timing of sending a resume is essential. In these cases you want the people receiving your information to remember that someone said it was coming, so send it as soon as possible. This is not the time to procrastinate. If you do, you might lose the opportunity to set up that all-important meeting.

Persistence is the word to remember when trying to get an interview. If you are responding to an advertisement and you don't hear back within a week or two, call to see what is happening. If after you call the first time, you don't hear back after another week or so (unless you've been specifically given a time frame) call back again. Don't be obnoxious and don't be a pain, but call.

If you're shy, you're going to have to get over it. Write a script ahead of time to help you. Don't read directly from the script, but practice, so it becomes second nature. For example: "Hello, this is Ellen Gray. I replied to an advertisement you placed in the newspaper for the high school guidance counselor. I was wondering who I could speak with to find out about the status of the position?"

When you get to the correct person, you might have to reiterate your purpose in calling.

Then you might ask, "Do you know when interviewing is starting? Will all applicants be notified one way or the other? Is it possible to tell me whether I'm on the list to be contacted?" Don't be afraid to try to get as much information as possible, once again making sure you are being pleasant.

You want to be friendly with the secretary or receptionist. These people are on the inside and can provide you with a wealth of information.

Be aware that there is a way that you can get your resume looked at, obtain an interview, and beat the competition out of the dream job you want. Remember we discussed the hidden job market?

While many positions in public schools and education are advertised, we know that there are jobs that are not advertised. Following this theory, all you have to do is contact a company and land the job you want *before* it is advertised.

"How?" you ask.

Take a chance. Make a call or write a letter and ask. You might even stop in and talk to the human resources department or one of the department heads. There is nothing that says you have to wait to see an ad in the paper. Call up and ask to speak to the human resources department, recruitment services, or hiring manager. Once again, write out a script ahead of time so you know exactly what you want to say. Ask about job openings. Make sure you have an idea of what you want to do and convey it to the person you are talking to.

If you are told there are no openings or you are told that the school, company, or organization doesn't speak to people regarding employment, unsolicited, be pleasant, yet persistent. Ask if you can forward a resume to keep on file. In many cases they will agree just to get you off the phone. Ask for the name of the person you

should direct your resume to, then ask for the address where it should be sent *and* the fax number. Thank the person you spoke with and make sure you get his or her name.

Now here's a neat trick: Fax your resume. Send it with a cover letter that states that a hard copy will be coming via mail. Why fax it?

Did you know that when you fax documents to a company they generally are delivered directly to the desk of the person you are sending it to? They don't go through the mailroom where they might be dumped into a general inbox. They don't sit around for a day. They are generally delivered immediately.

Now that your resume is in the hands of the powers that be, it's your job to call them, make sure they got it, and try as hard as you can to set up an interview. The individual's secretary might try to put you off. Don't be deterred. Thank her or him and say you understand his or her position. Say you're going to call in a week or so after the boss has had a chance to review your material. Send your information out in hard copy immediately. Wait a week or so and call back. Remember that persistence pays off.

Depending on the job, you sometimes might reach someone who tells you, "If I weren't so busy I would be glad to meet with you." They might tell you when their workload lightens or a project is done, they will schedule an interview. You could say thank you and let it go. Or you could tell them that you understand they're busy. All you are asking for is 10 minutes and not a minute longer. You'll even bring a stopwatch and coffee if they want. Guarantee them that 10 minutes after you get in the door, you will stand up to leave.

If you're convincing, you might land an interview. If you do, remember to *bring* that stopwatch. Introduce yourself, put the stopwatch down on the desk in front of you, and present your skills. It's essential that you practice this before you get to the appointment. Give the highlights of your resume and how hiring you would benefit the school, college, or company. When your 10 minutes are up, thank the person you are meeting with for his or her time and give him or her your resume, any supporting materi-

---

⭐ **Tip from the Coach**

While the following occurred when I was first trying to enter the music business, I think the concept illustrates how persistence can pay off in any industry. At that time I met and got to know a young man who was a comedian. He wasn't a very good comedian, but he said he was a comedian and he did have a good number of jobs and bookings, so I guess he was a comedian.

During this time I was trying to land interviews with everyone I could so I could get my own dream job in the music industry.

I made a contact with a booking agent whom I called and developed a business relationship with. Every week I'd call, and every week he would tell me to call him back. It wasn't going anywhere, but at least someone was taking my call. This went on for about three or four months.

One day when I called the owner got on the phone and said, "Do you know Joe Black? [Not his real name.] He said he has worked in your area?"

I said, "Yes, he works as a comedian."

"What do you know about him?" he asked.

"He's very nice," I answered.

"But what do you know about him?" the agent asked again. "Is he any good?"

"Well, he's not a great comedian, but he seems to keep getting jobs. He's booking himself," I replied.

"That's interesting," he said. "He has called me over 25 times looking for a job as an agent. What do you think?"

I was wondering why he was asking my opinion, because I had yet to get into his office myself. "If he can book himself, he can probably do a great job for your agency," I said. "You have great clients. I bet he would do a great job."

"Thanks," he said, "I might give him a call."

"What about me?" I asked.

"I still can't think of where you might fit in," he said. "Why don't you give me a call in a couple of weeks."

I waited a couple of weeks, called back and asked to speak to the owner.

"Hello," he said. "Guess who's standing next to me?"

He had hired Joe Black, the comedian, to work as an agent in his office.

"He had no experience, outside of booking himself, " the agent said. "But I figured if he is as persistent making calls for our clients as he was trying to get a job, he'd work out for us. Why don't you come in and talk when you have a chance. I don't have anything, but maybe I can give you some ideas."

I immediately said that I had been planning a trip to the booking agent's city the next week. We set up an appointment.

Did the agent ever have a job for me? No. But while I was in his office he introduced me to some of the clients he was booking, who introduced me to some other people, who later turned out to be clients of mine when I opened up my public relations company.

No matter in what industry you want a job, the moral of the story is the same. Networking and persistence always pay off.

als you have brought with you, and your business card. Then leave. If you are asked to stay, by all means, stay and continue the meeting. One way or the other, write a note thanking the person for his or her time.

If you have sold yourself or your idea for a position, someone may just get back to you. Once again, remember to follow up with a call after a week or two.

The Interview Process

You got the call. You landed an interview. Now what? The interview is an integral part of getting the job you want. There are a number of different types of interviews. Depending on the company and the job, you might be asked to go on one or more interviews, ranging from initial or screening interviews to interviews with department heads or supervisors you will be working with.

Things To Bring

Once you get the call for an interview, what's your next step? Let's start with what you should bring with you to the interview.

- ◎ Copies of your resume
  - ▫ While they probably have a copy of your resume, they might have misplaced it or you might want to refer to it.
- ◎ Letters of reference
  - ▫ Even though people have given you their letters of reference, make sure you let them know you are using them.
- ◎ References
  - ▫ When interviewing for jobs, you often need to fill in job applications that ask for both professional and personal references. Ask before

you use people as references. Make sure they are prepared to give you a good reference. Then when you go for an interview, call the people on your reference list and give them the heads up on your job-hunting activities.

- ◎ A portfolio of your achievements and other work.
  - ▫ Refer to Chapter 6 to learn how to develop your career portfolio
- ◎ Business or networking card
  - ▫ Refer to Chapter 6 to learn more about business cards.
- ◎ Other supporting materials
  - ▫ This might include a variety of materials, including copies of certifications, licenses, etc.

You want to look as professional as possible, so don't throw your materials into a paper bag or a sloppy knapsack. A professional-looking briefcase or portfolio is the best way to hold your information. If you don't have that, at the very least put your information into a large envelope or folder to carry into the interview.

Your Interviewing Wardrobe

You've landed an interview, but what do you wear? That depends to a great extent on the specific job for which you're interviewing. However, the rule of thumb is to dress for the job you want.

That doesn't mean that if you're pursuing a career where you will be wearing a uniform you go to the interview wearing a uniform. What it means is that you want to dress professionally, so interviewers will see you as a professional, no matter what level you currently are in your career.

First let's start with a list of what not to wear:

◎ sneakers
◎ flip-flops
◎ sandals
◎ micro-miniskirts or dresses
◎ very tight or very low dresses or tops
◎ jeans of any kind
◎ midriff tops
◎ skin-tight pants or leggings
◎ very baggy pants
◎ sweatshirts
◎ work-out clothes
◎ T-shirts
◎ heavy perfume, men's cologne, or aftershave lotion
◎ very heavy makeup
◎ flashy jewelry (this includes nose rings, lip rings, and other flamboyant piercings)
◎ tattoos (if you have large, visible tattoos, you may want to cover them with either clothing or some type of cover-up or makeup)

Now let's talk about what you should wear:

Men
◎ dark suit
◎ dark sports jacket, button down shirt, tie, and trousers
◎ clean, polished shoes
◎ socks

Women
◎ suit
◎ dress with jacket
◎ skirt with blouse and jacket
◎ pumps or other closed-toe shoes
◎ hose

Interview Environments

In most cases interviews are held in office environments. If you are asked if you want coffee, tea, soda, or any type of food, my advice is to abstain. This is not the time you want to accidentally spill coffee, inadvertently make a weird noise drinking soda, or get sugar from a donut on your fingers when you need to shake hands.

In some cases, however, you may be interviewed over a meal. Whether it is breakfast, lunch, or dinner, it is usually best to order something simple and light. This is not the time to order anything that can slurp, slide, or otherwise mess you up. Soups, messy sauces, lobster, fried chicken, ribs, or anything that you have to eat with your hands would be a bad choice. Nothing can ruin your confidence during an interview worse than a big blob of sauce accidentally dropping on your shirt—except if you cut into something and it splashes onto your interviewer's suit. Eating should be your last priority. Use this time to present your attributes, tell your story, and ask intelligent questions.

This is also not the time to order an alcoholic beverage. Even if the interviewer orders a drink, abstain. You want to be at the top of your game. If, however, the interviewer orders dessert and coffee or tea, do so as well. That way he or she isn't eating alone and you have a few more minutes to make yourself shine.

★ Words from the Wise

Never ask for a doggie bag at an interview meal. I don't care how good the meal is, how much you have left over, or how much you've had it drummed into your head that you shouldn't waste food. I don't care if the interviewer asks for a doggie bag. In case you're missing the message, do not ask for a doggie bag. I've seen it happen and I've heard the interviewers talking about it in a negative manner weeks later.

Words from the Wise

In your effort to tell people about your accomplishments, try not to monopolize the conversation talking solely about *you*. Before you go to an interview, especially a meal interview, read up on the news of the day in case someone at the table asks your opinion about the day's happenings. You want to appear as well rounded as possible.

The Inside Scoop

If you have been invited to a meal interview, generally the interviewer will pay the tab and tip. At the end of the meal, when you are leaving, thank the person who paid the check and tell him or her how much you enjoyed the meal and the company.

In some cases a company may invite you to participate in a meal interview to see how you will act in social situations. They might want to check out your table manners, whether you keep your elbows on the table or talk with your mouth full. They might want to see whether you drink to excess or how you make conversation. They might want to know if you will embarrass them, if you can handle pressure, or how you interact with others. They might want you to get comfortable so they can see the true you. If you are prepared ahead of time, you will do fine. Just remember this isn't a social meal. You are being scrutinized. Be on your toes.

During the meal, pepper the conversation with questions about the company and the job. Don't be afraid to say you're excited about the possibility of working with them, you think you would be an asset to the organization, and you hope they agree. Make eye contact with those at the table.

When the interviewer stands up after the meal, the interview is generally over. Stand up, thank the interviewer or interviewers for the meal, tell them you look forward to hearing from them, shake everyone's hand, and then leave.

Many organizations today pre-interview or do partial interviews on the phone. This might be to pre-screen people without bringing them into the office. It also might come about if the employer is interested in a candidate and that individual lives in a different geographic location.

Whatever the reason, be prepared. If the company has scheduled a phone interview ahead of time, make sure your "space" is prepared so you can do your best.

Here are some ideas.

◎ Have your phone in a quiet location. People yelling, a loud television, or music in the background is not helpful in this situation.
◎ Have a pad of paper and a few pens to write down the names of the people you are speaking to, notes about the conversation, and to jot down questions as you think of them.
◎ Have a copy of your resume near you. Your interviewer may refer to information on your resume. If it's close you won't have to fumble for words.

Tip from the Coach

Everyone has their own opinions on politics and religion. During an interview stay clear of conversations involving either subject.

○ Prepare questions to ask in case you are asked if you have any questions.

○ Prepare answers for questions that you might be asked. For example:

- □ Why do you want to work for us?
- □ What can you bring to the school, college, organization, company?
- □ What type of experience do you have?
- □ Why are you the best candidate?
- □ Where do you see yourself in five years?
- □ Why did you leave your last job?
- □ Did you get along with your last boss?
- □ What are you best at?
- □ What is your greatest strength?
- □ What is your greatest weakness?

Preparing for these questions is essential. While I can't guarantee what an interviewer might ask, I can pretty much guarantee that he or she probably will ask at least one of those questions or something similar.

Other Types of Interview Scenarios

When you think of an interviewing situation, you generally think of the one-on-one scenario where the interviewer is on one side of the desk and you are on the other. At some time during your career you may be faced with other types of interviews. Two of the more common ones you may run into are group interviews and panel interviews. What's the difference?

Group Interviews

A group interview is a situation where an organization brings a group of people together to tell them about the company and job opportunities. There may be open discussions and a question-

---

★ The Inside Scoop

I frequently receive calls from individuals who are distraught after going on interviews. It seems while they prepared for answering every question they could possibly think an interviewer might ask about the job they are applying for, they hadn't prepared for the unexpected.

"I prepared for answering every question," a man told me. "And then the interviewer threw me for a loop. He started asking me all kinds of questions that had nothing to do with the job I was applying for. I just couldn't come up with answers that made sense."

"What did he ask?" I questioned.

"He asked me what my favorite book was when I was a child. He asked me what I wanted to be when I was little. He asked me what my greatest strength was in my last job. Then he asked me what my biggest mistake was in my last job. I couldn't think of anything to say that quick."

Interviewers often come up with questions like this for a variety of reasons. They may want to see how you react to nontraditional questions. They may want to see how well rounded you are. On occasion, they might just be thinking about something at the time they are interviewing you and the questions just pop out of their mouth.

If this has happened to you in the past, instead of beating yourself up about not coming up with what you consider a good answer, prepare for next time. Know there generally isn't any right or wrong answer. When an interviewer asks you a question it's okay to take a moment to compose yourself and think about the best answer to give.

and-answer period. During this time, individual one-on-one interviews may be scheduled.

Companies use this type of situation not only to bring a group of potential employees together, but also to screen potential employees. What do you need to know? Remember that while this may not be the traditional interview setting you are used to, this is still an interview.

From the minute you walk in the door in these settings, the potential employer is watching your demeanor and your body language. He or she is listening to what you say and any questions you might ask. He or she is watching you to see how you interact with others and how you might fit into the company.

How can you increase your chances of being asked to a one-on-one interview?

◎ Actively participate in conversations and activities.
◎ Be a leader not a follower.
◎ Ask meaningful questions.

Panel Interviews

Basically, a panel interview is an interview where you are interviewed by a group of people at the same time. While you might run into this type of interview at any time in your career, they are most often used for higher-level positions. You might, for example, go through a panel interview if you are pursuing a position as a school administrator such as a principal or superintendent, or a college administrator such as a dean or college president. You might also go through a panel interview if you are going for a position as a college athletic director, director of public relations, fund-raising director, or similar jobs.

Why do employers use panel interviews? Every member of the panel brings something different to the table. Everyone has a different set of skills and experiences. Many employers feel that a panel can increase the chance of finding the perfect applicant for the job. It also is sometimes easier to bring everyone involved together for one interview instead of scheduling separate interviews.

The panel interview will rarely be the first interview you go through. Generally, after going on one or more one-on-one interviews, if you become one of the finalists, you will be asked to attend a panel interview.

Who is there? It can be any mixture of people depending on the job. If you are pursuing a job as a school administrator, for example, the panel might include the human resources or personnel director, board members, other administrators, and perhaps a teacher. There may be members of the search committee present. It all depends on the specific job.

How can you succeed in a panel interview? Start by relaxing. Looking *or* feeling stressed will not help in this situation. When you walk into the interview, smile sincerely and make sure you shake each person's hand with a firm handshake. You want each person to feel equally important.

Prepare ahead of time. Know what is on your resume or CV. It sounds simple, but when you're on the hot seat, it is very easy to get confused. You want to be able to answer every question about your background without skipping a beat.

★ Tip from the Coach

If the thought of participating in a panel interview stresses you out, think of it this way You have more than one chance to impress interviewers. While one member of the panel may not be impressed by your credentials, another may think you are the perfect candidate and after the interview be your cheerleader.

Research the school, college, university, or company. Have some questions prepared so you can show a true interest in the position for which you are interviewing. Instead of referring to notes you have written, try to have your questions seem part of the conversation.

One of the important things to remember when participating in a panel interview is to make eye contact with everyone. Start by looking at the person who asks you the question. Then, as you're answering, glance at the other people sitting around the table making contact with each of them. You want everyone there to feel that you are talking to them, personally.

Timing is everything in an interview. Whatever you do, don't be late. If you can't get to an interview on time, the chances are you won't get to a job on time. On the other hand, you don't want to show up an hour early either.

Try to time your arrival so you get there about 15 minutes before your scheduled time. Walk in and tell the receptionist your name and who your appointment is with. When you are directed to go into the interview, walk in, smile sincerely, shake hands with the interviewer or interviewers, and sit down. Look around the office. Does the interviewer have a photo on the desk of children? Is there any personalization in the office? Does it look like the interviewer is into golf, or fishing, or basketball, or some other

---

Tip from the Coach

Always prepare a response for the beginning of the interview when someone on an interview panel says, "Tell us about yourself." Have a long and short version of your response. Don't say, "I don't know what to tell you." Or, "Where should I start?" Begin with your short version and ask if they would like you to go into more detail.

---

hobby? Do you have something in common? You might say something like:

"What beautiful children."

"Is golf one of your passions, too?"

"Do you go deep sea fishing?"

"Those are amazing orchids. How long have you had them?"

"What an incredible antique desk. Do you collect antique furniture?"

Try to make the interviewer comfortable with you before his or her questions begin.

What might you be asked? You will probably be asked a slew of general questions and then, depending on the job, some questions specific to your skills and talent.

◎ Why should we hire you?

⊡ This is a common question. Think about the answers ahead of time. Practice saying them out loud so you feel comfortable. For example, "I believe I would be an asset to your school (college, university, company, or organization.) I have the qualifications. I'm a team player and this is the type of career I've always wanted to pursue. I'm a hard worker, a quick study, I have a positive attitude, and I'll help you achieve your goals."

Tip from the Top

If you have an extreme emergency and absolutely must be late, call and try to reschedule your appointment. Do not get there late and then come up with an excuse when arrive.

- You can then go on to explain one or two specifics. For example, "In my current position I developed a program to involve parents in their children's education. It really helped cut down on the dropout rate and our absentee rate has dropped dramatically. I would love the opportunity and challenge to do the same thing in an even bigger school system."

◎ What makes you more qualified than other candidates?

- This is another common question. Depending on the situation, you might say something like, "I believe my experience, first working as a teacher for four years, then as a summer school principal, and then as the assistant principal of a middle school in a community much like this, gives me a fuller understanding of the needs of students in this type of area. I brought my portfolio so you can actually see some of the projects in which I've participated. You indicated today one of the challenges you're facing here is keeping kids in school. In my current position I helped develop a program that would target solutions to that problem. As a matter of fact, I wrote a grant, which brought in $20,000 to support the program. I have copies of a couple of stories from the newspaper, which discussed the program. I'll leave them for you to review later."

◎ Where do you see yourself in five years?

- Do not say, "Sitting in your chair," or "In your chair." People in every job and every business are paranoid that someone is going to take their job, so don't even joke about it. Instead, think about the question ahead of time. It's meant to find out what your aspirations are and if you have direction?

- One answer might be, "I hope to be a successful member of the administrative team of this university. This is a wonderful institution, which is not only needed, but is an asset to the community. I would love to think that I can have a long career here."

◎ What are your strengths?

- Be confident, but not cocky when answering this one. Toot your horn, but don't be boastful. Practice ahead of time saying what your greatest strengths, talents, and skills are. "I'm passionate about what I do. I love working at something I'm passionate about. That's one of the main reasons I applied for this position. I am really good at finding interesting ways to teach others so they can not only understand a subject, but also get passionate about knowing more about it. I'm also a people person and a really good communicator. I pride myself in being able to solve problems quickly, efficiently, and successfully."

◎ What are your weaknesses?

- We all have weaknesses. This is not the time to share them. Be creative. "My greatest weakness is also one of my strengths. I'm a workaholic. I don't like leaving a project undone.

I have a hard time understanding how someone can not do a great job when they love what they do."

◎ Why did you leave your last job?
  ▫ Be careful answering this one. If you were fired, simply say you were let go. Don't go into the politics. Don't say anything bad about your former job, company, or boss. If you were laid off, simply say you were laid off, or, if it's true, that you were one of the newer employees and unfortunately, that's how the layoff process worked. You might add that you were very sorry to leave because you really enjoyed working there, but on the positive side, you now are free to apply for this position. If you quit, simply say the job was not challenging and you wanted to work in a position where you could create a career. Never lie. Don't even try to stretch the truth. I've mentioned it before and I'm going to reiterate it. This is a transient society. People move around. You can never tell when your former boss knows the person interviewing you. In the same vein, never say anything during an interview that is derogatory about anyone or any other school, company, facility, or organization. The supervisor you had yesterday might just end up moving to your new company and end up being your new boss. It is not unheard of.

◎ Why do you want to work in education? (Depending on the specific area of the industry, the question might be, "Why do you want to work as a teacher?" "Why do you want to work in a private school instead of a public school?" "Why do you want to work with children with special needs?" "Why do you want to teach history?" And so on.)

◎ What do you think is the biggest problem in education at this time?

◎ What is your philosophy of education?

◎ If you had to pick the most important advancement in education, what would it be?

◎ When did you decide you wanted to work in education?
  ▫ Think about questions like this ahead of time and come up with answers. There is no right or wrong answer for these types of questions. You just want to be able to come up with answers without saying, "Uh . . . let me think. Well, I'm not sure."

◎ Are you a team player?
  ▫ Whether you're working at a school, college, or other type of organization, companies want you to be a team player, so the answer is, "Yes, it's one of my strengths."

◎ Do you need supervision?
  ▫ You want to appear as confident and capable as possible. Depending on the specific job and responsibilities, you might say, "I work well with limited supervision." Or "No, once I know my responsibilities, I have always been able to fulfill them."

◎ Do you get along well with others?
  ▫ The answer they are looking for is, "Yes, I'm a real people person." Do not give any stories about times when you didn't get along with someone. Do not say anything like, "I get along better with women" or

"I relate better to men." Even if it's true, don't make any type of comment which can come back to haunt you later.

- Every now and then, you get a weird question or a question that you just don't expect. If you could be a car, what type of car would you be and why? If you were an animal, what animal would you be? If you could have dinner with anyone alive or dead, who would it be? These questions generally are just meant to throw you off balance and see how you react.

- Stay calm and focused. Be creative but try not to come up with any answer that is too weird.

- An interviewer might ask what was the last book you read, what newspapers you read, or what television shows are your favorites. Be honest, but try not to say things like, "I don't have time to read" or "I don't like reading." You want to appear well rounded.

◎ What type of salary are you looking for?

- This is going to be discussed in more detail in a moment, but what you should know now is that this is an important matter. You don't want to get locked into a number before you know exactly what you will be responsible for. You might say something to the effect of, "I'm looking for a fair salary for the job. I really would like to know more about the responsibilities before I come up with a range. What is the range, by the way?" You might turn

---

Tip from the Top

Try not to discuss salary at the beginning of the interview. Instead wait until you hear all the particulars about the job and you have given them a chance to see how great you are.

---

the tables and say something like, "I was interested in knowing what the salary range is for this position." This turns the question back to the interviewer.

What They Can't Ask You

There are questions it is illegal for interviewers to ask. For example, they aren't permitted to ask you anything about your age, unless they are making sure you are over 18. They aren't supposed to ask you about marriage, children, or relationships. Interviewers are not supposed to ask you about your race, color, religion, national origin, or sexual preference. If an interviewer does ask an illegal question, in most cases it is not on purpose. He or she just might not know that it shouldn't be asked.

Your demeanor in responding to such questions can affect the direction of the interview. If you don't mind answering, then by all means, do so. If answering bothers you, try to point the questions in another direction, like back to your skills and talents. If you are unable to do so, simply indicate in a nonthreatening, nonconfrontational manner that those types of questions are not supposed to be asked in interviews.

What You Might Want to Ask

Just because you're the one being interviewed doesn't mean you shouldn't ask questions. You want to appear confident. You want to portray someone who can fit in with others comfortably. You want to ask great questions. Depending on the specific job, here are some ideas:

- ◎ What happened to the last person who held this job? Was he or she promoted or did he or she leave the organization?
  - ☐ You want to know whose shoes you're filling.
- ◎ What is the longevity of employees here?
  - ☐ Employees who stay for a length of time generally are happy with the organization.
- ◎ Does the company promote from within as a rule or look outside?
  - ☐ This is important because companies that promote from within are good companies to build a career with.
- ◎ Is there a lot of laughing in the workplace? Are people happy here?
  - ☐ If there is, it means it's a less stressed environment.
- ◎ How will I be evaluated? Are there periodic reviews?
  - ☐ You want to know how and when you will know if you are doing well in your supervisor's eyes.
- ◎ How do you measure success on the job? By that I mean, how can I do a great job for you?
  - ☐ You want to know what your employer expects from employees.
- ◎ What are the options for advancement in this position?
  - ☐ This illustrates that you are interested in staying with the company.
- ◎ Who will I report to? What will my general responsibilities be?
  - ☐ You want to know what your work experience and duties will be like.

Feel free to ask any questions you want answered. While it is perfectly acceptable to ask questions, don't chatter on incessantly. You want to give the interviewer time to ask you questions and see how you shine.

It's normal to be nervous during an interview. Relax as much as you can. If you go in prepared and answer the questions you're asked, you should do fine. Somewhere during the interview, if things are going well, salary will come up.

Salary and Compensation

No matter how much you want a job, unless you are doing an internship, the good news is, you're not going to be working for free. Compensation may be discussed in a general manner during your interview or may be discussed in full. A lot has to do with the specific job. One way or another, salary will generally come up sometime during your interview. Unless your interviewer brings up salary at the beginning of an interview, you should not. If you feel an interview is close to ending and another interview has not been scheduled, feel free to bring up salary when asked if you have any questions.

A simple question such as "What is the salary range for the job?" will usually start the ball rolling. Depending on the specific job, your interviewer may tell you exactly what the salary and benefits are or may just give you a range. In many cases salary and compensation packages are only ironed out after the actual job offer is made.

Keep in mind that many jobs in education, especially in schools and many colleges and universities, may be unionized. What that means to you is that minimum earnings (as well as working conditions) are negotiated and set by a specific union.

Let's say you are offered a job and a compensation package. What do you do if you're not happy with the salary? What about the benefits? Can you negotiate? You certainly can try. Sometimes, you can negotiate better terms as far as salary, sometimes better benefits, and sometimes both. A lot of it depends on how much they want you, how much of an asset you will be, and what they can afford.

When negotiating, speak in a calm, well-modulated voice. Do not make threats. State your case and see if you can meet in the middle. If you can't negotiate a higher salary, perhaps you can negotiate extra vacation days. Depending on the company and specific job, compensation may include salary, vacation days, sick days, health insurance, stock options, pension plans, or a variety of other things. When negotiating, look at the whole package.

You might do some research ahead of time to see what similar types of jobs are paying. Depending on the specific job, information on compensation may also have been in the original advertisement you answered.

Over the years I have seen many people who are so desperate to get the job of their dreams that once offered the job, they will take it for almost anything. Often, when questioned about salary, they ask for salary requirements far below what might have been offered. Whatever you do, don't undersell yourself.

Accepting a job offer below your perceived salary "comfort level" often results in you resenting your company, coworkers, and even worse, whittles away at your self-worth.

It is perfectly acceptable to ask for a day or two to consider an offer. Simply say something like "I appreciate your confidence in me. I'd like to think about it overnight if that's okay with you. Can I give you a call tomorrow afternoon?"

In some situations, when you are dealing with certain high-level jobs in education, such as a superintendent or a college president, you might have someone like an attorney negotiate your contract, including working conditions and earnings.

Things to Remember

In order to give yourself every advantage in acing the interview, there are a few things you should know. First, practice ahead of time. Ask friends or family members for their help in setting up practice interviews. You want to get comfortable answering questions without sounding like you're reading from a script.

Many people go on real "practice interviews." In essence what this means is going on interviewers for jobs you might not want in order to get experience in interview situations. Some people think that it isn't right to waste an interviewer's time. On the other hand, you can never tell when you might be offered a job, which you originally didn't plan on taking, but which turns out to be something you want.

Here are some other things to remember to help you land an offer.

◎ If you don't have confidence in yourself, neither will anyone else. No matter how nervous you are, project a confident and positive attitude.

◎ The one who looks and sounds most qualified has the best chance at getting the job. Don't answer questions in monosyllables. Explain your answers using relevant experiences. Use your experiences in both your work and personal life to reinforce your skills, talents, and abilities when answering questions.

◎ Try to develop a rapport with your interviewer. If your interviewer "likes" you, he or she will often overlook less than perfect skills because you "seem" like a better candidate.

◎ Smile and make sure you have good posture. It makes you look more successful.

◎ Be attentive. Listen to what the interviewer is saying. If he or she asks a question that you don't understand, politely ask for an explanation.

◎ Be pleasant and positive. People will want to be around you.

◎ Turn off your cell phone and beeper *before* you go into the interview.

◎ When you see the interview coming to a close, make sure you ask when a decision will be made and if you will be contacted either way.

◎ When the interview comes to a close, stand up, thank the interviewer, shake his or her hand, and then leave.

Here are some things you should not do:

◎ Don't smoke before you go into your interview.

◎ Don't chew gum during your interview.

◎ Don't be late.

◎ Don't talk negatively about past bosses, jobs, or companies.

◎ Don't say *ain't*, *heh*, *uh-huh*, *don't know*, *got me*, or other similar things. It doesn't sound professional and suggests that you have poor communication skills.

◎ Don't wear heavy perfume or men's cologne before going on an interview. You can never tell if the interviewer is allergic to various odors.

◎ Don't interrupt the interviewer.

◎ While you certainly can ask questions, don't try to dominate the conversation to try to "look smart."

◎ Don't swear, curse, or use off-color language.

Thank-You Notes

It's always a good idea to send a note thanking the person who interviewed you for his or her time. Think a thank-you note is useless? Think again. Take a look at some of the things a thank-you note can do for you.

A thank-you note after an interview can

◎ show that you are courteous and well mannered

◎ show that you are professional

◎ give you one more shot at reminding the interviewer who you were

◎ show that you are truly interested in the job

◎ illustrate that you have written communication skills

◎ give you a chance to briefly discuss something that you thought was important, yet forgot to bring up during the interview

◎ help you stand out from other job applicants who didn't send a thank-you note

Try to send thank-you notes within 24 hours of your interview. You can handwrite or type them. While it's acceptable to e-mail or fax them, I suggest mailing.

What should the letter say? It can simply say thank you or it can be longer, touching on a point you discussed in the interview or adding in something you may have forgotten.

Waiting for an Answer

You've gone through the interview for the job you want. You've done everything you can.

Now what? Well, unfortunately, now you have to wait for an answer. Are you the candidate who was chosen? Hopefully you are!

If you haven't heard back in a week or so (unless you were given a specific date when an applicant would be chosen), call and ask the status of the job. If you are told that they haven't made a decision, ask when a good time to call back would be.

If you are told that a decision has been made and it's not you, thank them and say how you appreciated the consideration. Request that your resume be kept on file for the future. You might just get a call before you know it. If the school, college, or organization is a large one, ask if there are other positions available and how you should go about applying for them if you are interested.

If your phone rings and you got the job, congratulations! Once you get that call telling you that you are the candidate they want, depending on the situation, they will either make an offer on the phone or you will have to go in to discuss your compensation package. If an offer is made on the phone, as we previously discussed, you have every right to ask if you can think about it and get back to them in 24 hours.

If you are satisfied with the offer as it is, you can accept it.

Depending on the job, you may be required to sign an employment contract. Read the agreement thoroughly and make sure that you are comfortable signing it. If there is anything you don't understand, ask. Do not just sign without reading. You want to know what you are agreeing to.

Interviewing for jobs is a skill. Practice until you feel comfortable answering every type of question and being in a variety of situations. The more prepared you are ahead of time, the better you'll usually do. The more you do it, the more comfortable you'll be going through the process.

Mastering the art of interviewing can make a huge difference in your interview. Remember the intangible essentials that can help you win the job:

- enthusiasm
- excitement
- passion
- interest
- confidence

Enthusiasm is key when interviewing for a job. You want to be enthusiastic at the interview.

"But I don't want them to think I'm desperate," people always tell me.

My response is always the same. You don't want to appear desperate, but you don't want there to be a question in your interviewer's mind that you want the job.

What else? Yes, you want to be excited about the possibility of working at the job for which you are interviewing.

Passion is essential. Make sure you let your passion shine. It can make the difference between you getting the job or someone else getting it.

Anything else? You definitely want to appear interested. What does that mean? You want your interviewer to know without a shadow of a doubt that you are interested not only in the job, but in the concept of working at that particular job.

And finally, you want to appear confident. As we have already discussed, if you don't believe you are the best, neither will anyone else.

9

MARKETING YOURSELF FOR SUCCESS

What Marketing Can Do for You

Who hasn't heard of Coca-Cola, Pepsi, and Dr Pepper? What about McDonald's, Burger King, and Wendy's? Here's a question: Do you know what those companies have in common with Las Vegas, Disneyworld, the Rolling Stones, and every other successful corporation and person? It's the same thing that hot trends, major sports events, blockbuster movies, top television shows, hot CDs, mega-superstars, and even hot new toys have in common. Do you know what it is yet?

Here's the answer. Every one of them utilizes marketing. Do you want to know the inside track on becoming successful and getting what you want, no matter what segment of education you're interested in pursuing? It's simple; all you have to do is utilize marketing.

Many people think that marketing techniques are reserved for businesses, products, or celebrities. Here's something to think about: From the moment you begin your career until you ultimately retire, you are a product. It doesn't matter what direction your career is going, what level you're at, or what area you want to pursue.

There are thousands of people who want to work in various segments of education. Some make it, and some don't. Is it all talent? A lot of it has to do with talent, but that is not everything. We all have heard of talented individuals who haven't made it in their chosen field. Is it skills? We have all heard of people who are skilled, yet don't make it either.

So if it isn't just talent or skills, what is the answer? What is the key to success? As we've discussed previously, probably a lot of it may also have to do with luck and being in the right place at the right time. Some of it may be related to working hard and having a strong passion. One of the factors that appear to be related to success is how one individual sets himself or herself apart from another individual in the way they were marketed or conversely marketed themselves.

Here's something you should know: When major corporations want to turn a new product into a hot commodity, they develop and implement a successful marketing plan. No matter which segment of education you want to work and succeed in, marketing can help *you* become one of the hottest commodities around too.

While most people can understand how marketing can help a product succeed, or a celebrity become more popular, they often don't think about the possibility of marketing themselves if they are pursuing a career in an industry such as education.

When I give seminars and we start discussing this area, there are always a number of attendees who inevitably ask, "Does this relate to me?" "Can't I just look for a job, interview, get it, and forget it?" they ask. "Do I need to go through this extra process? Why do I have to market myself?"

Here's the answer in a nutshell: If you aren't marketing yourself and someone else is, they will have an advantage over you. One of the tricks to success is taking advantage of every opportunity. Marketing yourself is an opportunity you just can't afford to miss.

What is marketing? On the most basic level, marketing is finding markets and avenues to sell products or services. In this case, you are the product. The buyers are employers.

To be successful, you not only want to be the product, you want to be the *brand*. Look at Nabisco, Kelloggs, McDonalds, Coke, Pepsi, and Disney. Look at Orange County Choppers, Martha Stewart, NASCAR, American Idol, and Michael Jordan.

Look at Donald Trump. One of the most successful people in branding, Trump, a master marketer, believes so strongly in this concept that he successfully branded himself. Although he made his mark in real estate, Trump also has successful television shows, a successful line of hotels, casinos, clothing, water, ice cream, meats, books, seminars, and even Trump University. He continues to illustrate to people how he can fill *their needs*. Then he finds new needs he can fill. If you're savvy, you can do the same.

If you know or can determine what you can do for an employer or what can help them, you can market yourself to illustrate how you can fill those needs. If you can sell and market yourself effectively, you can succeed in your career; you can push yourself to the next level, and you can get what you want.

Is there a secret to this? No, there really isn't a secret, but it does take some work. In the end, however, the payoff will be worth it.

Do you want to be the one who gets the job? Marketing can help. Want to make yourself visible so potential employers will see you as desirable? Marketing can help. Do you want to set yourself apart from other job candidates? Guess what? Marketing can help. It can also distinguish you from other employees. If you have marketed yourself effectively, when promotions, raises, or in-house openings are on the horizon, your name will come up. Marketing can give you credibility and open the door to new opportunities.

If you're pursuing a career as a teacher or professor, marketing is just as important as if you are going into the business or administration end of education. Of course you need the education, knowledge, skills, and talent. But that's not all.

Do you want to stand out from every other teacher in your field? Do you want to set yourself apart from other professors? Do you want to set yourself apart from other administrators and business people? You know what you have to do? Market yourself!

Do you want to become more visible? Get the attention of the media? Do you want to get the attention of recruiters, headhunters, industry insiders, and other important people? Do you want to open the door to new opportunities? Do you want to catch the eye of board members, human resources directors or personnel officers of schools and colleges who want you to be part of their team? Market yourself!

"Okay," you're saying. "I get it. I need to market myself. But how?"

> ⭐ **Tip from the Top**
> Effective marketing focuses on the needs of the customer (in this case the employer). You want to show employers how you can fill their needs, not what they can do for you. What does this mean to you? You not only want to show potential employers how good you are, you want to show them how your skills, talents, and package can help them.

That's what we're going to talk about now. To begin with, understand that in order to market yourself effectively, you are going to have to do what every good marketer does. You're going to have to develop your product, perform market research, and assess the product and the marketplace.

Are there going to be differences between marketing yourself for a career in the business or administration segments of the industry and a career as a teacher or professor? Yes, of course there may be some differences, but in general, you're going to use a lot of the same techniques.

Read over this section and see which techniques and ideas will work best for you. As long as you are marketing yourself in a positive manner you are on the right track.

The Five Ps of Marketing and How They Relate To Your Career

There are five Ps to marketing, whether you're marketing your career, a hot new restaurant, a new product, a school, your talent, or anything else. They are:

◎ product
◎ price
◎ positioning
◎ promotion
◎ packaging

Let's look at how these Ps relate to your career.

◎ *Product*: In this case, as we just mentioned, the product is *you*. "Me," you say. "How am I a product?" *You* are a package complete with your physical self, skills, ideas, and talents.

◎ *Price*: Price is the compensation you receive for your work. As you are aware, there can be a huge range of possible earnings for any one job. One of your goals in marketing yourself is to sell your talents, skills, and anything else you have to offer for the best possible compensation.

◎ *Positioning*: What positioning means in this context is developing and creating innovative methods to fill the needs of one or more employers or potential clients. It also means differentiating yourself and/or your talent and skills from other competitors. Depending on your career area, this might mean differentiating yourself from other employees, teachers, professors, administrators, businesspeople, journalists, marketing people, deans, and so on.

◎ *Promotion*: Promotion is the development and implementation of methods that make you visible in a positive manner.

◎ *Packaging*: Packaging is the way you present yourself.

Putting Together Your Package

Now that we know how the five Ps of marketing are related to your career, let's discuss a little more about putting together your package.

The more you know about your product (*you*), the easier it is to market and sell it. It's also essential to know as much as possible about the markets to which you are trying to sell. What do you have to offer that a potential buyer (*employer*) needs? If you can illustrate to a market (*employer*) that you are the package that can fill their needs, you stand a good chance to turn the market into a buyer.

Assess what you have to offer as well as what you think an employer needs. We've already discussed self-assessment in a prior chapter. Now review your skills and your talents to help you determine how they can be used to fill the needs of your target markets.

While all the Ps of marketing are important, packaging is one of the easiest to change. It's something you have control over.

How important is packaging? Very! Good packaging can make a product more appealing, more enticing, and make *you* want it. Not convinced? Think about the last time you went to the store. Did you reach for the name-brand products more often than the bargain brands?

Still not convinced? How many times have you been in a bakery or restaurant, and chosen the beautifully decorated deserts over the simple un-iced cake? Packaging can make a difference—a big difference—in your career. If you package yourself effectively, people will want your package.

★ Tip from the Coach

While you can't tell a book by its cover, it is human nature to at least look at the book with an interesting cover first. You might put it back after looking at it, but you at least gave it a first shot. That is why it is so important to package yourself as well as you possibly can.

Want to know a secret? Many job candidates in every industry are passed over before they get very far in the process because they simply don't understand how to package themselves. What does this mean to you?

It means that if you can grasp the concept, you're ahead of the game. In a competitive world this one thing can give you the edge. Knowing that a marketing campaign uses packaging to help sell products means that you will want to package yourself as well as you can. You want potential employers, recruiters, headhunters, board members, and others to see you in the most positive manner possible. You want to illustrate that you have what it takes to fill *their* needs.

So what does your personal package include?

People base their first impression of you largely on your appearance. Whether you are going for an interview for a hot job or are currently working and trying to move up the ladder of success, appearance is always important.

It might seem elementary, but let's go over the elements of your appearance. Personal grooming is essential. What does that mean?

- Your hair should be clean and neatly styled.
- You should be showered with no body odor.
- Your nails should be clean. If you polish them, make sure that your polish isn't chipped.
- If you are a man, you should be freshly shaved and mustaches and beards should be neatly styled.
- If you are a woman, your makeup should look natural and not overdone.
- Your breath should be clean and fresh.

Good grooming is important no matter what segment of the industry you are pursuing.

Tip from the Top

Make sure you have mints or breath strips with you when you go to interviews, meetings, or even teaching. Nothing can turn off people faster than someone breathing funky breath in their face.

Words from a Pro

Even if you are interviewing for an entry-level job, dress professionally. You want your interviewer to see that you are looking for a *career*, not just a job.

Now let's discuss your attire. Whether you're going on interviews, are in a networking situation, or are already on the job, it's important to dress appropriately. What's appropriate? Good question.

Appropriateness to a great extent depends on what area of the industry you're involved in and your specific job. If you're working in the business or administrative end of the industry, you, of course, want to look professional at all times.

While teachers often have leeway for casual dressing on certain days during the year, it's important to remember that dressing professionally can help your career in a number of ways, from establishing credibility to maintaining respect to establishing yourself as an authority figure.

Always dress to impress. Employers want to see that you will not only fit in, but that you will not embarrass them when representing the school, college, organization, or company. So what should you do? What should you wear?

If you are going on an interview, dress professionally. If you're a man, you can never go wrong in a suit and tie, or a pair of dress slacks with a sports jacket, dress shirt, and tie. Women might wear a suit, a professional looking dress, a skirt and jacket, skirt and blouse, or perhaps a pantsuit. Once you're hired learn the company's dress policy. It's okay to ask. No matter what the policy is, observe what everyone else is wearing. If the policy is casual and everyone is still dressed in business attire, dress in business attire.

"But I'm going for a job as a physical education teacher (or coach, etc.)," you say. "Why would I get dressed up?"

The answer is simple. You want to make a good impression. You want to look like you care, and you want to look like you're serious about your career. You want to look professional.

You might also want to think about your image when you're *not* working. Why is this important? If you project an unprofessional image off the job, it can possibly affect your career in a negative manner.

Words from the Wise

Strong perfume, cologne, and aftershave often make people *not* want to be near you. Many people are allergic to strong odors. Many just can't stand the smell. You don't want to be known as the one who wears that stinky stuff. If you wear scents, go light.

The Inside Scoop

It's always easier to make yourself look more casual than it is to make yourself appear dressed more professionally. If in doubt about what to wear, err on the side of looking professional.

This isn't to say that you have to wear a suit all the time or even be dressed up. What it means is that you never want to be in a position where you leave home looking sloppy and then run into someone who could be helpful to your career.

Communication Skills

Your communication skills, both verbal and written, are yet another part of your package. What you say and how you say it can mean the difference between success and failure in getting a job or succeeding at one you already have. You want to sound articulate, polished, strong, and confident.

Do you ever wonder how others hear you? Consider using a tape recorder to record yourself speaking, and then play it back.

Is this scary? It can be if you have never heard yourself. Here's what to remember: No matter what you think you sound like, it probably isn't that bad. You are probably your own worst critic.

When you play back your voice, listen to your speech pattern. You might, for example, find that you are constantly saying "uh" or "uh-huh." You might find that your voice sounds nasal or high pitched or that you talk to quickly. If you're not happy with the way you sound, there are exercises you can do to change your pitch, modulation, and speech pattern.

There are even methods to change your accent, if you have one. Do you need to change your accent? Only if *you* feel it's a hindrance to your career. If, for example, you are an aspiring television or radio education reporter, you might feel a very heavy accent might limit your career. If you are a teacher you also want to make sure your students can understand you. If you are a corporate trainer, you want to make sure an accent isn't standing in the way of your success. This is something you have to decide for yourself, no one else can make this decision. If you do feel you need to change your accent, look for a speech therapist, speech coach, or vocal coach.

Because you can't take words back into your mouth after you say them, here are some *don'ts* to follow when speaking.

- ◎ Don't use off-color language.
- ◎ Don't swear or curse.
- ◎ Don't tell jokes or stories that have either sexual, ethnic, or racial undertones or innuendoes.

> ⭐ **Words from the Wise**
> Don't say words like "ain't." It makes you sound stupid, even if you're not.

- Don't interrupt others when they are speaking.
- Don't use poor grammar or slang.
- Don't talk about people.

We've discussed your verbal communication skills, so now let's discuss the importance of your written communication skills. Here's the deal: Written communication skills are important in every industry. If you are pursuing a career in any segment of education, they are even more important. At the very least you will need the ability to write letters and reports.

If you are uncomfortable with your writing skills, either pick up a book to help improve them, or consider taking some extra writing classes at a local school or college.

Your body language can tell people a lot about you. The way you carry yourself can show others how you feel about yourself. We've all seen people in passing that were hunched over or looked uninterested or just looked like they didn't care.

Would you want someone like that teaching your children? Would you want someone like that representing your college? Would you want someone who looked like that working for *you?* Well, generally, neither do most employers.

What does your body language illustrate? Does it show that you are confident? That you are happy to be where you are? Do you make eye contact when you're speaking to someone? Are you smiling? What about your demeanor? Common courtesy is mandatory in your life and your career. Polite expressions such as "please,"

"thank you," "excuse me," and "pardon me" will not go unnoticed.

Your personality traits are another part of your package. No one wants to be around a whiner, a sad sack, or people who complain constantly. You want to illustrate that you are calm, happy, well balanced, and have a positive attitude.

You want to show that you can deal effectively with others, are a team player, and can deal with problems and stress effectively. You might be surprised to know that in many cases employers will lean toward hiring someone with a bubbly, positive, and energetic personality over one with better skills who seems negative and less well balanced.

We've discussed education in an earlier chapter. The education you have is an important part of your package. Get the best education you can. Don't stop at the minimum requirements. Continue learning throughout your career. Education, both formal and informal, not only helps you increase knowledge and build new skill sets, but it helps you make new contacts and build your network.

Last but not least in your package are your skills and talents. These are the things that make *you* special. What's the difference between skills and talents?

Skills can be learned or acquired. Talents are things that you are born with and can be embellished. Your personal package includes both.

What you must do is package the product so the buyer wants it. In this case, as we have discussed, the product is you and the buyer might be a potential employer, recruiter, headhunter, human resources director, and so on.

Now that you know what goes into your package, and you're working on putting together your best possible package, what's next?

Marketing Yourself like a Pro and Making Yourself Visible

How can you market yourself? If you're like many people, you might be embarrassed to promote yourself, embarrassed to talk about your accomplishments, and embarrassed to bring them to the attention of others. This feeling probably comes from childhood when you were taught "it wasn't nice to brag."

It's time to change your thinking. It's time to toot your own horn! Done correctly, you won't be bragging. Done correctly you are simply taking a step to make yourself visible. You are taking a step to help let potential employers know that you are the one who can fill their needs.

Want to know the payoff to doing this? You can move your career in a positive direction quicker. Career success can be yours, but you need to work at it.

Visibility is important in every aspect of business and the education industry is no exception. No matter the segment of the industry in which you want to succeed, visibility can help you attain your goals. To start with, it can help set you apart from others who might have similar skills and talents.

How can you make yourself visible?

◎ Tell people what you are doing.
◎ Tell people what you are *trying* to do.

Tip from the Coach

Be positive about yourself and don't be self-deprecating, even in a joking manner. The truth is when you're self-deprecating you will start believing it and so will the people with whom you are speaking.

◎ Share your dreams.
◎ Live your dreams.
◎ Send out press releases.
◎ Toot your own horn.
◎ Make it happen.

When you make yourself visible you will gain visibility in the workplace, the community, the media, and more. This is essential to get what you want and what you deserve in your career, whether it's the brand new job or a promotion pushing you up the career ladder.

We'll discuss later how you can you tell people what you're doing without bragging, but first let's discuss when it's appropriate to toot your own horn. Here are some situations.

◎ When you get a new job.
◎ When you get a promotion.
◎ When you get a good review.
◎ When you are giving a speech.
◎ When you are giving a presentation.
◎ When you are going to be (or have already appeared) on television or radio.
◎ When you have a major accomplishment.
◎ When you receive an honor or an award.
◎ When you chair an event.
◎ When you graduate from school, college, or a training program.
◎ When you obtain professional certification.
◎ When you volunteer on a project with a not-for-profit or charity organization.

And the list goes on. The idea isn't only to make people aware of your accomplishments, but to make yourself visible in a positive manner.

How do you do it? Well, you could shout your news from a rooftop or walk around with a sign, but that probably wouldn't be very effective.

> ### ⭐ Tip from the Top
> A press release is not an ad. Ads cost money. There is no charge to send press releases to the media. Press releases are used by the media to develop stories or are edited slightly or published as is.

> ### ⭐ The Inside Scoop
> Press releases and news releases are the same thing. The phrases are used interchangeably.

One of the best ways to get the most bang for your buck is by using the media.

"I don't have money for an ad," you say.

Here is the good news. You don't have to take out an ad. You can use publicity, and publicity is free. Newspapers, magazines, and periodicals *need* stories to fill their pages. Similarly, television and radio need to fill airspace. If you do it right, your story can be one of the ones filling that space, and it won't cost you anything.

How do you get your news to the media? The easiest way is by sending out press or news releases.

There are also many books, classes, seminars, and workshops that can help you learn how to write effective news releases. Basically, however, you should know that news releases are developed by answering the five Ws. These are:

◎ Who
  ▫ Who are you writing about?
◎ What
  ▫ What is happening or has happened?

◎ When
  ▫ When did it happen or is it happening?
◎ Where
  ▫ Where is it happening or has it happened?
◎ Why
  ▫ Why is it happening or why is it noteworthy or relevant?

While it would be nice for everyone to have his or her own personal press agent or publicist, this is not generally the case. So, until you have one, you are going to have to be your own publicist. In order to market yourself, you'll have to find opportunities to develop press releases and then send them out. You want your name to be visible in a positive manner as often as possible.

Let's look at a possible scenario. Let's say Will Strauss just received his teaching degree in December but hasn't yet found a teaching job. Until he does he has located a part-time job as a reporter for a local newspaper.

While watching television one night Strauss heard a story that noted that many of the students in the local high school had poor written communication skills.

"I can't wait until I find a job as a high school English teacher," Strauss said to himself. "I bet I can change that."

Strauss knew how important written communications skills are. He thought about the television story for a bit, decided to do something about it and came up with a plan of action.

> ### ⭐ Words from a Pro
> Many of the stories you read in newspapers and magazines or hear on the radio or television are the direct result of press releases. Don't make the mistake of not sending out press releases because you *think* the media won't be interested.

Strauss talked to his editor about the possibility of the paper and the local school partnering to give students who want to participate a chance to learn how to write better. He developed a pilot program called Write-Right where he would give weekly workshops to interested students on various aspects of writing.

To make the program interesting, Strauss suggested taking the participants to a couple of professional sports games and giving them the opportunity to interview the players, coaches, or management and then report about the experience in a special section in the paper. To increase interest, he thought about also partnering with the local entertainment venue and arranging for the participants to meet the people in charge as well as going to a few concerts, possibly interviewing some of the name acts, and reporting about that too.

Strauss's editor loved the idea and brought it to the publisher. Together they brought it to the school. Strauss became the coordinator of the project and had feature stories in his paper as well as other media in the area. He also spoke to a number of the civic groups in the area about the program and how important it was for everyone to learn good communication skills.

In this scenario Strauss was gaining visibility in a number ways. Not only would his editor and publisher see him in a different light, but he also would be gaining visibility in the community from people who might not have otherwise known him. More importantly, people in various school systems learned who he was, what he was doing, and some of his capabilities.

As Strauss's ultimate goal was to work as a high school English teacher, this would be extremely helpful in networking and making important contacts. When a teaching position be-

> ### Tip from the Coach
> Contacts are an important part of your career. Once you make them, don't risk losing your relationships. Stay in contact by periodically sending e-mails, cards, and letters, making periodic calls, and arranging to meet for lunch, coffee, or just to get together and talk.

came available, Strauss would standout among others seeking the job. Strauss would already have something that other candidates wouldn't have on their resume.

Think it can't happen this way? Well, it can! While you might not live this exact scenario, you can potentially create your own scenario with a similar outcome if you are creative and think outside of the box.

On the next page is an example of a press release that Will or his paper might send out to further market the project. Note that in marketing the project, the press release is also helping market Will.

What does this press release do? In addition to publicizing Strauss's radio appearance, it gets his name in the news. It gets his message out. It exposes his career accomplishments, and it helps keep him in the pubic eye in a positive way. Strauss, using this avenue to market

> ### The Inside Scoop
> Always be ready for the media. Keep stock paragraphs on your computer so you can turn out press releases quickly when needed. As a matter of fact, you might want to keep stock press releases and bios on hand so you're always ready when the media calls.

NEWS FROM WRITE-RIGHT

P.O. Box 2022
Some City, NY 11111
Media: For additional information, contact:
Will Strauss, 111-888-8888

For Immediate Release:

Will Strauss, of Some City, NY, will be a guest on WRAN's popular talk show, *Life Lessons,* on Tuesday, February 19, at 8:00 p.m. He will be discussing a pilot program he is coordinating called Write-Right, involving helping high school students improve their written communication skills.

Strauss graduated from State University with a teaching degree in December. While looking for his dream job as a high school English teacher, he took a job as a part-time reporter with the *Valley Record*.

Strauss heard a report on television noting that over 60 percent of the student population at Anytown High had less than minimum written communication skills. What that meant was they couldn't write an essay, they couldn't write a report, and they could barely write a letter.

Knowing how important written communication skills are, when Strauss heard the report he knew he wanted to do something. Before long he had developed a plan of action, spoke to his editor, Randy Imus, and *Valley Record* publisher Susan Wynan, and together they went to the school with the pilot program.

Strauss and a number of other reporters give weekly workshops to interested students on various aspects of writing. Participants take part in writing exercises and then have their work critiqued.

As part of the program Strauss has arranged to have participants attend a number of pro sports games and will give each student the opportunity to interview either players, coaches, or someone from team management. He has also arranged to have participants visit the Encore Entertainment Arena with an opportunity to interview those in top management as well as acts booked into the arena. Participants will then write articles bout their experiences, which will appear in a special section in the paper.

Over 100 students have already signed up to participate in the new Write-Right program, which is being held after school hours as an extracurricular activity.

"I'm excited to see such a positive reaction to the program," noted Strauss. "I can't wait to see how it progresses."

-30-

Voice of Experience

It's difficult to proofread your own press releases to catch errors. Always have someone else read them, not only for errors but to make sure they make sense.

Tip from the Coach

When working on your basic media database, make sure you find out the publication's deadline. The deadline is the day by which you need to get the information to the publication so your news can be considered for the next issue.

himself, puts himself in a different light than those who are not doing so.

"Well, that's a nice story," I can hear you saying. "But in the real world does *that* kind of thing happen?"

You might not hear about it all the time, but those situations do happen and they can happen to you. The key here is that in order for them to occur, you're going to have to start thinking outside of the box.

Make sure your press releases look professional by printing them on press or news release stationary. This can easily be created on your computer. Have the words "News" or "News From" or something to that effect someplace on the stationery so the media is aware it is a press release. Also make sure to include your contact information. This is essential in case the media wants to call to ask questions about your release. In many instances the media just uses the press release as a beginning for an article. Once you pique their interest, they use the press release as background and write their own story.

You've developed a press release. Now what? Whether it's about getting a promotion, being named employee of the month, or anything else, developing and writing a great press release is just the first step. Once that's done, you have to get the releases to the media.

How do you do this? You have a few options. You can print the press releases and then send or fax them to the media, or you can e-mail them. Either way, it's essential to put together a media list so you can reach the correct people. Look around your area. Get the names of your local media. Then find regional media. If your stories warrant it, national or trade media should also be included. Don't forget any Web or online publications.

Call each media outlet and ask to whom press releases should be directed. Sometimes

Tip from the Top

Be sure to add in either the symbol -30- or the number sign #, centered at the end of your press release. This lets the editor know that the press release is completed.

Words from the Wise

Remember that just because you send a press release doesn't mean it will get into the publication. Small local publications are likely to eventually use your press releases. Larger publications are more discriminatory. Do not call the media and insist that they use your release. This will make you look like an amateur and they will probably ignore your releases from that day forward.

⭐ Words from a Pro

Make it easier to issue press releases by setting up sheets of labels. That way, when you're ready to send out a mailing, you need only to place the labels on envelopes.

⭐ Tip from the Top

If you're e-mailing press releases find out what format publications accept *ahead* of time. If you're sending out printed press releases, you might also call to find out what font is preferred. Many smaller publications just scan in your release and certain fonts scan better.

it may just be "News Editor," "Education Editor," or "Business Editor." Sometimes it will be a specific person. Get their contact information. Put together a database consisting of the name of the publication or station, contact name or names, address, phone and fax numbers, e-mail, and any other pertinent information.

Becoming an Expert

Want another idea to make yourself visible? Become an expert. You probably already are an expert in one or more areas, either in or out of the education industry. Now it's time for you to exploit it.

Many people are used to the things they know well. They don't give enough credence to being great at them. It's time to forget that type of thinking!

One of the wonderful things about being an expert in any given area is that people will seek you out. Everyone knows how to do something

better than others. What you have to do is figure out what it is.

"Okay," you say. "You're right. Let's say I'm a gourmet chef. But what does that have to do with education?"

Well, it might have nothing to do with education on the surface. However, if it can help you gain some positive attention and visibility, it will give you another avenue to get your story out. This will help you achieve the career success you desire. So with that in mind, it has everything to do with it.

Let's begin by determining where your expertise is. Sit down with a piece of paper and spend some time thinking about what you can do better than anyone else in or out of education. What subject or area do you know more about than most? Do you volunteer in an interesting area? Are you a gourmet chef? Can you teach almost anyone how to pitch a ball? Can you teach senior citizens how to use a computer? Can you spell words backward?

Need some help? Can't think of what you're expertise is? Here are some ideas to get you started.

⭐ The Inside Scoop

Send your press releases to all applicable publications and stations. The idea with press releases is to send them consistently. Keep in mind that while you don't want to write a press release about *nothing,* anytime you have *anything* noteworthy to send out a press release about, you should.

- Are you a gourmet cook?
- Do you bake the best brownies?
- Are you a sports trivia expert?
- Are you a master gardener?

- Do you design jewelry?
- Can you speak more than one language fluently?
- Do you love to shop?
- Do you know how to coordinate just the right outfit?
- Do you know how to write great songs?
- Can you put together events with ease?
- Do you know how to write great press releases?
- Do you know how to pack a suitcase better than most people?
- Are you an expert organizer?
- Do you know how to arrange flowers?
- Are you an expert in building things?
- Are you a great fund-raiser?
- Have you set a world record doing something?
- Do you volunteer teaching people to read?
- Do you know about helping children with special needs?
- Do you volunteer reading books for the blind?
- Do you have special skills or talents that others don't?

Are you getting the idea? You can be an expert in almost any area. It's the way in which you exploit it that can make a difference in your career.

You want to get your name out there. You want to draw positive attention to yourself. You want others to know what you can do. That way you can market yourself in the areas in which you are interested.

Find ways to get your name and your story out there. How? Developing and sending out press releases is one way, but what else can you do?

You can become known for your expertise by talking about it. How? Most areas have civic or other not-for-profit groups that hold meetings. These groups often look for people to speak at their meetings. You can contact the president of the board or the executive director to find out who sets up the meeting speakers. In some areas, the chamber of commerce also puts together speaker lists.

You might be asking yourself, "Unless I'm a rocket scientist, why would any group want to hear me speak about anything? What would anyone want to know about me knowing how to pack a suitcase?" or "Why would anyone be interested in my organizing ability?"

Here's the answer: They might not be, *unless* you tailor your presentations to their needs. If you create a presentation from which others can learn something useful or interesting, they usually will. For example, if you're speaking to a group of business people, you might do a presentation about "The Stress Free Bag: Packing Easily For Business Trips," "Organize Your Career, Organize Your Life," "Helping Children Feel Good About Themselves Through Sports," or "Using Cooking to Build Teamwork."

Whatever your subject matter is when you speak in front of a group, whether it be 20 or 2,000 people, you will gain visibility. When you are introduced, the host of the event will often mention information about your background to the audience. Make sure you always have a short paragraph or two with you to make it easy for the emcee to present the information *you* want to convey.

For example, based on information you provide, the emcee might introduce you like this: "Good evening, ladies and gentlemen. Our luncheon speaker today is Lucy Jones. Some of you might know her from her weekly column in the *Town Times* about reading to your children. Today, she will be helping you understand more how to help your children feel good about themselves and how to help them increase their self-esteem. Lucy was a graduate of our local high school and then left us for a bit to go to college. She graduated from State University in May with an elementary teaching degree and is hoping to find a teaching job right here in town. Please join me in welcoming Lucy Jones."

As you can see, Lucy is getting exposure, which can help her gain career visibility. Someone at the luncheon may know of an upcoming teaching opening in town. Someone may know someone from another community who is looking for elementary school teachers. Lucy may make contacts and increase her network. The important thing to remember is to use every occasion as an opportunity to get what you are looking for in your career.

On a local level, you will generally get no fee for most of these types of presentations. The benefit of increased visibility, however, will usually be well worth it. When you are scheduled to do a presentation, make sure you send out press releases announcing your speech. If it was a noteworthy event, you might also send out a release after the event as well. Many organizations will also call the media to promote the occasion. Sometimes the media will call you for an interview before the event. Once again, take advantage of every opportunity.

⭐ Tip from the Coach

If you aren't comfortable speaking in front of large groups, consider joining Toastmasters or the Dale Carnegie Institute. Both will help you gain experience in a nurturing and safe environment.

⭐ Words from a Pro

The media works on very tight deadlines. If they call you, get back to them immediately or you might lose out.

It's exciting once you start getting publicity. Take advantage of this too. Keep clippings of all the stories from the print media. Make copies. If you have been interviewed on television or radio, get clips. Keep these for your portfolio. Every amount of positive exposure will help set you apart from others and help you market yourself for career success.

I can almost hear some of you saying, "Oh, no! I'm not getting up to speak in public."

Here's the deal. If you don't feel comfortable speaking in public, you don't have to. These ideas are meant to be a springboard to get you thinking outside of the box. Use any of them to get you started and then find ways you *are* comfortable in marketing yourself.

More Strategies to Market and Promote Yourself

If you aren't comfortable speaking in public, how about writing an article on your area of expertise instead?

What about writing articles or columns on a given subject? The idea, once again, is to keep your name in the public's eye in a positive manner. While it's helpful to write about something in your career area, it is not essential.

For example, you might write an article about what life is like as a new teacher or a day in the life of a school guidance counselor. You might write an article on collecting quilts or cookbooks. You might write articles about organizing your office, your schedule, or your life. You might write an article on stress management or laughter or humor. If you can tailor your articles in some manner to focus on your career area, all the better. If not, that's okay as well.

If you look at similar types of articles or stories in newspapers, you will notice that if the article is not written by a staff reporter, at the end of the article there generally is a line or two about the author. For example, "Gina Lawson is an assistant principal at Summers Town Middle School."

How do you get your articles in print? Call the editor of the publication you are interested in writing for and ask! Tell them what you want to do, and offer to send your background sheet, resume or bio, and a writing sample. Small or local publications might not pay very much. Don't get caught up on money. You are not doing this for cash. You are doing it to get your name and your story before the public.

Don't forget to tell media editors about your expertise. You can call them or send a short note. Ask that they put you on their list of experts for your specific area of expertise. Then when they are doing a story on something that relates to your subject area, it will be easy to get in touch with you.

Remember that if you don't make the call or write the note, no one will know what you have to offer. You have to sometimes be assertive (in a nice way) to get things moving.

Consider teaching a class, giving a workshop, or facilitating a seminar in your area of expertise. (You can do this even if you are a teacher or are looking for a formal teaching position.) Most people want to learn how to do something new and you might be just the person to give them that chance. Every opportunity for you is an opportunity to become visible

The Inside Scoop

Don't get caught up in the theory that if you help someone do something or learn how to do something, it will in some way take away opportunities from you. Help others when you can.

and move your career forward. Can you give people the basics of writing a press release or doing publicity? Offer to teach a class at a local college or school. Can you easily explain how to understand what you see when watching a game on television? Offer to teach a workshop? Do you think you can illustrate the basics of putting together a fund-raiser? Suggest a workshop! What a great way to get your name out!

There are a plethora of possibilities. You just need to use your imagination.

What can your expertise do for you? It will get your name out there. It will give you credibility and it will give you visibility. Of course, when you're at meetings or speaking to the media, it's up to you to network. Tell people what you do. Tell people what you want to do. Give out cards. This technique works effectively no matter what area of education in which you want to succeed. As a matter of fact, this technique can help you succeed in any venture.

Join professional associations and volunteer to be on committees or to chair events that they sponsor. Similarly, join civic groups and not-for-profit organizations, volunteering to work on one or two of their projects.

"I don't have time," you say.

Make time. Volunteering, especially when you chair a committee or work on a project is one of the best ways to get your name out there, obtain visibility, and network.

The radio and television talk show circuit is yet another means to generate important visibility. Offer to be a guest on radio, cable, and television station news, variety, and information shows.

"Who would want me?" you ask.

You can never tell. If you don't ask, no one will even know you exist in many instances. Check out the programming to see where you might fit. Then send your bio, resume, or CV with a letter to the producer indicating that you're available to speak in a specific subject area. Pitch an idea. A producer just might take you up on it.

Here's a sample pitch letter to get you started.

Lisa Ford, Producer
WGAT Radio
Talk Tonight Show
P.O. Box 3333
Anytown, NY 44444

Dear Ms Ford:

How many of your listeners are looking for a career? How many are looking for something to do where they can make a difference? I'm betting there are many!

As far back as I can remember I have wanted to work as a teacher. I wanted to make a difference. I know that it is a dream many have. I got lucky. My dream is coming true.

Five years ago I graduated from college and became a high school health education teacher. The job is challenging, yet rewarding.

Unfortunately, all too often in the past few years, I've seen young people from our school and schools in the surrounding areas end up in the hospital emergency room in critical condition because they have been driving while under the influence of alcohol or drugs. Some make it, while others do not.

It is now my mission to help educate young people on the seriousness of these actions.

I would love to share some of my stories with your listeners. I regularly listen to your program and believe that the subject matter fits well into your show's format.

I have included my background sheet for your review. Please let me know if you require additional information.

I look forward to hearing from you.

Sincerely,
Gina Hastings

Wait a week or so after sending the letter. If you don't hear back in that time, call the producer and ask if he or she is interested in your proposal. If there is no interest, say thank you and request that your background sheet can be kept on file.

Remember that people talk to each other, so every person you speak in front of, who reads an article about you, who hears you on the radio, or sees you on television has the potential of speaking to other people who might then speak to others.

As we've discussed, networking is one of the best ways to get a job, get a promotion, and advance your career. Even if your expertise is in something totally unrelated to education, just getting your name out can help boost your career.

If your expertise happens to be in something related to education, that's even better. Whatever your expertise, exploit it and it will help your career move forward.

Tip from the Top

Many people lose out because they just don't follow up. They either feel like a nuisance or feel like they are being a pain. No matter how awkward and uncomfortable you feel, call and follow up on things you are working on. Be polite, but call to see what's happening.

More Ways to Market Yourself

Here's another idea that can get you noticed: A feature story in a newspaper or magazine. How do you get one of these? Well, everyone wants see a story about himself or herself or their product or service in print, so you have to develop an angle that will catch attention. Then contact a few editors and see if you can get one of them to bite.

Before you call anyone, however, think out your strategy. What is your angle? Why are *you* the person someone should talk to or do a story about? Why would the story be interesting or unique or entertaining to the reader?

How do you develop an angle? Come up with something unique that you do or are planning to do. What is the unique part of your package? Were you the one who was so afraid to speak in high school that you skipped the class where you had to give a report, yet today you are the spokesperson for a college? Were you the one who succeeded despite severe adversities? Do you have a human interest story?

Send a letter with your idea and a background sheet, bio, CV, or resume. Wait a week and then call the editor you sent your information to. Ask if he or she received your information. (There is always a chance it is lost, if only on a reporter's desk.) If the answer is no, offer to send it again and start the process one more time. Sometimes you get lucky. Your angle might be just what an editor was looking for or he or she might need to fill in a space with a story.

Opening Up the Door to New Opportunities

If you keep on doing the same old thing, things might change on their own, but they probably won't. It's important when trying to create a more successful career to find ways to open the door to new opportunities.

Start to look at events that occur as new opportunities to make other things happen. If you train yourself to think of how you can use opportunities to help you instead of hinder you, things often start looking up.

Do you want to be around negative people who think nothing is going right, people who think they are losers? Probably not. Well neither does anyone else. Market yourself as a winner, even if you are still a winner in training.

The old adage "misery loves company" is true. One problem people often have in their career and life is that they hang around other people who are depressed or think that they're not doing well. Remember that negative energy attracts negative results, so here's your choice. You can either stay with the negative energy, help change the negative energy, or move yourself near positive energy. Which choice do you want to make?

Work on developing *new* relationships with positive people. Cultivate new business relationships. When doing that, don't forget cultivating a business relationship with the media. How? Go to events where the media is present. Go to chamber of commerce meetings, not-for-profit organization events, charity functions, entertainment events, sports events, meetings, and other occasions.

★ Tip from the Coach

If you don't think you're worth something, usually neither will anyone else. In the same vein, if you don't think you're the best, neither will anyone else. Maintain a positive attitude, illustrating that you are marketing the best.

Walk up, extend your hand, and introduce yourself. Give out your business cards. Engage in conversation. If a reporter writes an interesting story about anything, drop him or her a note saying you enjoyed it. If a newscaster does something special, drop a note telling him or her. The media is just like the rest of us. They appreciate validation.

Don't just be a user. One of the best ways to develop a relationship with the media or anybody else is to be a resource. Help them when you can.

Want to close the door to opportunity? Whine, complain, and be a generally negative person who no one wants to be near. Want the doors of opportunity to fly open? Whatever level you are in, more doors will open if you're pleasant, enthusiastic, and professional.

Dreams can come true. They can either happen to you or happen to someone else. If you want it bad enough and market yourself effectively, you will be the winner.

It's essential in marketing yourself and your career to move out of your comfort zone, even

> ### ⭐ Words from the Wise
>
> Many people go to networking events and social occasions where they meet people and make important contacts. They then proceed to "forget" who they met. It's essential to keep track of business cards, names, people you meet, and where you met them. In order to do this, after any event where you make contacts, make it a habit to write notes about who you met, where you met them, and any other pertinent details. Do it quickly. While you think you can't possibly forget meeting someone important to your career, you would be surprised how easy it is to forget details.

if it's just a little bit. Take baby steps if you need to, but learn to move out of your comfort zone. Find new places to go, new people to meet, and new things to do

You can be the number one factor in creating your own success. Don't let yourself down! Market yourself and reap the rewards of a great career.

10

SUCCEEDING IN THE WORKPLACE

Learning As You Go

You got the job! Now what? Are you ready to succeed?

"Well," you say, "I guess so."

No matter what segment of education you are pursuing, there are things you can do that can help you increase your chances of success, things you can do that can turn your job into the career of your dreams.

"Can't I worry about that later?" you ask.

You don't need to worry about it at all. You need to take action. Lots of people have jobs. You don't just want a job. You want a great career! It doesn't matter if you want to be a teacher, an administrator, work in support services, the business side of the industry or anywhere in between. In order to succeed and move up the career ladder you sometimes have to do a little extra, do more than is expected of you, and put some effort into getting what you want.

No matter how it looks, there are very few overnight successes. Appearances can be very deceiving. While it may appear that some individuals get their foot in the door one day and zoom to the top rung of the career ladder the next, it generally doesn't happen like that.

While there are exceptions, more than likely the people you *think* are overnight successes have been working at it and preparing for their dream career for some time. Many of them were probably in the same position you are now.

What looks like someone who just became an overnight success is generally a person who had a well-thought-out plan, did a lot of work, had some talent, a bit of luck, and was in the right place at the right time.

Unfortunately, just getting your foot in the door is not enough. It's essential once you get in to take positive actions to climb the ladder to success. If you don't take those actions, someone else will.

Once you get your foot in the door you want to create your perfect career. Getting a job is a job in itself. However, just because you've been hired doesn't mean your work is done. It's essential once you get in to learn as you go.

If you look at some of the most successful people, in all aspects of life and business, you'll see that they continue the learning process throughout their life. If you want to succeed you'll do the same.

Learning is a necessary skill for personal and career growth and advancement. Many think that your ability and willingness to learn is linked to your success in life. This doesn't necessarily mean going back to school or taking traditional classes, although for many jobs you are going to have to continue your education. In many cases, it means life learning.

What's life learning? Basically, it's learning that occurs through life experiences. It's learning that occurs when you talk to people, watch others do things, work, experience things, go places, watch television, listen to the radio, hear others talking, or almost anything else. Every experience you have is a potential learning experience.

Not only that, but almost everyone you talk to can be a teacher. If you're open to it, you can usually learn something from almost everyone you come in contact with.

"What do you mean?" you ask.

Look for opportunities. Be interested. Everything you learn might not be fascinating, but it might be helpful, maybe not today or tomorrow, but in the future. Sometimes you might learn something work related, sometimes not. It doesn't matter. Use what you can. File the rest away until needed.

How do you learn all these things? Observe what people say or do. Sometimes you might see that someone has a skill you want to master. You might, for example, see another teacher who has a unique method of teaching something.

Don't be afraid to ask others how to do something. Whether it's simple or complicated, most people are flattered when someone recognizes they're good at something and ask for their help.

Challenge yourself to learn something new every day. Not only will it help improve your total package, but it will make you feel better about yourself as well. Whether it's a new word, new skill, new way to do something, or even a new way to deal better with people, continue to learn as you go.

How else can you continue to learn? Take advantage of internships, formal and informal education, company training programs, in-service programs and volunteer opportunities. Many companies, schools, colleges, and universities have formal volunteer programs. If yours does, take advantage of it. If yours doesn't, you might want to get your company involved in one.

What can you learn? The possibilities are endless. You might learn a new skill, or a better way to get along with others. You might learn how to coordinate events or run organizations. You might learn almost anything. And as a bonus, if you volunteer effectively you not only will get some experience, you might obtain some important visibility.

Don't discount books as a learning tool. As the saying goes, reading is fundamental. Are you a teacher's aide who aspires to be a teacher? An administrative assistant in a college fund-raising and development office who aspires to move up the career ladder? Look for a book. Read more about it.

Are you working in the student activities department of a college but yearn to work in workforce development? Look for a book. See if it's a career area you want to pursue. Are you interested in learning more about doing publicity or public relations for a college or school system? Find a book. Need help improving your leadership skills? Check out some books for ideas? Want to know more about the lives of teachers? Look for a book! Want to know more about any aspect of the education industry? There are tons of books on all aspects of education. The more you read, the more you'll know. Books often hold the answer to many of your questions. They give you the opportunity to explore opportunities and learn about things you didn't know.

Trade journals offer numerous possibilities as well. They'll keep you up-to-date on industry trends and let you know about industry problems and solutions. What else can you find in the trades? You might discover advertisements for job openings, notices for trade events, and current news.

How do you find trade journals? You might check with your local library. You can also surf the net to check out journals specific to the area of education in which you're interested.

Go to your local newsstand and library to see what's available. If your library doesn't have the periodical you are looking for, try your local community college or university.

If you are already working in some aspect of education, these trades may also be available in your workplace. For example, schools, colleges, and universities often subscribe to many of the trades related to education.

National bookstore chains such as Borders or Barnes and Noble also often carry some of the more popular trade publications. Be sure to check out the online versions of trade publications. While many trade Web sites require subscriptions to access some areas, they still often carry the latest news and job openings in the free section.

How about workshops, seminars, and other courses? In addition to learning new skills in or out of the area you are pursuing in education, there are a number of added benefits in going to these events. First, you'll have the opportunity to meet other people interested in the same subject area you are. You also be able to network. Instructors, facilitators, even other students in the class are all potential contacts that might be instrumental in your career.

"But," you say, "I'm busy enough without doing extra work. Is this really necessary? Do I have to take classes?"

No one is going to make you do anything, but you should be aware that they can help take your career to a new level. Classes, workshops, and seminars will help give you new ideas and help you to look at things from a different perspective.

★ Tip from the Top

Be sure to keep up with any continuing education you may be required to take to keep any certification or licenses you might have. If you aren't sure what you need, talk to your supervisor or contact the trade association or union related to your career area.

> ⭐ **Words from the Wise**
>
> In some situations, having additional education or training may help you get a better job, a promotion, or even higher compensation. It will also open up more opportunities.

Additionally, if you are either a teacher or an administrator you will want to take courses to keep up with changes and advances in your industry. In certain areas you will also be required to take continuing education to remain certified.

Whether you are taking workshops, seminars, or classes, are learning new techniques, or are honing your skills, the results will help you in your quest to be the best at what you do. If you continue to navigate your way through formal and informal learning experiences throughout your life and career you will be rewarded with success and satisfaction.

Workplace Politics

In order to succeed in your career in education, it is essential to learn how to deal effectively with some of the challenging situations you'll encounter. Workplace politics are a part of life. And depending what area of education you are pursuing, the *workplace* can be almost anyplace.

The real trick to dealing with workplace politics is trying to stay out of them. No matter which side you take in an office dispute, you're going to be wrong. You can never tell who will be the *winner* or *loser*, so try to stay neutral and just worry about doing your job. Is this easy? No. But for your own sake, you have to try.

Will keeping out of it work all the time? Probably not, and therein lies the problem. There's an old adage that says the workplace is a jungle. Unfortunately that's sometimes true.

If you think you're going to encounter politics only in the office, think again. As we just mentioned, in education the *workplace* can be almost anyplace. It can be in a classroom, an administration office, or any part of a school or college or university. It can be a corporate office. It can even be in the community in which you work.

What all this means is that no matter in what part of education you are working, you often may have additional challenges. In many cases workplace politics may be expanded to every area of your life, including your personal relationships and your family. With this in mind, let's learn more about them.

Why are there are politics in the workplace? Much of it comes from jealousy. Some coworkers might think you have a better chance at a promotion or are better at your job than they are at theirs. Someone might think you slighted him or her. Believe it not, someone just might not like you. In any business setting there are people who vie for more recognition, feel the need to prove themselves right all the time, or who just want to get ahead. There really is nothing you can do about workplace politics except to stay out of them to the best of your ability.

In certain segments of education, feelings of jealousy sometimes escalate. There are many reasons for this. Some coworkers may feel they are more talented than you in their area of the industry.

Often, jealousy surfaces when someone doesn't understand why *you* got the job or the promotion and he or she did not. Some may not understand why you are a department head and they can't get a promotion.

Sometimes people may want to protect themselves from feeling like failures or may just be frustrated with their career (or lack of it).

> ## ★ Words from the Wise
>
> We've all heard of someone about whom others say, "You know, he (or she) is such a nice man (or woman). He (or she) never says a bad word about anyone." These people stay out of office politics. They stay out of office squabbles, and they stay out of trouble in the workplace. If you can keep this in mind and try to follow their lead, you will be ahead of the game. It may not be easy, but before you decide to speak about someone, remember that office politics and gossip can be problematic.

In these situations many lash out and talk about others. Whether what is said is the truth or not, these words can hurt. Worse than that, your words can come back to haunt you—big time.

Office Gossip

Gossip is a common form of office politics. Anyone who has held a job has probably seen it, and perhaps even participated in it in some form. Have you? Forget the moral or ethical issues. Gossip can hurt your career.

Here's a good rule of thumb: Never say anything about anyone that you wouldn't mind them hearing and knowing it came from you. If you think you can believe someone who says, "Oh, you can tell me, it's confidential," you're wrong.

"But she's my best friend," you say, "I trust her with my life."

It doesn't matter. Your friend might be perfectly trustworthy, but trust is not always the problem. Sometimes people slip and repeat things during a conversation. Other times a person might tell someone else whom they trust what you said and ask him or her to keep it confidential, but then that person tells another person and so it goes down the line. Eventually, the person telling the story doesn't even know it's supposed to be confidential and might even mention it to a good friend or colleague of the person everyone has been gossiping about.

The reason people gossip is because it makes them feel like part of a group. It can make you feel like you're smarter or know something other people don't. Most of the time, however, you don't even know if what you're gossiping about is true. Yet once a gossip session gets started, it's difficult to stop.

Most people are good at heart. After gossiping about someone else, they often feel badly. It might just be a twinge of conscience, but it's there. Is it worth it? No. Worse than that, it's safe to assume that if you are gossiping about others, they are gossiping about you.

How do you rise above this? Keep your distance. People generally respect that you don't want to be involved. Don't start any gossip, and if someone starts gossiping around you, just don't get involved.

How do you handle the conversation?

Suppose someone says to you, "Did you hear that Dr. Tobin got so drunk that he fell over at the party? Imagine a principal acting like that."

You respond, "No. Have you tasted that great new flavored coffee at the coffee shop?"

They might want to keep the conversation going and say, "Yeah, it's great. You should have seen Dr. Tobin. I don't know how he can show his face around this school."

All you have to do is either change the subject again or say, "I made a decision a long time ago not to get involved in gossip. It can only get me in trouble."

Every now and then you hear through the grapevine that people are gossiping about you. It's not a good feeling, but you might have to deal with it. What do you do? You have a few options:

◎ You can ignore it.
◎ You can confront the person or people who are gossiping about you.
◎ You can start gossiping about the person or people gossiping about you.

What's your best choice? Well, it's definitely not gossiping about the person who is gossiping about you. Ignoring the gossip might be your best choice, except that suppressing your feelings of betrayal and anger can be stressful. So how about confronting the person or people who are gossiping about you? If you're certain about who has been spreading the gossip and you can do this calmly and professionally, it often resolves the situation.

Whatever you do, don't have a public confrontation and don't confront a group. Instead, wait until the person is alone. Calmly approach him or her and say something like this: "John, I didn't want to bring this up in front of anyone else because I didn't want to embarrass you, but I've heard that you've been talking to others here at school about my performance and discussing my personal life. I've always had respect for you so I really questioned the people who told me it was happening. I'd just like to know if it's true."

Words from a Pro

Do you like to be around negative people? Probably not. Well, neither does anyone else. We all have bad days when we complain and whine that nothing is going right. The problem comes when it occurs constantly. If you want to succeed in your career, try to limit the negativity, at least around your colleagues. While they say misery loves company, in reality, after a while people won't want to be around you. Eventually, they'll start to avoid you. On the other hand, most people like to be around positive people who make them smile and laugh. If you can do this, you'll have an edge over others.

At this point John probably will be embarrassed and claim that he doesn't know what you're talking about. He might ask you who mentioned it.

"Who told you that?" he'll ask. "I want to straighten them out."

Do not give out any names. It's better to let him start questioning the trust of all the people he's been talking to and gossiping with.

While he might tell a couple of people you confronted him on the gossip subject, John will probably find someone else to gossip about in the future.

In many segments of education gossip may often lead to bigger problems. Depending on

Voice of Experience

Use coffee breaks or meetings at the water cooler or teacher's lounge to your advantage. Instead of gossiping, try using the situations as opportunities. A few pleasant words or a smile can often win over even those with conflicting opinions.

Tip from the Top

It is never a good idea to speak badly about your employer, your colleagues, your students or your supervisors, no matter what. When you do, people on the outside start doubting your loyalties.

⭐ The Inside Scoop

At one point when I was substituting, I had a two-week assignment filling in for a teacher who had a family emergency. During that time I remember going into the teacher's lounge each day for lunch and hearing a number of the teachers talking about how "stupid" a couple of students were. I wondered how far they would go trashing their students. Didn't they know that insulting their students evidenced their own inability to teach effectively? I commented that perhaps the students just needed someone to give them some extra help or explain things in a different way, but was told, "I just didn't understand." Although distressed, I said nothing more to them. In the course of my two-week stay I learned (from listening to others) that these particular teachers had a reputation for "trashing" their students. Their attitude, and their idle chatter, were often overheard by other teachers and the administration and had not gone unnoticed. Many teachers avoided them and they neither had the respect of the administration nor of their students. I found out later that two of the teachers did not receive tenure that year.

Am I sure it was because of their attitude and their gossiping about students? Of course, I can't be 100 percent positive, but I have pretty strong feelings that their attitude didn't help.

⭐ Tip from the Coach

Remember the philosophy that on the ladder to success, real successful people pull others up the ladder with them; the ones who try to push others down the ladder will never be real successes themselves.

It's essential to your success and your career not to spread rumors in the workplace or out. Don't talk about the inside information you have, whether it's good or bad. If anyone pumps you for information learn to simply say, "Sorry, that's confidential."

Money, Money, Money

How upset would you be if you found out that a coworker who had a job similar to yours was making more money than you? Probably pretty upset. Whether it's what you're making, what your coworker is making, or what someone else is making, money is often a problem in the workplace. Why? Because everyone wants to earn more. No matter how much money people are paid for a job, they don't think they're getting enough. If they hear someone is getting paid better than them, it understandably upsets them.

Here's the deal. If you know you're making more than someone else, keep it to yourself. If you're making less than someone else, keep it to yourself. No matter what your earnings are, keep it to yourself. Don't discuss your earnings with coworkers. The only people in the workplace you should discuss your earnings with are the human resources department and your supervisors.

In certain situations earnings or salary caps are determined by state law. Additionally, earnings of some such as administrators in public

your work environment, you might be privy to private stories about students, teachers, administrators, and other coworkers.

Here's the deal: Office gossip is bad enough, but gossiping about students is not only in poor taste but may breach confidentiality. Gossiping about what happens in the workplace, what you hear, or what you know (even if it is true) can ruin your career, especially if it leads to embarrassment of powerful people.

schools or colleges may be public record. Sometimes your earnings may become not only public but also newsworthy. For example, a superintendent or school administrator may have his or her earnings scrutinized during a highly contested budget vote.

Sometimes a consultant or corporate trainer negotiates a good contract. There may be any number of circumstances involving salaries and compensation packages.

Here's the deal. If you've just landed a huge contract it's okay to be happy; it's okay to be ecstatic. But it probably isn't a good idea to walk around gloating, especially around colleagues who may not have negotiated the great salary you did.

Why would one person be earning more than another in a similar position? There might be a number of reasons. Compensation for many positions is negotiated, and the person might be a better negotiator. He or she might have more experience, more education, seniority, different skills, or more responsibilities. Even where salary is fixed by statute, an employer may classify two similar employees in different positions, which would affect salaries.

In the corporate or business segment of education, some employees may have skills or attributes that employers feel they need to prosper. A corporate trainer, for example, may have demonstrated that he or she can train employees more effectively than others. A sales person may sell more than others. There are any number of scenarios.

"But it's frustrating," you say.

I understand, but being frustrated won't help. Worry about your own job. Don't waste time comparing yourself to your coworkers, colleagues, or others in positions you consider similar. Definitely don't whine about it in your workplace. It will get on people's nerves.

> ### ⭐ Tip from the Coach
> It's very easy to start comparing your earnings with those of others who are making more and start feeling sorry for yourself. Try not to compare yourself, your job, or your earnings to anyone else. Instead of concentrating on what "they're making," try to concentrate on how you can get "there."

What can you do? Make sure you are visible in a positive way. Make sure you're doing a great job. If you're already doing a great job, try to do a better job. Keep notes on projects you've successfully completed, ideas you've suggested which are being used and things you are doing to make things better in the school, college, or company. Then, when it's time for a job review, you'll have the ammunition to ask for the compensation you deserve.

If you're in a situation where salaries are mandated, such as a public school, use your experience and successes to land a promotion, which will result in increased earnings.

Dealing with Colleagues

Whatever area of education you choose to work in, you're going to be dealing with others. Whether they are superiors, subordinates, or colleagues, the way you deal with people you work with will impact your opportunities, your chances of success, and your future.

Many people treat colleagues and superiors well, yet treat subordinates with less respect. One of the interesting things about careers in education is that, like other industries, career progression doesn't always follow a normal pattern. What that means is that with the right set of circumstances someone might jump a number of rungs up the career ladder quicker than expected. The end result could be someone who is a subordinate might technically become either a colleague or even a superior. It's essential to treat everyone with whom you come in contact with dignity and respect. Aside from this being common courtesy, you can never tell when the person making you coffee today will be making a decision about your future tomorrow.

Want to know a secret about dealing effectively with people? If you can sincerely make every person you come in contact with feel special, you will have it made. How do you do this? There are a number of ways.

When someone does or says something interesting or comes up with a good idea mention it to them. For example, "That was a great idea you had at the meeting, Kevin. You always come up with interesting ways to solve problems."

Sometimes you might want to send a short note instead. For example:

Donna,

While I'm sure you're ecstatic that the press conference is over, I hope you know how impressed everyone was with the event. You handled the coordination like a seasoned pro. No one would ever have guessed that this was the first time you ever put a press conference together.

Everything was perfect. But the real coup was getting the story about the college's new culinary program on every major television station in the area. You did a great job. I'm glad we're on the same team.

Debbie

If another employee does something noteworthy, write a note. If a colleague receives an award or an honor, write a note. It doesn't make you any less talented or skilled and your words can not only make someone else's day, but help you build a good relationship with a colleague as well.

Everyone likes a cheerleader. At home you have your family to cheer you on. In your personal life you have friends to cheer. If you can be a cheerleader to others in the workplace it often helps you to excel as well.

Never be phony and always be sincere. Look for little things that people do or say as

The Inside Scoop

A number of years ago I was talking to someone about the possibility of a new job.

"It's a really good opportunity, but I'm not sure I'm going to take it," the man told me.

"Why not?" I asked.

"The woman who is the department head used to be a teacher's aide when I first started teaching," he replied. "We had a decent working relationship, but I never let her forget she was only an aide. Not only that, it would just be uncomfortable working with my former aide knowing she has climbed the career ladder faster and I'm still at this level."

"From what you told me, your career dream was to be a great teacher. You didn't want to be an administrator," I said. "The woman who was originally your teacher's aide wanted to be a department head. That was her dream. Not yours. Before you turn down the job, think about what you really want. If you decided to take the job, clear the air with the woman. She might not even have any issues."

The man ended up taking the job. He did clear the air with the woman before starting the job. He did tell me that from that moment on, he always tried to treat all people respectfully.

You can never tell who you're going to run into again down the line in your career, or your life. Always treat everyone with respect and dignity.

> ⭐ **Tip from the Coach**
>
> In an attempt to build themselves up, many people try to tear others down. Unfortunately, it usually has the opposite effect.

well. "That's a great tie, John." "Nice suit, Amy. You always look so put together." "New semester registration was so busy this morning. We are really lucky to have you coordinating things down there."

Notice that while you're complimenting others, you're not supposed to be self-deprecating. You don't want to make yourself look bad, you want others to look good. So, for example, you wouldn't say, "Nice suit Amy. You always look so put together. I couldn't coordinate a suit and blouse if I tried," or "Great job on the press conference. I never could have coordinated an event like that," or "Registration was so busy this morning. We are really lucky to have you coordinating things down there. If they left registration solely in my hands, everyone would still would be there."

The idea is to build people up so they feel good about themselves. When you can do that, people like to be around you, they gain self-confidence and they pass it on to others. One of them might be you. Best of all, you will start to look like a leader. This is a very important image to be building when you're attempting to move up the career ladder.

Dealing with Your Superiors

While you are ultimately in charge of your career, superiors are often the people who can help either move it along or hold it back. Depending on what area of education in which you are involved, your superior might be a supervisor,

boss, a director, department head, principal, superintendent, board of directors, college or university president, or others.

Try to develop a good working relationship with your superiors, whoever they are. A good boss can help you succeed in your present job as well as in your future career.

One of the mistakes many people make in the workplace is looking at their bosses as the enemy. They get a mindset of *us* against *them*. Worse than that, they sit around and boss-bash with other colleagues.

Want to better your chances of success at your job? Make your boss look good. How do you do that?

◎ Don't boss-bash.
◎ Speak positively about your boss to others.
◎ Do your work.
◎ Cooperate in the workplace.
◎ If you see something that needs to be done, offer to do it.
◎ Volunteer to help with projects that aren't done.
◎ Ask if your boss needs help.

"But what if my boss is a jerk?" you ask. It's still in your best interest to make him or her look good. Believe it or not, it will make you look good.

While we're on the subject, let's discuss bad bosses. With any luck, your boss will be a great person who loves his or her job. But every now and then you just might run into a bad boss.

He or she might be a jerk, a fool, or an idiot.

"I could do a better job than him," you say. Well you might be able to, but not if you can't learn to deal with people so you still have a job. In many cases your boss has already proven himself or herself to the organization and is therefore more of a commodity than you are at this point. So just how do you deal with a bad boss and come out on top?

Let's first go over a list of *don'ts*.

◎ Don't be confrontational. This will usually only infuriate your boss.

◎ Don't shout or curse. Even if you're right, you will look wrong.

◎ Don't talk about your boss to coworkers. You can never tell who is whose best friend or who is telling your boss exactly what you're saying.

◎ Don't send e-mails to people from your office about things your boss does or says.

◎ Don't talk about your boss to students, teachers, parents, colleagues, clients, etc. It's not good business and it's not really ethical.

◎ Don't, and I repeat don't, cry in your workplace. No matter how mad your boss or supervisor makes you, no matter what mistake you made, no matter what nasty or obnoxious thing someone says about you, keep your composure until you're alone. Bite your lip, pinch yourself, or do whatever you have to do to keep the tears under control.

Now let's go over a list of *dos* that might help.

◎ Do a good job. It's hard to argue with someone who has done what they are supposed to do.

◎ Be at work when you are scheduled to be there, and always be on time.

◎ Attend all scheduled meetings.

◎ Keep a paper trail. Keep notes when your boss asks you to do things and when you've done them. Keep notes regarding calls that have been made, dates, times, etc. Keep lesson plans. Keep a running list of projects you've completed successfully. Do this as a matter of course. Keep it to yourself. Then, if and when you need something to jog your memory, you can refer to it.

◎ Wait until there is no time constraint to finish something and there is no emergency and ask your supervisor if you can speak to him or her. Then say you'd like to clear the air. Ask what suggestions he or she can give you to help you do a better job.

⊡ You might, for example, say, "Dr. Jones, I just wanted to clear the air. We're on the same team and if there is something I can be doing to do a better job or be a better teacher, just let me know. I'll be glad to try to implement it."

◎ Think long and hard before you decide to leave your job. If your supervisor is as much of a jerk as you think, perhaps he or she will find a new job or be promoted.

No matter what type of boss or supervisor you have, learning to communicate with him or her is essential. Everyone has a different

***

⭐ **Words from the Wise**

Do not put anything in e-mail that you wouldn't mind someone else reading. No matter what anyone tells you, e-mail is not confidential. Furthermore, be aware that in many situations your e-mails, private or business, may be classified as company property. What this means is management may have the right to access your e-mail.

⭐ Tip from the Top

Check out your school or company's policy on private e-mail. Be aware that in many situations private e-mails are not allowed. Whatever you do don't use your company e-mail address when looking for a new job.

communication style and it's up to you to determine what his or hers is.

Does your boss like to communicate through e-mail? Some organizations today communicate almost totally through e-mail. Everything from the daily, "Good Morning," until, "See you tomorrow," and everything in between will be in your inbox. If this is the way it is at your office, get used to it. E-mail will be your communication style. The good thing about it is you pretty much have a record of everything.

Other bosses communicate mainly on paper. He or she may give you direction, tell you what's happening, or ask for things via typed or handwritten notes. Sometimes communications may be in formal memos; other times memos may be informal or even on sticky notes.

It's important to realize that you have a choice in your career. You can sit there and hope things happen or you can make them hap-

⭐ Tip from the Coach

If you carry a personal cell phone, set it to the vibrate mode while in the office. Getting constant calls from friends in the office, even on your cell phone, is inappropriate. While we're on the subject, never take a call on your personal cell phone during a business meeting or during class.

pen. You can either be passive or proactive. In order to succeed in your career, being proactive is usually a better choice.

You can go to work and let your supervisor tell you what to do, or you can do that little bit extra, share your dreams and aspirations, and work toward your goals. No matter what segment of the industry you are pursuing, supervisors can help you make it happen.

Ethics, Morals, and More

We all have our own set of ethics and morals. They help guide us on what we think is right and wrong. In your career you may be faced with situations where a person or group of people want you to do something you know or feel is wrong. In return for doing it, you may be promised financial gain or career advancement.

Would you do it? "Well," you might say, "that depends on what I'd have to do and what I'd get." Here's the deal. No matter what anyone wants you to do, if you know it's wrong, even if you only think it *might* be wrong, it probably is a bad idea.

"But they told me no one would know," you say. Most people are not that good at keeping secrets and if *they* get caught, you're going down too. If you're just getting started in your career, you might be looking at ending it for a few dollars. If you're already into your career, are you really prepared to lose everything you worked that hard to get.

"But they told me if I did this or did that, they'd remember me when promotions came up," you say. How do you know someone isn't testing you to see what your morals are? And exactly what are you planning on doing after you do whatever the person asked you to do and he or she doesn't give you the promotion? Report them? Probably not.

It's important to realize that people move around. They move from job to job and location to location. It is not unheard of to learn that someone took a job on the other side of town or the other side of the country.

What this means is that while every supervisor you have may not know every other supervisor, there is a chance that some of them may know other people in the industry. With this in mind, do you really want to take a chance on doing something stupid or unethical? Probably not.

And forget getting caught. Do you want to build a great career, a long-term career that you can be proud of, on unethical activities? Once again, the answer is probably not.

How do you get out of doing something you don't want to do? You might simply say something like, "My dream was to work in education. I am not about to mess it up for something like this." Or, "I've worked so hard to get where I am now, I really don't want to want to lose what I have." What about, "No can do. Sorry." How about, "Sorry, I'm not comfortable with that."

But what do you do if a supervisor wants you to do something unethical? How do you handle that? You can try any of the lines above, but if your job is on the line you have a bigger problem to deal with. In cases like this, document as much as you can. Then, if you have no other choice go to human resources, a higher supervisor, or someone else you think can help.

"What do I do if I see something going on around me?" you say. What if I'm not involved but I see a supervisor or coworker doing something that I know is wrong? Then what?"

This is a tough one as well. No one likes a tattletale, but if something major is going on, you have a decision to make.

Do you say something? Bring it to the attention of a higher up? Mention it to the alleged wrongdoer? Or just make sure you're not involved and say nothing?

Hopefully, at the time, you'll make the right choice. It generally will depend on the position you hold, your responsibilities, and the alleged crime. It's a difficult decision. If you decide to say something, be very sure that you are absolutely, positively certain you are correct about your information.

What do I do if I see someone abusing or not treating a student correctly? What then?

In cases like this you need to make a choice as well. If you think someone is mistreating or abusing a student, or you are told it is happening, it is your responsibility to say something. In certain states it is not only your moral and professional responsibility, but your legal responsibility as well.

Accountability

No one is perfect. We all make mistakes. No matter how careful anyone is, things may happen. Accept the fact that sometime in your career you are going to make one, too. In many cases it's not the mistake itself that causes the problem, but the way we deal with it.

The best way to deal with a mistake is to take responsibility, apologize, try to fix it, and go on. Be sincere. Simply say something like, "I'm sorry. I made a mistake. I'm going to try to fix it and will make sure it doesn't happen again." With that said, it's very difficult for anyone to argue with you.

If, on the other hand, you start explaining mitigating circumstances, blame your coworkers, your secretary, your boss, or make excuses, others generally go on the defensive. Similarly, when you're wrong, just admit it and go on.

People will respect you, you'll look more professional, and you'll have a lot less turmoil in your life.

For example, "I was wrong about the school budget marketing campaign. You were right. Good thing we're a team." Or, "I am so sorry I was late today. I know we had a parent-teacher meeting scheduled. I'll make sure it doesn't happen again. Thanks for covering for me."

Okay, you're taking credit for your mistakes, but what happens if someone else makes a mistake and you're blamed or you're the one who looks like you're unprepared? Let's say, for example, you are working in the fund-raising and development office of a college and find that the name of a major benefactor has inadvertently been spelled wrong on an engraved plaque that is supposed to be presented at a luncheon in 45 minutes. What do you do? Blame the engraver? Blame your assistant? Blame your secretary?

The benefactor probably doesn't care or want to know if you have an incompetent staff. It's not his or her problem. The best thing to do in these types of situations is also to acknowledge the problem, apologize, and see what you can do to fix it quickly. "I'm sorry. I should have triple checked the spelling on your plaque before I brought it to the luncheon. I've already called the engraver to rectify the situation and asked him to make a new plaque. I personally will get you the new plaque with the correct spelling tomorrow. I hope you can forgive me." The result? What could have been a major faux pas is now just a minor inconvenience that no one will probably even remember a few weeks down the line.

In work, as in life, many people's first thoughts when there is a problem are to cover themselves. So when things go wrong, most people are busy reacting or coming up with excuses.

Here's something to remember. The most successful people don't come up with excuses. Instead, when something goes wrong, their first thoughts are how to fix the problem, mitigate any damages, and get things back to normal. If you can do this and remain cool in a crisis, it will enhance your position, whether you are working in the business, administration, creative, or talent areas of an industry.

Time, Time Management, and Organization

Here's a question for you. What is one thing that every person on the planet has the same amount of? Do you know what it is?

Here's a hint. I have the same amount you have. Bill Gates has the same amount I have. Oprah Winfrey has the same amount Bill Gates has. William Shakespeare had the same amount Oprah Winfrey has. Do you know what it is yet?

Every person in this world, no matter who they are or what they do, has the same 24 hours a day. You can't get less and you can't get more, no matter what you do. It doesn't matter who you are or what your job is. You don't get more time during the day if you're young, old, or in-between. You don't get more time if you're a millionaire or you're making minimum wage. You wouldn't even get more time if you were a Nobel Prize winner who had discovered a cure for cancer.

With all this in mind, it's important to manage your time wisely. That way you can fit more of what you need to fit into your day and get the most important things accomplished.

To start with, let's deal with your workday. Try to get to work a little earlier than you're expected. It's easier to get the day started when you're not rushing. On occasion you might also want to stay late. Why? Because when superi-

---

The Inside Scoop

The time period before everyone else gets in or after everyone has left the workplace is usually less formal and less stressed. If you make it a habit to come in right before the big brass comes in and leave either when they leave or just afterward, you will generally become visible in a more positive manner to higher ups. More than that, however, you will often have the opportunity to ask a question, make a comment, or offer a suggestion. If someone questions you about what you're doing at work so early simply say something like, "Preparing for the day ahead," or "Getting some project started before it gets busy," or "Finishing up a few things so I can devote tomorrow to new projects."

---

ors see you bolting at 5 p.m. (or whenever your workday ends) it looks like you're not really interested in your job.

You also want to be relaxed before dealing with your job, not stressed because you got stuck in a traffic jam and started worrying that you were going to be late getting to work.

No matter what your career choice in education, in order to be successful you will need to learn to prioritize your tasks. How do you know what's important?

If your boss or supervisor needs it now, it's important. If it's dealing with a life or death situation, it's important. If a student or his or her parent needs something and you can do it, it's important. If you promised to do something for someone, it's important. If something is happening today or tomorrow and you need to get a project done, it's important. If things absolutely *need* to get done now, they're important.

Generally what you need to do is determine what is most important and do it first. Then go over your list of things that need to get done and see what take precedence.

The more organized you are the easier it will be for you to manage your time. Make lists of things you need to do. You might want to keep a master list and then a daily list of things you need to do. You might also want a third list of deadlines that need to be met.

It's important to remember that just making lists won't do it. Checking them on a consistent basis to make sure the things that you needed to do actually got done is the key.

Here's an example of the beginnings of a master list. Use it to get you started on yours.

◎ Call Kate Bennett to set up appointment.
◎ Prepare lesson plans.
◎ Prepare report for department head meeting Thursday.
◎ Check class schedule for certification program.
◎ Confirm in-service meeting time.
◎ Talk to Dr. Lynn regarding board meeting.
◎ Dinner with Sandy R., Monday, 7:00 p.m.

Writing things down is essential to being organized. Don't depend on your memory, or anyone else's. Whatever your job within the education industry, it is sure to be filled with a lot of details, things that need to get done, and

---

Words from the Wise

In prioritizing, don't forget that you must fit in the things you promised others you would do. Don't get so caught up in wanting to be liked, or wanting to agree, or even wanting to be great at your job, that you promise to do something you really don't have time to get done. Doing so will just put you under pressure.

just plain stuff in general. The more successful you get, the busier you will be and more things you'll have to remember. Don't depend on others to remind you. Depend on yourself.

If you want to you can input information into your Blackberry or other electronic device. However, always keep a backup.

Here's an idea if you want to be really organized. Keep a notebook with you where you can jot things down as they occur. Date each page so you have a reference point for later. Then make notes. Like what?

◎ The dates people called and the gist of the conversation.
◎ The dates you called people and the reason you called.
◎ Notes on meetings you attend. Then when someone says something like, "Gee, I don't remember whether we said May 9 or May 10," you have it.
◎ Names of people you meet.
◎ Things that happened during the day.

After you get used to keeping the notebook it will become a valuable resource. You might, for example, remember someone calling you six months ago. "What was his name," you ask yourself. "I wish I knew his name." Just look in your notebook.

"It seems like a lot of trouble," I hear you saying.

Well it is a little extra effort, but I can almost guarantee you that once you keep a notebook like this for a while you won't be able to live without it. You won't be looking for little sheets of paper on which you have jotted down important numbers and then misplaced. You won't have to remember people's names, phone numbers, or what they said. You won't have to

remember if you were supposed to call at 3:00 p.m. or 4:30 p.m., as you'll have everything at your fingertips.

A Few Other Things

It's important to realize that while of course you want to succeed in your career, everything you do may not be successful. You might not get every job you apply for. You might not get every promotion you want. Every idea you have may not work out. Every project you do may not turn out perfectly. And every job may not be the one you had hoped it would be.

It also is essential to remember that none of these scenarios mean that you are a failure. What they mean, simply, is that you need to work on them a little bit more. Things take time. Careers take time—especially great careers.

Be aware that success is often built on the back of little failures. If you ask most successful people about their road to success, many will tell you it wasn't always easy. And no matter what it looks like, most people are not overnight successes.

While some may have it easier, others may have had one or more rejections or failures before they got where they were going. What you'll find is, those who are now successful didn't quit. After keeping at it and plugging away they landed the jobs they aspired to, got the promotions, received good work reviews, and got where they are today.

You might not get the promotion you wanted right away. You might not have the job of your dreams yet. That does not mean it won't happen. Keep plugging away and work at it and success will come to you.

Most successful people have a number of key traits in common. They have a willingness to take risks, a determination that cannot be undone, and usually an amazing amount of confidence in themselves and their ideas.

Can they fail? Sure. But they might also succeed, and they usually do. What does this have to do with you? If you learn from the success of others, you can be successful too. If you emulate successful people, you too can be on the road to success.

Don't be so afraid of not getting things right that you don't take a chance at doing it a better way or a different way. Don't get so comfortable that you're afraid to take a risk. Don't get so comfortable that you don't work toward a promotion or accept a new job or new responsibilities. Be determined that you know what you want and how to get it, and you will.

If you want to succeed in your career and your life, I urge you to be confident and be willing to take a risk. Success can surprise you at any time.

Take advantage of opportunities that present themselves, but don't stop there. Create opportunities for yourself to help launch your career to a new level by using creativity and innovative ideas.

Know that you not only can *have* success in your career in education, but that you *deserve* success. And if you work hard enough you can achieve your goals and dreams.

Whether your dream is to be a great teacher or top administrator, to work in a private school or public school, to work in a community college or large university, or to work for a corporation or any type of business in the education industry, your success is waiting. The more you work toward success, the quicker it will come.

11

Succeeding as a Teacher

We've discussed a multitude of things throughout this book that can help you in your quest for a great career in education. We've talked about a variety of jobs and career options in various areas of the industry. We've discussed making your job into a career. We've investigated ways to get past the gatekeeper, some unique ways to obtain interviews, and interview tips.

We've discussed developing resumes, cover letters, and putting together action plans. We've talked about job search strategies and tools for success. We've discussed why marketing is so important and how you can market yourself.

You may have picked up this book for many reasons. I'm assuming if you're still reading you've decided you want to work in some segment of the education field. While there is a wide array of career options you might choose from in education, and we've talked about a number of them throughout the book, what I would like to do now is take some time to focus on teaching.

If teaching is not your career choice, you can skip over this chapter if you wish. However, while much of this information is specific to those becoming teachers or those who are already teachers, even if teaching is not your career choice, you might find some of the information helpful in your career as well.

Many young people grow up dreaming of a career as a teacher. Some grow up, change their dreams, and go on to careers in other fields, while others grow up and follow their original dream.

Which scenario is yours? While I'm betting I know the answer, let's be sure. Here are some things you might want to think about.

How many times have you read a story in the newspaper about a teacher who did something wonderful with his class and wished it were you? How many times have you seen a teacher leading her class on a field trip, answering the questions of her excited students and wished it were you? How many times have you turned on the news and watched as a teacher achieved a goal with his or her class and wished it were you? How many times have you learned something new and wished you could share the knowledge with someone? How many times have you seen teachers in the office supply store getting ready for the first week of school and wished it were you? How many times do you wish you were developing a lesson plan or standing before a room filled with students, teaching your class?

I'm betting if you are reading this section of the book, there's a good chance you see yourself in one of these scenarios.

There certainly is nothing wrong with wishing. It definitely can't hurt. As a matter of fact, it sometimes helps you focus more clearly on what you want. But wishing alone can't make something happen. In order to succeed it's essential to take some positive steps.

There are bad teachers. There are good teachers. And then there are great teachers. The question is, how do you become the latter? Later in this section we're going to cover some things you can do to increase your chances of being that great teacher. But before we do that, let' make sure teaching is for you.

How Do You Know If Teaching Is for You?

Have you decided you want to become a teacher? Has it been your life's calling for as long as you can remember? Some people know from the time they are quite young that they are going to be teachers when they "grow up." Others made the decision when they were in high school or in college. There are also many who make the decision *after* they have already been in another career but then realize a career in teaching is their *real* dream.

Perhaps a special teacher impacted your life and you wanted to do the same for someone else. Or maybe you never had a really good teacher and wanted to make sure others did.

Many people go into teaching because they have a genuine desire to help others learn. Some have parents or other family members who were teachers and decide to follow in their footsteps.

Whatever the reasons you have chosen this profession, know that as a teacher your work will have a tremendous impact on others.

And while everyone has his or her own reason for deciding to enter the field, if you haven't made your decision yet, read on.

★ The Inside Scoop

While I didn't always like school or many of my teachers, the day I walked into my social studies class when I was a junior, I hit the jackpot. The teacher I had was a wonderful woman who, by her love of teaching, made others love learning. Although she taught social studies and history, she always added in "things we would need in later life," many of which I still remember and use today.

A number of years after I graduated, the teacher was being recognized for a community service award. I attended the event and after the ceremony went to congratulate her and tell her how she was my favorite teacher of all time. She modestly told me that there were other good teachers.

"Not like you," I said. "You made everything so interesting. I actually remember most of what you taught, and that was years ago. It's because of you I began reading biographies. I still do today. What made you become a teacher in the first place?" I asked.

She told me that teaching had always been her passion, even before she was a teacher. She loved sharing information with people, she loved finding new ways to explain things to them, and she loved knowing that she was making a difference. She told me how lucky she felt that she was to have had the opportunity to teach as a vocation as well as an avocation, and how lucky she was that she got to do what she had always wanted to do with her life.

If you have the same passion, chances are you, too, can be the best teacher someone had.

I've often been asked by people making career choices if I thought teaching was the right choice for them, or if I thought they would be good teachers? If you are wondering the same thing, you might want to ask yourself a few questions.

The Inside Scoop

Many people make the decision to become a teacher after having a deep personal experience—either positive or negative—with a teacher. I once asked an elementary school teacher why she chose a career in that field and she told me that she had a learning disability when she was growing up and did not have a very easy time in school. She went on to tell me how a number of teachers had called her stupid and told her she was too dumb to learn. Another teacher had asked her if she was retarded when she didn't understand something. No teacher had ever stepped in when her classmates were making fun of her.

When she was in sixth grade, however, things changed. During a class, the teacher asked the girl to answer a question about a story she had just asked them to read. The girl didn't know the answer and the teacher realized something was wrong. She asked the girl to stay after class, and when they were alone, the girl blurted out, "I'm stupid. Everyone says so. I'm sorry, but this is the best I can do." The kind teacher told her she was not stupid. As a matter of fact, the teacher told her she thought she was very smart. She told the girl that perhaps she just needed to learn things in a different way and she was going to help her. The teacher brought the problem to her supervisors and made sure the girl was tested. It turned out she was dyslexic.

While she didn't have an easy time, once she was diagnosed and used some alternative ways to look at things, she actually started liking school and doing better. That teacher made a huge difference in that girl's life. She decided that even if it was hard, she was going to find a way to help other children. Her goal was never to have a child feel stupid again. From that moment on she was determined to work hard and find a way to become a teacher.

◎ Do I really *want* to become a teacher? This sounds like it should be easy to answer, but in some cases people become teachers for the wrong reasons. Perhaps someone else tells them it's a good idea or it is someone else's dream. Perhaps someone thinks a career as a teacher is a good choice because they have heard that teachers can always find a job. Or they might want to be a teacher because teachers have the summer off. Or they might not really know what they want to do and teaching seems like the easiest choice. None of these are good reasons.

◎ Do I have a genuine desire to work with children and young people and help them learn?

◎ Am I passionate about becoming a teacher?

◎ Do I want to make a positive impact in a child's life?

◎ Do I want to share a love of learning with others?

◎ Do I want to help others discover their potential?

◎ Do I truly like to be around children and young people?

◎ Am I nurturing?

Words to the Wise

As a teacher it is essential that you choose your words wisely. Remember that the words you say to someone can make a big impact on his or her life. Words you might say in passing can be the words a child remembers for the rest of his or her life.

The Inside Scoop

When I was in my last year of high school I had an English teacher who, after reading one of my short stories, gave me an F and told me, "You are a horrible writer. You can't write your way out of a paper bag and you'll never be able to." He went on to tell me that he would be surprised if I succeeded at anything.

I never knew what caused that outburst because I thought my short story was pretty good, but I always remembered his words. Every time I wrote anything after that I remembered him telling me I couldn't write and questioned my abilities.

When I went to college I took a class in short story writing. One day, when given an assignment to write a short story, I decided to use the same story I had written in high school. Other than retyping it, I didn't change a thing.

The next week the professor handed back our papers. At least he handed back every paper but mine. He said, "If you don't mind, I would like you to read this story to the class."

I panicked, remembering the failing grade I received in high school for the same story. The words of that teacher came flooding back and I got that horrible feeling in the pit of my stomach you get when you fear something it going to go very wrong. I was about to be embarrassed again, and it was my own fault. I used the same horrible story.

"I don't really want to read it," I said.

"Please," the professor told me. "We all want to hear it."

I read the story. When I finished I heard applause. Applause? Why was everyone clapping? I didn't understand.

"Now that's a great story," the professor said.

Great story? The last time I handed that same story in, I failed. I was told that I couldn't write my way out of a paper bag. What was happening?

I never really figured it out. However, I began to have a lot more confidence in my writing abilities after that. The story would end there if a number of years later—after I had graduated from college and had already written and published a number of books—I hadn't heard from that horrible teacher again.

"Hi Shelly," he said when I picked up the phone. "This is _____. How have you been doing?"

Before I had a chance to answer, he continued. "I applied for a job as your mother's assistant and I haven't heard back. You know I'm retired and it would be the perfect the job. I was, after all, an English teacher for over 20 years. Do you think you can put in a good word for me?"

It goes without saying that I did put a word in for him, and it wasn't good. It didn't really matter because my mother remembered the incident as well and when she received his resume, she put it in the "No" pile.

◎ Do I have patience?

◎ Am I prepared to find new or innovative ways to teach children?

◎ Am I ready to be a life learner? Am I interested in learning more than is required of me?

◎ What are my core values? There are certain core values that good teachers should have. Are you responsible? Are you kind, compassionate and caring? Do you have integrity? Can you keep a confidence? Are you committed to your students?

Now that you've answered those questions, have you decided that a career in teaching is for you? Are you ready to make that commitment?

If so, know that whatever area of teaching you choose, whether you decide to be an elementary school teacher, junior or middle school teacher, high school teacher, or any other educator, you will truly be making a difference in the lives of others.

What Should I Teach?

How do you know what grade level you should teach? How do you know what your specialty should be? The answer to those questions depends to a great extent on you and your expertise. Do you love working around young children? Do you find them fun to be around? Does it make you smile to see young children's eyes shine when they learn something new? Then teaching elementary school is probably for you.

Do you want to be the one who gives young children their first school experience? Perhaps you might love teaching kindergarten. Do you want to be the one who teaches young children to read and write? Perhaps it would give you joy to teach first or second grade.

Do you find it challenging and exciting to teach a specific subject area? Would you rather specialize in a subject such as language arts or math or the sciences than in an age group? Then you might consider teaching middle or high school students.

One of the ways to help you determine what you would enjoy is to observe teachers teaching various grade levels and subject areas. You might, for example, sit in a few classes or you might volunteer to assist in classrooms for a set amount of time. Many people make the determination while in college.

Some people also become substitute teachers to get hands-on experience and see how they actually feel in certain types of classroom situations.

★ The Inside Scoop

After you decide if you want to teach elementary or secondary school, there are a wide array of teaching specializations you can choose from depending on your interests and your passions. These include:

- art
- music
- English
- language arts
- social studies
- home economics
- family and life science
- gifted education
- special education
- sciences
- reading
- physical education/health
- ESL (English as a second language)
- foreign language
- technology

Focus on finding out what age groups and subject areas give you joy. Elementary school teachers generally teach most subjects to their class. Middle and high school teachers generally specialize in a specific subject area.

Just because you teach a grade one year, does not mean that you have to teach that same grade for the rest of your career. Based on your certification and, of course, job availability, you might teach another grade.

Your Road to Becoming a Teacher

Becoming a good teacher takes time, education, experience, and a great deal of commitment. Are you ready?

Let's start with some general requirements. If your dream is to work as a teacher in a public school in the United States, you're going to need to be licensed and/or certified. Licensing/ certification evidences that individuals have completed the proper educational requirements, have passed all necessary testing, have the required experience, and have met any other requirements of the specific state, or the specific position. As a rule, licensure/certification is granted by either the state department of education (sometimes called the state board of education), or by a state licensure or credentialing advisory group or similar agency.

There are a number of different types of licenses/certifications for which you might apply as a teacher. You may, for example, become licensed to teach early childhood grades, which includes preschool through third grade; elementary grades, which includes first through sixth or eighth grade; the middle grades, which includes fifth through eighth grade; secondary-education, which includes seventh through 12th grade; a special subject such as reading, math, art, or music, which includes kindergarten through 12th grade; or special education, dealing with children with learning disabilities or other challenges. Though the specific requirements for licensure/certification differ by state, there are some similarities. All states require teachers who want to work in general education to have a minimum of a bachelor's degree as well as to have completed an approved teacher-training program. This program includes a prescribed number of subject and education credits and supervised practice teaching.

Tip from the Top

The more areas in which you are licensed/certified the more employable you will be.

Tip from the Coach

Technology is such a useful tool in enhancing learning today that it is essential for teachers to be computer literate, be familiar with various software programs, and know how to do research online. If you are not already totally comfortable with computer technology, take classes and get comfortable. It is essential to your career as a teacher.

Certain states also require technology training as well as the maintenance of a minimum grade point average. In order to maintain licensure, some states also require their teachers to continue their education, obtaining a master's degree in education within a specific period of time after they begin teaching.

How do you find out exactly what you need? Call your state department of education and ask. You can also surf the Web to check out requirements.

What else do you need to know? In addition to education requirements, most state also require applicants to take and pass competency exams in basic skills, including reading, writing, and teaching. Additionally, most states require the teacher to exhibit proficiency in his or her subject.

In some areas, in order to get a provisional or temporary license, school systems require teachers to satisfactorily demonstrate teaching performance over an extended period of time. After that time period has been satisfactorily completed, the teacher will be granted a permanent license. Continuing education is also required in most states for renewal of certification and/or teaching licenses.

"What do I do if I get licensed in one state and want to move?" you ask. "Do I have to start all over?"

Not necessarily. Many states have reciprocity agreements. What that means is that if you are licensed/certified in one state, another state may honor your certification or licensing from that state.

"What do I do if I have a bachelor's degree and want to teach, but I don't have the necessary education for licensure?" you ask. "What then?"

Here is something you might not know. Many states offer something called an alternative licensure program. These programs offer an alterative method of licensure for individuals who want to become teachers, and have a bachelor's degree, but have not completed the traditional education program. These programs were created for a number of reasons, including:

◎ To help ease the shortage of teachers in certain subject areas such as math and science.
◎ To help urban or rural areas fill teaching positions that they might otherwise have difficulty filling.
◎ To attract college graduates who didn't complete the educational program, yet want to teach.
◎ To attract career changers to the profession.

Tip from the Coach

There are some tests that are used by more than one state such as the PRAXIS Series Teacher Licensure and Certification Assessments, a series of tests measuring skills and subject knowledge. At this time, PRAXIS is the licensing exam required by 44 states. Visit http://www.ets.org/praxis to learn more. This site also provides resources about each state's licensing requirements, information on educational conferences and events, and tests for assessment of new teachers.

Other licensing exams include the CSET (California Subject Examinations for Teachers), the NYSTCE (New York State Teacher Certification Examinations), TExES (Texas Examinations of Educator Standards), and INTASC (Interstate New Teacher Assessment and Support Consortium).

Speak to your adviser about what exams you will be required to take.

Tip from the Top

The National Board Certification is a credentialing option for teachers. This certification does not replace a state license; rather it enhances it. The National Board Certification (NBC) is a voluntary, advanced teaching credential that has national standards for what accomplished teachers should both know and be able to do. Individuals who successfully go through the National Board Certification process will receive National Board Certification.

Alternative licensure is granted in a number of different ways, depending on the specific state and circumstances. Some states, for example, allow individuals to work under the supervision of experienced teachers for one or two years while they are taking required education courses. Others allow students to obtain their master's degree in education and then grant licensure.

If you are interested in alternative licensure programs, contact your state department of education to get more information.

Student Teaching

Generally, one of the requirements you are going to have to fulfill in order to become a certified/licensed teacher is to go through a period of student teaching. For those who have been dreaming of becoming a teacher, this can truly be a very exciting time.

Student teaching is designed to help provide you with experience in the field. You generally will be assigned to a class within the cooperating school that works in conjunction with the college you are attending. Using a hands-on approach, student teaching helps develop your skills in classroom management, instructional planning, and the application of effective teaching methods.

The length of student teaching assignments varies by state and by the specific program in which students are enrolled. Generally, student teaching is done in the last semester of your college program.

While every situation may be different, as a rule you will be assigned a cooperating teacher. In some cases you may have more than one. As the student teacher, you will then assume the schedule of that teacher.

To begin with you may observe the classes. After a few weeks you will be given various responsibilities for the class. Within the scope of this position, you will plan lessons, classroom activities, and assist with the evaluation of students.

While responsibilities will depend on the specific situation, they may include:

◎ planning and developing concise lesson plans
◎ submitting and discussing lesson plans with your cooperating teacher prior to presenting lessons
◎ developing unit plans
◎ executing lesson plans using effective teaching techniques
◎ learning about students
◎ developing and maintaining ethical interpersonal relationships with students

◎ taking part in parent-teacher conferences
◎ participating in in-service conferences
◎ participating in supervisory duties
◎ participating in extracurricular activities
◎ fulfilling requests made by cooperating teachers

During this process you will be evaluated by a variety of people, including your cooperating teacher, principal, and supervisory liaisons from your college. Some student teachers mistakenly look at these people as adversaries, worrying about what they are going to say and what type of evaluations they will give. Smart student teachers, instead, look at these people as allies who can help make them the best teacher possible.

How are student teachers evaluated? What are cooperating teachers, principals, and supervisors looking for?

In most cases student teachers are observed in the classroom. Cooperating teachers, principals, and supervisors are looking for many things. They want to be sure that the student teacher has not only grasped general teaching methods but can perform them in an effective, interesting, and motivating manner. They want to see that student teachers can handle the classroom and handle any disciplinary problems.

They want to see that student teachers have created a diverse learning environment for all types of learners. And they want to make sure that student teachers have good communications skills with students, parents, and colleagues.

It's important to recognize in this process that while it's essential to "know what is in the book," it also is necessary to add your own innovative spin to teaching. Teaching has changed over the years. There are many new technologies and methods that can be incorporated. Just teaching by the book might be shortchanging your students and short changing you. The trick in student teaching, as in full-fledged teaching, is to take what you have learned throughout your education and find your own connection in the classroom.

How can you be a better student teacher?

◎ Obtain a copy of the faculty handbook (if there is one) and familiarize yourself with its contents.
◎ Make sure you know the rules, regulations, and procedures that apply to the faculty.
◎ Try to introduce yourself to your cooperating teacher *before* the day you begin your student teacher assignment. Ask what his or her teaching philosophy is and share yours.
◎ Remember that while you are not a full-fledged teacher, you must still be professional at all times.
◎ Dress neatly and appropriately.
◎ Speak appropriately to students, parents, and faculty.
◎ Act appropriately. While you are still a student, you are on your way to becoming a teacher.
◎ Be on time for everything, including classes, meetings, etc.
◎ Remember that as a teacher you will be a role model. Act appropriately.
◎ Keep a journal to monitor your progress. You might also jot down questions for your cooperating teachers as well as any ideas you may have.
◎ Take criticism constructively. Use it to become a better teacher.
◎ Do things in a timely fashion.
◎ Your lesson plans will most likely be reviewed by your cooperating teacher. Leaving this to the last minute puts him or her under pressure.

⭐ **Tip from the Top**
In most situations student teaching is not a paid experience.

◎ Be pleasant and positive.
◎ Be prepared for everything.
◎ Use your own creativity to develop interesting ways to present subject matter to students.
◎ If you don't understand something, don't be afraid to ask your cooperative teacher or advisor. He or she is there to help.

Breaking into Teaching

So you've gone through your student teaching, you have your bachelor's degree, and you're licensed/certified to be a teacher. Now what? I'm assuming that now you are a teacher you want to be the very best teacher you can be. I'm assuming you want to be a respected member of the teaching community. And, I'm assuming you want to be successful. What can you do to increase your chances?

In order to succeed, you need to act in a professional manner all the time and in every situation. That means in school, in the classroom, and in the community in which you work.

How can you be professional? Present yourself professionally. Be reliable and responsible. If you say you're going to be someplace, be there. If you say you're going to call someone, call them. If someone calls you and leaves a message, call them back in a timely basis. If you say you're going to do something, do it.

It goes without saying that you should be at school in your classroom on time. But it goes much further. If you have a meeting scheduled, be there on time—not 10 minutes late. If you have an appointment with a student, a parent, your principal, or a colleague, whether in person or on the phone, be where you say you're going to be at the time you say you're going to be there.

If you have a report due on Monday morning, make sure it is handed in Monday morning, not Monday afternoon or some time on Tuesday.

In case I'm not making myself clear enough, be on time for everything. There is nothing worse for your career than being known as the teacher who is habitually late.

It is totally unprofessional to drink or use drugs when you are on duty as a teacher. (Not to mention that it also is against the law to use illegal drugs.) It is not fair to your class, to your school, or even to you. You might *think* that you are doing a better job, but no matter what you have heard, you will not do a better job if you are under the influence.

In that same vein, it's important to remember that teachers are often role models for young people. What does that mean? Youngsters often look up to teachers. They admire them. In many cases they may try to emulate them. Right or wrong, that's the way it is.

What does that have to do with you? Like it or not, your life as a teacher will often be scrutinized more closely than others. Using illegal drugs or drinking to excess at any time may not only send a negative message to your students, it also sends a message to school systems or school boards, which may use this as a reason not to give you tenure or a promotion.

"It's not fair," you say.

Here's the deal. To begin with, everything isn't fair. When you decide to be a teacher, especially if you are living in a smaller, rural area where everyone knows everyone, you need to realize that—like it or not—your life will probably be scrutinized more closely than others.'

Here's something else you should know. It doesn't matter what level you're at in your career. If you're just starting your career as a teacher, people in authority will use any negative thing you do as a reason why you shouldn't move up the career ladder. If you are at the top, people will say you should know better, you're a professional. The lesson here is, remember that if you want a career as a successful teacher and want to take advantage of everything the career affords, act professionally.

Are you ready to *be* a teacher? Are you ready to make it? Be honest with yourself. If you're not ready, take the steps you need to prepare.

Here's something else for you to think about. Every successful teacher, no matter what grade they teach, no matter what their area of specialization, no matter who they are, no matter where they are in their career at this moment, had to start somewhere. While, of course, everyone has a slightly different set of circumstances, most teachers have been where you are

---

★ The Inside Scoop

During a seminar, we were going over the section on being professional at all times. A man raised his hand and said, "I can see being professional in school, but this is *just* a job. They don't own me when I'm not working."

Being a teacher is not just a job. You are teaching people's most precious commodity: their children. Parents do not want to hear that their child's teacher was arrested for drunk driving, got into a fight with someone at a bar, or was just acting like an idiot.

I've mentioned it before and will reiterate, as a teacher you are a role model. You need to act professional at all times.

today. They've had to take the step from student teacher to full-fledged teacher, they've had to find their first job, and they've had to go through their first day of school as a teacher.

As they climb the ladder of success, most teachers have to face similar challenges as well. They have to face the challenges of larger class sizes or a lack of funding for the opportunity to be wired for the ever-evolving technology needed to help improve education. They face the challenges of teaching students with complex family issues, and teaching students who may not see the value in education. Some face the challenges of worrying about teaching in unsafe schools.

Teachers worry about having job security, getting tenure, and doing a good job. They worry about making a difference to each and every child. Teachers who are climbing the career ladder not only have to build a successful career, but sustain it.

You want everything about you to stand out from others in a positive manner. You want to be well informed and keep up on changes and current trends in education and teaching methods. To give yourself the best chances at success in teaching, learn as much as possible about all aspects of teaching and the educational process.

It is imperative to learn everything you can about the administrative end of education, even if you don't want to take that career path but want to continue your career as a successful classroom

The Inside Scoop

While most schools do their hiring during the months of July and August, there are often openings throughout the year. Teachers may leave for personal reasons or may be terminated, and the opening needs to be filled.

If you are looking for a teaching job, keep your eye on the classifieds. Don't forget to look online. Check out traditional jobs sites such as monster.com and hotjobs.com. Then check out education-oriented career Web sites. Public and private school Web sites may also list job openings.

teacher. That way you'll be informed about things that may affect you and your career.

Read as much as you can find about every aspect of teaching and education. Go to the library and the bookstore and find books on the administrative end of the industry. Look for books about other teachers who have succeeded. Read trade publications. Find other magazines and periodicals with articles about teaching and education. Scour the Web for information.

If you just find one piece of information in a book, or magazine, or on the Internet that you

Tip from the Top

Make it part of your daily routine to learn at least one new thing every day. Learn something new every opportunity you get.

Voice of Experience

During interviews, the hiring committee might ask your philosophy of education. What this means is what are your beliefs in regard to education. You might have written a paragraph or two covering this topic while in college. While there is no right or wrong answer, you should be aware that hiring committees generally like to see that you have a broad or mainstream philosophy.

> ### The Inside Scoop
> Tenure is a form of job security for teachers who have successfully gone through a probationary period. It protects teachers from being terminated for most reasons with the exception of moral issues.

> ### Tip from the Coach
> There are hundreds of opportunities between the point where you might currently be in your career and where you want to be. Becoming a highly successful teacher is a journey. Some people get there faster than others. While your final destination may be that of a respected, tenured teacher or an administrator, you can have a successful career getting there. The important thing to remember is to look at every opportunity as a way to get where you want to go.

can use to help teach something in a better way, or one thing that you can relate to your career, it will be worth it. And don't stop there. Look for workshops, seminars, and classes that may be of value. Why? You will gain valuable information, learn new skills and have the opportunity to network and make important contacts.

Success as a Teacher

Some teachers start their careers in the classroom and then work toward building a career in education by being promoted to administrative positions. Some want to be promoted to positions as department heads. Others become supervisors, assistant principals, principals, or even superintendents.

Some individuals, however, don't seek success in administrative promotions. Instead they want to continue classroom teaching. They prefer working hands-on with students in classrooms. Success to these individuals may be making a difference in the lives of their students or seeing a student have a "light-bulb moment." It might be getting tenure and knowing his or her job is secure. It might mean successfully teaching a difficult subject or being thanked by a student for making a difference in his life. It might mean teaching a group of children who were classified as low achievers and helping them score better on tests than the rest of the school. It might mean being named Teacher of the Year.

Only you can decide what success means to you and go after it. It is your decision and your decision alone.

How do you succeed in the classroom? Great teachers don't just appear one day. They develop over time. Basic teaching skills are just the beginning. You need to develop a variety of other skills in order to develop yourself as a great teacher.

You need to develop your people skills. You need to develop your teaching personality. You need to know you are going to be great and begin to have confidence in yourself.

What else can you do? Try to remember some of the great teachers you had. What did they do to earn that position?

Need some ideas? Here is a list of things to try. Use this as a springboard to get you started, and then add in your own ideas.

◎ Greet your students at the door as they walk into class. It will make your students feel important.
◎ Smile at your students during the day, no matter what. No one likes a sad sack, and smiling will put your students in a better mood and help create a better learning environment.

- Turn every occasion you can into a learning opportunity in your classroom.
- Find ways to help your students relate current events that are happening in the world, in the school, or in their lives to lessons you are teaching.
- Use a variety of methods of learning to be sure that lessons are interesting.
- Ask questions that will encourage your students to share their ideas.
- Include every student in discussions, not just a select few.
- Make sure your voice is loud enough so the entire class can hear you.
- When teaching a lesson, try to make a point that students can relate to or make a personal connection to so they will remember.
- Bring in guest speakers to speak to your students on occasion.
- Realize that everyone does not learn in the same way, and develop alternative methods of teaching lessons.
- Find ways to inspire and motivate every student, not just the ones who are doing well.
- If one teaching method is not working effectively, come up with a new one in a timely fashion.
- Be prepared for class. Have lesson plans completed, handouts photocopied, and a great idea on how to teach each lesson.
- Make every child feel special.
- Treat every child with respect and understanding.
- Develop good relationships with the rest of the faculty. Whether you stop into another teacher's classroom or sit with a teacher for coffee or lunch, get to know everyone. By doing this you will

not only have support, you will have people to discuss new ideas and teaching strategies with.
- Establish a good relationship with parents. Get them involved whenever possible.
- Contact parents immediately if you see a problem with their children. Don't leave it alone and hope the problem goes away.
- Get involved in the community. Volunteer and help where you can.
- Get your class involved in the community. Try to develop a program where students can see that helping others can make a difference.
- Speak well about your school, your students, the administration, and the rest of the faculty.

Here are some other tips that will help you succeed as a teacher.

- Be a team player. Step in and help other faculty members and administration when needed.

The Inside Scoop

The No Child Left Behind Act (NCLB) is a piece of educational reform legislation, which was signed into law on January 8, 2002. The NCLB was designed to help close the gap between the highest and lowest achievers. The NCLB was created to ensure that all students receive the education that they deserve regardless of gender, race, age, and socioeconomic status. The program federally mandates that by the 2013–14 school year all students will read and perform math at grade level. To learn more about the NCLB, visit http://www.ed.gov/nclb.

- Set goals for yourself. Where do you want to be at the end of the school year? What do you want to be dong in five years? What are your priorities?
- Project a positive, neat image. Keep up your appcarance. Just because you got tenure does not mean you should come to work looking sloppy or poorly groomed.
- Make sure you have good people skills.
- Keep your sense of humor. It will help in every situation.
- Believe in yourself. No one will believe in you unless you do so first.

Here is a list of things *not* to do.

- Don't touch students in an inappropriate manner or in a way that might be misconstrued.
- Don't overlook problems students may have with substance abuse, sexual abuse, or abuse of any type.
- Don't date students.
- Don't leave students unsupervised.
- Don't gossip.
- Don't break confidentialities.
- Don't promise students you won't tell anyone about a situation that you may bc mandated to report to authorities.

Whether you choose to teach elementary school, middle school, or high school; whether you choose to teach in a specialized area of instruction; whether you choose to teach in a pub-

lic school or private school, you can have a long and successful career. Work toward your goals. No matter what you teach, be the best you can be and both you and your students will thrive.

12

SUCCESS IS YOURS FOR THE TAKING

Do You Have What It Takes?

There is an old adage that says, "Give a man a fish; he'll eat for a day. Teach a man to fish; he'll eat for a lifetime." There is no question that education is the key to a better life. Whether in this country or in a country on the other side of the world, education can make a big difference in the way people live.

On the most basic level, education is the pursuit of knowledge. Yet education gives people more than knowledge. It gives them hope and strength to live their dreams and do more.

Imagine knowing that the job you have will help others have better lives. Imagine working in an industry that really makes a difference. Imagine knowing you are not only living your dream, you are succeeding. If you are reading this book you don't have to imagine one more second. You are closer than ever to your dream career in education.

This book was written for every single person who aspires to work and succeed in the education field in any capacity. If this is you, and you know who you are, I need to ask you a very important question.

Do you have what it takes?

"What do you mean, do I have what it takes?" you ask.

Do you have what it takes to be successful in this field?

"Well, I think so," you say.

You think so? That's not good enough. You have to know so! Why? Because if you don't believe in yourself, no one else will.

"Okay," you say. "I get it. I *know* I can be successful."

That's good. That's the attitude you need to succeed!

With that out of the way, let's go over a couple of other facts that can help you in your quest for success in education. You have to remember that no matter what comes your way, you can't give up. Whatever you have to deal with, when you achieve your goals you most likely will feel it was worth it. There may be stumbling blocks. You may have to take detours. There may even be times you encounter a fork in the road and must make a choice. But if you give up, it's over.

Here's another fact you should know. When you share your dreams and goals with others about working in any aspect of education, there will always be some people who insist on telling you their version of the statistics of the industry.

They may try to tell you how difficult it is to teach in today's society; how kids today are not like kids used to be years ago. They may tell you that it's difficult to get a job unless you want to work in the inner city or that teachers don't get paid enough.

There might be people who quote statistics on everything from burnout in teachers to high stress levels of those working in administration. And the list will go on. It probably doesn't matter what area of education (or any other industry for that matter) in which you are trying to create a career, there will be people who will try to make you feel like if you go for your dreams, statistically, you will stand absolutely *no* chance of success.

If you listen to those people and start believing them, you probably will become one of their statistics. If you pay attention to them, a career in any aspect of the education probably isn't for you. I'm willing to bet that no matter what career you choose and in what industry, some people will probably have something negative to say about it.

However, if you have gotten to this section of the book, I'm guessing you aren't going to let anyone negatively influence you. I am also betting that you are still going to go after your dream.

Here's something to think about. Let's look at a few analogies. Statistically, it's difficult for most people to lose weight, yet there are many people who do. Statistically, most people who play the lottery don't win, yet there are always winners. Statistically, the chances of winning the Publishers Clearing House Sweepstakes aren't great, yet someone always wins. Will it be you? Not if you don't enter.

With those analogies in mind, I stand behind what I have said throughout this book. No matter what the statistics are, someone has to succeed. Why shouldn't it be you? Someone has

to be at the top. Why shouldn't it be you? If you give up your dream, someone else will be there to take it. You will be standing on the outside looking in and watching someone doing what you want. I don't think that's your dream.

Will it be easy? Not always. But the industry is full of educators, teachers, and trainers who teach in public and private elementary schools, middle schools and high schools, colleges and universities, and outside of the traditional classroom environment. It's full of people who do corporate and business training in a wide array of industries.

The industry is full of people working in the business and administration segments of schools and colleges. It's full of people working in various educational trade associations and organizations, and is full of education reporters, journalists, writers, and columnists. It is full of people doing research, developing curriculum, and more. The industry is huge. It is jam packed with wonderful and fulfilling opportunities. Why shouldn't you live your dream and be part it?

Many are concerned about their chances for success. Often they are concerned that there are too many variables. Will there be jobs? Will you have to move to a different geographic location? Will you be good enough? Will you get burned out? Will you be able to actually make a difference? And the list goes on.

Many are concerned that in certain parts of the industry, success (or failure) is too dependent on other people. What you need to know is that while it is true that others can affect your career, they can't stop it unless you let it happen. You are in the driver's seat. You can make it happen! What I am saying, in essence, is that the decision to keep on working toward your goal is yours.

You have the power. Are you going to quit?

Here's what I want you to remember. Whether you are dreaming of success as a preschool teacher, elementary school teacher, middle school teacher, high school teacher, adult education teacher, or college professor; whether you are dreaming of success as a teacher in a non-classroom setting in any other area; whether you are dreaming of success as a department head, principal, superintendent, commissioner of education, or any other administrator; whether you are dreaming of success as a school librarian, child life specialist, nurse, curriculum development specialist, school psychologist, guidance counselor, employment counselor, or in any other support area.

Whether you are dreaming of success as a school speech pathologist, media center specialist, resource teacher, educational therapist, grant writer, educational resource coordinator, or student personnel coordinator.

Whether you are dreaming of success as an in-house corporate trainer, a corporate training consultant, or a trainer or educator in any other area of the corporate world. Whether you are dreaming of success in any area of the business segment of the industry.

Whether you are dreaming of success as a college or university professor, marketing director, public relations director, fund-raising or development director, grant writer, IT director, registrar, director of activities, student admissions administrator, student affairs director, director of alumni affairs, or in any other area of a college or university.

Whether you are dreaming of success as an educational journalist, reporter, or author, or editor, writer, or even the owner of an education-oriented Web site.

Whether you are dreaming of success in collegiate athletics as a coach, recruiter, or development officer; are dreaming of success in the research and development of better curriculums, educational materials, and examinations; or are dreaming of success in any other area of education.

Whether you want to be in the forefront of the industry, behind the scenes, or somewhere in between, know this: You *can* do it and do it successfully as long as you don't give up.

Throughout your journey, always keep your eye on the prize: the great career you are working toward in education.

Sometimes your dream may change. That's okay. As long as you are following *your* dreams, not those of others, you usually are on the right road.

Whatever segment of the education industry in which you are interested, your choices are huge. What is going to be your contribution to this important industry?

What path do you want to follow? Where do you envision yourself? What do you see yourself doing? Seize your opportunity. It's there for you. Grab onto your dream to start the ball rolling.

Over the years, I've talked to many people who are extremely successful in a variety of careers. One of the most interesting things about them is that most were *not* surprised at all that they were successful. As a matter of fact, they expected it.

Words from the Wise

Throughout all history, the great wise men and teachers, philosophers, and prophets have disagreed with one another on many different things. It is only on this one point that they are in complete and unanimous agreement. We become what we think about.

—Earl Nightingale

While researching this area I found that many teachers knew from the time they were youngsters that they were going to be teachers, and they knew they were going to be great at their job. A good number of these individuals even knew what their classroom would look like and even envisioned their desk. Interestingly enough, many of them told me that when they grew up and became teachers their classrooms and their desks looked similar to the ones they had imagined years back. This type of thing seems to be true of many people in various industries who are successful, as well.

I want to share a story with you. While it isn't about someone in the educational field, it does help illustrate the point of just how important a positive focus can be in your career.

One night I was on the road with one of the acts I represented and we were sitting backstage before the concert. I was talking to one of the singers and we were discussing some of the other hot artists in the industry. The singer was telling me a story of another artist who was on the charts.

"We knew he was going to be a star," he said about the other artist. "When he was still in school, he told everyone he was going to be a star and that's all he talked about."

"Doesn't everyone say that?" I asked.

"Sometimes they do," he continued, "But what made him different was he was specific about what he was going to do and when. He told everyone he was going to have a hit record before he graduated. (At the time the man hadn't even recorded anything yet.) He started acting like a star and then dressing the part of a star. He went on and on about it so much that he almost had to become a star to save face. Funny thing was, he did have a hit before he graduated and he did turn into a huge star."

This is not an isolated story. There are probably hundreds like it in every industry. Stories like this do help prove the point of just how important a positive focus and believing in yourself can be to your career. What's really interesting is that in many cases, way before successful people even plan their success, they expect it.

Is it the planning and the work that creates the reality, or is it the dream that puts them on the road to success? I think it's a combination.

And in case you're thinking that you're only supposed to expect success in the education industry if your career aspirations are to be a teacher or administrator, think again. You are supposed to expect success in whatever area of the industry you pursue. Every job is important. Every job can make a difference to someone.

Are you ready for success? Are you really ready?

Do you know what you're going to say when you're being interviewed as Teacher of the Year? Can you imagine the feeling you will have as you accept the award?

Can you imagine how proud you will feel as principal when your school garners top accolades? Can you almost feel the excitement you will experience when you help a student with a learning disability read his first book? Can you imagine the feeling when one of your students writes the winning essay for a national essay contest?

Can you imagine how proud you will be when a student you had in first grade, your very first year of teaching, graduates from medical school? Can you imagine the feeling you will have when a student comes up to you and tells you he is becoming a teacher because of the difference you made in his life?

Have you chosen the perfect suit you're going to wear to the meeting when you are named superintendent of schools? Can you see the press release in the newspaper when you are named principal of the high school?

Can you hear the introduction you are given when you are presenting a paper at a major education conference?

Can you almost see what you will be wearing when you sign an employment contract? Can you picture what your office will look like? Do you know what you're going to say?

If not, you should—at least in your mind. Why? Because if you claim something, you're often closer to making it happen.

Over the years I have heard many similar stories from people who are very successful in their careers of choice. Was it that they knew what they wanted to do and focused on it more than others? Was it that they had a premonition and things just worked out? Were they just lucky? Were they more talented than others? Was it visualization? Or was it that a positive attitude helped create a positive situation? No one really knows. The only thing that seems evident is that those who expect to be successful usually have a better chance of achieving it. Those who have a positive attitude usually have a better chance of positive things happening.

We've covered visualization earlier in the book. Whether you believe this theory or not, one thing is for sure: it can't hurt. So start planning your acceptance speech for becoming Teacher of the Year. Start planning the party you are going to have when your book on education is published.

Plan on what you will say when you win the Pulitzer Prize for finding a way for all children to succeed. Plan your celebration for your promotion or for when you achieve the career of which you've been dreaming. Plan for your success, and then get ready for it to happen.

⭐ Tip from the Coach

Before writing my first book, I mentioned to a number of people that I wanted to write a book and was looking for a publisher. Their response was always the same: "It is very difficult to get a publisher. It's very hard to write a book. Don't get your hopes up."

While my book wasn't yet written, I had already seen it in my mind. I knew what it would look like; I knew what it was going to say.

I had a plan and told everyone the same story. I was going to send out queries to publishers whose names started with A and go through the alphabet until I reached Z and knew I would find a publisher. The book would be a reality no matter what anyone thought.

By the time I got to the Fs, I had sold my book idea. I wasn't surprised, because I not only knew it would happen, I expected it. That first book, *Career Opportunities In The Music Industry*, is now in its fifth edition. Shortly after that I sold other book ideas. The rest is history. Over 25 books later my dream has turned into reality.

Creating a Career You Love

While working toward your perfect career, it's important to combine your goals with your life objectives. The trick to success in any industry is not only following your interests, but also following your heart. If you're working toward your dream, going that extra mile and doing that extra task won't be a chore.

And when you run into obstacles along the way, they won't be problems, just steppingstones to get you where you're going.

By now you have read some (if not all) of this book. You've learned that there are certain things you need to do to stack the deck in your favor, whether you want your success to be in the classroom, in administration, or the business segment of the industry.

You know how to develop your resume and/or a CV, captivating cover letters, career portfolios, business cards, and other tools. You know how to get past the gatekeepers. You know what to do in interviews, and what not to do.

You know how important it is to help develop a plan and know how essential it is to have a good attitude.

You know that it is crucial to read everything before you sign it so you can protect yourself, and you know how important good communication skills are no matter what segment of education you are pursuing.

You know a bit about what it's going to be like as a teacher and how you can increase your chances of success.

You've learned how to network and how to market yourself. You've learned some neat little tips and tricks to get your foot in the door. You've learned that you need to find ways to stand out from the crowd.

Most of all, you've learned that it's essential to create a career you love. You've learned that you don't ever want to settle and wonder "what if?"

Creating the career you want and love is not always the easiest thing in the world to accomplish, but it is definitely worth it. In order to help you focus in on what you want, you might find it helpful to create a personal mission statement.

Your Personal Mission Statement

There are many people who want a career in various areas of the education industry. Some will make it and some will not. I want you to be the one who makes it. I want you to be the one who succeeds.

Throughout the book, I've tried to give you tips, tricks, and techniques that can help. I've tried to give you the inspiration and motivation to know you can do it. Here's one more thing that might make your journey easier.

Create your personal mission statement. Why? Because your mission statement can help you define your visions clearly. It will give you a path, a purpose, and something to follow. Most importantly, putting your mission statement in writing can help you bring your mission to fruition.

What's a mission statement? It's a statement declaring what your mission is in your life and your career. How do you do it? As with all the other exercises you've done, sit down, get comfortable, take out a pen and a piece of paper, and start writing. What is your mission?

Remember that your mission statement is for *you*. You're not writing it for your family, your friends, or your employer. It can be changed or modified at any time.

Think about it for a moment. What do you want to do? Where do you want be? What's the path you want to take? What are your dreams? What is your mission?

There is no one right way to write your mission statement. Some people like to write it in paragraph form. Others like to use bullets or numbers. It really doesn't matter as long as you get it down in writing. The main thing to remember is to make your statement a clear and concise declaration of your long-term mission.

Your mission statement might be one sentence, one paragraph, or even fill two or three pages. It's totally up to you. As long as your mission statement is clear, you're okay.

Here are some examples of simple mission statements.

- ◎ High school teacher
  - ▫ My mission is to use my education, skills, and talent to become a high

school English teacher in a school where I can really make a difference to students. I want to instill a love of literature and a love of writing.

◎ Special education teacher
  ▫ My mission is to use my education, skills, talent, patience, and compassion to become a special education teacher. I want to provide new experiences to children in my classroom. I want to help maximize the success of every child and give them confidence in themselves.
  ▫ It is also my mission to eventually write a book about innovative methods of teaching children with special needs.

◎ Teacher
  ▫ My mission is to find ways to inspire and motivate students so they want to learn.

◎ Principal
  ▫ To use my education, skills, training, and experience to be the best high school principal I can. I want to create a safe environment where each student feels supported, inspired, and motivated so they can get a diverse education. I also want to create an environment where the faculty feels supported and feels free to develop innovative learning strategies.

◎ College history professor
  ▫ My mission is to become one of the most sought-out professors at the college. I want to make history interesting for everyone. I want to use innovative teaching methods so students look forward to coming to my class instead of finding ways to

stay away. I want to teach history so that long after my students have graduated they still remember things I have taught.
  ▫ Eventually I want to develop a documentary titled *Where Were You When...*, documenting where people were and what they were doing when they heard of major milestones in current history.

◎ Education reporter
  ▫ My mission is to get my bachelor's degree in communications with a minor in education. After completing my education I want to become an education reporter for a major newspaper or periodical. I want to be a major force in reporting educational issues in the country and the world.
  ▫ My mission also includes getting my master's in education and then becoming a professional speaker discussing educational subjects.

◎ Educational Web site owner
  ▫ I want to use my education, training, skills, and experiences as a teacher to develop and start the premier Web site for educational resources. I want it to be the place every teacher, administrator, parent, and student goes when they need anything related to education.
  ▫ I expect to build the Web site into such a great resource that five years after its launch it will be sold to one of the major Web companies for $100 million dollars!

◎ University marketing director
  ▫ My mission is to use my skills and talent to create a career as a

successful marketing executive large college. As a matter of fact, I want to be the director of marketing for one of the largest, most prestigious universities in the country.

◎ Fund-raising and development director
  ⊡ My mission is to use my talents, skills, and passions to create a career in fund-raising and development for colleges and universities. I want a career as a fund-raising and development director in a large university where I can create unique development programs.

What do you do with your mission statement? Use it! Review it to remember what you're working toward. Use it as motivation. Use it to help you move in the right direction.

You would be surprised how many successful people have their personal mission statement hanging on their wall, taped to their computer, or in their pocket. I know individuals who keep a copy of their mission statement in their wallet, taped to their bathroom mirror, stuck on their computer monitor, and placed in the inside of a desk drawer, or in another location where they can regularly glance at it.

Where ever you decide to place your mission statement, be sure to look at it daily so you can always keep your mission in mind. It makes it easier to keep focused on your ultimate goal.

Success Strategies

We have discussed marketing, promotion, and publicity. Used effectively, they can help your career tremendously. Here's what you have to remember! Don't wait for someone else to recognize your skills, accomplishments, and talents; promote yourself. There are many keys to success. Self-promotion is an important one.

Don't toot your own horn in an annoying or obnoxious manner, but make sure people notice you. You want to standout in a positive way. Don't keep your accomplishments a secret. Instead claim them proudly.

We've all been taught to be modest. "Don't boast," your mother might have said as you were growing up. But if your goal is success in your career, sometimes you can just be too quiet for your own good.

Your ultimate challenge is to create buzz. You need to create spin. You need others to know what you've done and what you're doing in the future. Some people aren't willing or able to do what it takes. If you want to succeed, it's imperative that you get started. Buzz doesn't usually happen overnight, but every day you wait is another day you're behind in the job.

Begin to think like a publicist. Whatever segment of education you're working in, you need to constantly promote yourself or no one will know you exist. While others may help, the responsibility really is on *you* to make your career work and make your career successful.

No matter what segment of the industry you are in, or what level you are at, continue to look for opportunities of all kinds. Search out opportunities to move ahead in your career and then grab hold of them.

You need to be aware that in your life and career, on occasion, there may be doors that

> ⭐ **The Inside Scoop**
>
> Don't procrastinate when an opportunity presents itself. Someone else is always on the lookout just like you, and you don't want to miss your chances.

close. The trick here is not to let a door close without looking for the window of opportunity that is always there. If you see an opportunity, jump on it immediately. It is usually there just waiting for you!

Throughout the book we've discussed the importance of networking. Once you become successful, it's important to continue to network. Just because you landed a new job as a teacher, doesn't mean you don't want to meet other teachers, principals, and school administrators. Just because you just landed a job as a school administrator doesn't mean you don't want to meet other administrators in the education industry. Just because you got a job handling the publicity or marketing or fund-raising for an educational institution doesn't mean you don't want to meet other executives in the industry. Just because you got a job as an education reporter doesn't mean you shouldn't know other reporters, writers, editors, and publishers.

If you've landed a new job, keep networking. Continue meeting people. Continue getting your name out there. You can never tell who knows who and what someone might need. There are always new opportunities ahead and if you don't keep networking you might miss some of them. Keep nurturing your network and developing contacts. This is also true as your career progresses. Keep on networking, meeting people, and making contacts. It is essential to the success of your career.

Don't be afraid to ask for help. If you know someone who can help you in your career, ask. The worst they can say is no. The best that can happen is you might get some assistance. Of course, if you can help someone else, do that as well.

Always be prepared for success. It might be just around the corner. Whatever segment of the industry you are pursuing, continue honing your skills. Keep taking classes, attending seminars, and going to workshops.

Education has changed over the years and continues to change and evolve. Keep up with the trends, read the trades, and make sure you know what is happening today.

Don't get caught in the thought pattern of "that's not how they did it in the old days." Get used to the idea that in our ever-changing world, there will be change. Instead of pushing change away or making believe it doesn't exist, embrace it. You might just come up with a better or more effective way to do things.

Stay as fit and healthy as you can. Try to eat right, get sleep, exercise, and take care of yourself. After all your hard work, you don't want to finally succeed and be too sick or tired to enjoy it.

Whatever facet of the industry you are involved with, you are going to be selling yourself. You might be selling yourself to a to a hiring committee at a school or a human resources manager in a college, university, or other educational institution. You might be selling yourself to partners in an educational consulting group. You might be selling yourself to a university's board of directors. You might even be selling yourself to students or parents.

What else? You might be selling or pitching your story for publicity or a variety of other situations. Take a lesson from others who have made it to the top and prepare ahead of time.

That way when you're in a situation where you need to say something, you'll be ready.

Sales skills are essential. Know that you are the best and know how to sell yourself the best way possible. Come up with a pitch and practice it until you're comfortable.

Always be positive. A good attitude is essential to your life and your professional success. Here's the deal. We've discussed this before. People want to be around other people who are positive. If there is a choice between two people with similar talents and skills and you have a better outlook than anyone else, a more positive type of personality and passion, you're going to be chosen. You're going to get the job. You're going to succeed.

Change the way you look at situations and the situations you look at will change. What's

---

Tip from the Coach

They say it takes approximately 21 days to break one habit and form a new one. With that in mind, if there is any habit you have that bothers you, is detrimental to your career, or any part of your life for that matter, know that not only can you change it, but you can do so fairly quickly. If, for example, you find yourself speaking over others when they are talking, begin today by consciously making an effort to listen, and then speak. You will find that if you continue to do that on a daily basis, soon it will become a habit.

Similarly, if you are told that you are negative at work, start today by consciously making an effort to be positive. Before you make a comment about something, stop, think about what you are saying, and try to put a positive spin on it. Continue doing this and a few weeks later you will find that not only will your attitude be perceived more positively, it will be more positive.

Words from the Wise

Keep all professional conversations professional and positive. Don't complain. Don't whine. Don't be negative.

---

that mean? If you look at a situation as a problem, it will be a problem. If, on the other hand, you look at a situation as an opportunity, it becomes one.

If, when looking at the education industry, all you see are the trials and tribulations of trying to succeed, all you will have are trials and tribulations. If, on the other hand, you look at the road to success in this industry as a wonderful and exciting journey, it will be.

Keeping Things Confidential

Privacy and confidentiality are crucial when working in many parts of the education industry. What this means is that it is your responsibility to keep students' names and issues private and confidential when required.

Climbing the Career Ladder

Generally, whatever you want to do in life, you most likely are going to have to pay your dues. Whatever segment of the education industry you've chosen to pursue, most likely you're going to have to pay your dues as well. Now that we've accepted that fact, the question is, how do you climb the career ladder? How do you succeed?

How do you go, for example, from a job as a first-year teacher to a tenured teacher? How do you move up to become a department head? How do you go from a position as a teacher to an assistant principal, principal, or even superintendent of schools?

How can you move from a coordinator to a job as the assistant director of a department? How do you go from a job as an assistant director to the full-fledged director of a department? How do you go from education reporter for a local weekly paper to becoming a successful education reporter for a major publication?

How do you go from being a new professor to one of the most sought after professors on campus? How do you go from a job as a publicity assistant at a university to their director of public relations?

There are many things you're going to have to do to climb the career ladder, but it can be done. We've covered a lot of them. Work hard, keep a positive attitude, and act professionally at all times. Stay abreast of the business, network, and hone your skills and talents so you can back up your claims of accomplishments.

Look for a mentor who can help you move your career in the right direction and propel you to the top of your field. Join trade associations and the unions. Read the trades, take seminars, classes, and workshops, and take part in other learning opportunities. Continue your education when you can. Be the best at what you do. Keep your goal in mind.

Look at every opportunity with an open mind. When you're offered something, ask yourself:

◎ Is this what I want to be doing?
◎ Is this part of my dream?
◎ Is this part of my plan for success?
◎ Is this opportunity a stepping-stone to advancing my career?
◎ Will this experience be valuable to me?

Fortunately or unfortunately, job progression in education doesn't always follow the normal career path. A coordinator in the marketing department of a university may get a break and end up director of public relations. An unknown author may get a mention on *Oprah* about his book on some aspect of education and be catapulted to a bestseller and tremendous success. An innovative teaching method discussed in the media might catapult the career of a new teacher who developed the method. It all depends. If it can happen to someone else, it might happen to you. That is one of the greatest things about your career. You just never know what tomorrow might bring.

You never know when a chance meeting is going to land you a great job, or someone passing through town might read about one of your accomplishments in a local newspaper and recruit you for a position in a larger or more prestigious school or situation. You never know who will tell a headhunter, recruiter, or human resources director about you, who then gives you a call. You really never know when success will come your way. It can happen at any time.

It should be noted that success means different things to different people. There are many people who work in education who are not well-known teachers; there are many people who don't work in large, prestigious schools, colleges, or companies; there are many people in education who never become directors of departments or administrators. Yet these people are all still successful. They are earning a living, doing what they love, living their dream, and helping others live theirs as well.

And it's like that in all segments of education. There are thousands of individuals working in education and the peripheral fields who may not be the ones you hear of, might not be the ones winning the awards, but they are successful just the same.

There are administrators of small schools, colleges, and universities who, while they aren't in charge of mega-institutions, are earning very good livings doing their jobs just the same.

There are marketing professionals, publicists, fund-raisers, grant writers, child advocates, accountants, attorneys, and others who might not be working for large prestigious schools or universities, but are working in the education industry just the same. That doesn't preclude them from having a successful career in education. To the contrary, one of the best things about working in education is that almost every job has some sort of an impact on others. Every job can make a difference, even if it's just a little one. And that little difference can make a big difference in the lives of others.

Risk Taking—Overcoming Your Fears

Everyone has a comfort zone from which they operate. What's a comfort zone? It's the area where you feel comfortable both physically and psychologically. Most of the time you try to stay within this zone. It's predictable, it's safe, and you generally know what's coming.

Many people get jobs, stay in them for years, and then retire. They know what's expected of them. They know what they're going to be doing. They know what they're going to be getting. The problem is that it can get boring, there's little challenge, and your creativity can suffer.

Stepping out of your comfort zone is especially important to your career. Wanting to step out of your comfort zone is often easier said than done, but every now and then you're going to have to push yourself.

The key to career success in the education industry as well as your own personal growth is the willingness to step outside of your comfort zone. Throughout your career you're going to be faced with decisions. Each decision can

> **Tip from the Coach**
> If you're starting to feel comfortable in your career or are starting to feel bored, it's time to step out of your comfort zone and look for new challenges.

impact your career. Be willing to take risks. Be willing to step out of your comfort zone.

Is it scary? Of course, but if you don't take risks you stand the chance of your career stagnating. You take the chance of missing wonderful opportunities.

Should you take a promotion? Should you stay at the same job? Should you go to a different school? Should you go to a different company? Should you go back to school? Should you move? Should you take a chance?

How do you make the right decision? Try to think about the pros and cons of your choices. Get the facts, think about them, and make your decision.

"What if I'm wrong?" you ask.

Here's the good news. Usually you *will* make the right decision. If by chance you don't, it's generally not a life and death situation. If you stay at the same job and find you should have left, for example, all you need to do is look for a new job. If you change jobs and you're not happy, you can usually find a new job as well.

> **Tip from the Top**
> Try to treat everyone from subordinates to superiors to colleagues to students to parents the way you want to be treated—with respect and dignity.

Most things ultimately work out. Do the best you can and then go on.

If your career is stagnant, do something. Don't just stay where you are because of the fear of leaving your comfort zone and the fear of the unknown.

Some Final Thoughts

No matter where you are in your career, don't get stagnant. Always keep your career moving. Once you reach one of your goals, your journey isn't over. You have to keep set new goals and move on to reach them.

Keep working toward your goal. It can happen. Don't settle for less than what you want. Every goal you meet is another steppingstone toward an even better career no matter what segment of the industry you are pursuing.

While I would love to promise you that after reading this book you will become the teacher of the year, your state's commissioner of education, the dean of a large medical school, the president of a prestigious university, the superintendent of schools, the principal of the school where you currently work, a sought after corporate trainer, the director of your department, or will win the Nobel Peace Prize for discovering a more effective way to help children learn, unfortunately I can't.

What I can tell you is that the advice in this book can help you move ahead and stack the deck in your favor in this industry. I've given you the information. You have to put it into action.

There are numerous factors that are essential to your success. You need to be prepared. There's no question that preparation is neces-

> ### ⭐ Words from the Wise
> Persevere. The reason most people fail is because they gave up one day too soon.
> —Shelly Field

sary. Talent in your field is critical as well. Being in the right place at the right time is essential, and good luck doesn't hurt. Perseverance is vital to success, no matter what you want to do, what area of the industry you want to enter, and what career level you want to achieve.

Do you want to know why most people don't find their perfect job? It's because they gave up looking *before* they found it. Do you want to know why some people are on the brink of success, yet never really get there? It's because they gave up.

Do you want to know what single factor can increase your chances of success? It's perseverance! Don't give up.

Have fun reading this book. Use it to jumpstart your career and inspire you to greater success and accomplishments. Draw on it to achieve your goals so you can have the career of your dreams. Use it so you don't have to look back and say, "I wish I had." Use it so you can say instead, "I'm glad I did."

I can't wait to hear about your success stories. Be sure to let us know how this book has helped your career by logging on to http://www.shellyfield.com. I would also love to hear about any of your own tips or techniques for succeeding in any aspect of education. You can never tell. Your successes might be part of our next edition.

APPENDIX I

TRADE ASSOCIATIONS, UNIONS, AND OTHER ORGANIZATIONS

Trade associations, unions, and other organizations can be valuable resources to you for career guidance as well as professional support. This listing includes many of the organizations related to the education industry. Namcs, addresses, phone numbers, e-mail, and Web sites (when available) have been included to make it easier for you to obtain information. Check out Web sites to learn more about organizations and what they offer.

Academy for Educational Development (AED)
c/o Stephen F. Moseley, President
1825 Connecticut Avenue, NW
Washington, DC 20009-5721
(202) 884-8000
web@aed.org
http://www.aed.org

Academy of Security Educators and Trainers (ASET)
c/o Dr. Richard W. Kobetz
PO Box 802
Berryville, VA 22611-0802
(540) 554-2540
http://www.asetcse.org

Accrediting Commission of Career Schools and Colleges of Technology (ACCSCT)
2101 Wilson Boulevard, Suite 302
Arlington, VA 22201-3062
(703) 247-4212
info@accsct.org
http://www.accsct.org

Accrediting Council for Continuing Education and Training (ACCET)
1722 N Street, NW
Washington, DC 20036-2907
(202) 955-1113
http://www.accet.org

American Academy of Teachers of Singing (AATS)
c/o Jan Eric Douglas
777 West End Avenue
New York, NY 10025-5551
(212) 666-5951
info@americanacademyofteachersofsinging.org
http://www.americanacademyofteachersofsinging.
   org

American Alliance for Health, Physical Education, Recreation and Dance

1900 Association Drive
Reston, VA 20191-1598
(800) 213-7193
http://www.aahperd.org/aahperd

American Art Therapy Association (AATA)

5999 Stevenson Avenue
Alexandria, VA 22304-3304
(888) 290-0878
info@arttherapy.org
http://www.arttherapy.org

American Association for Adult and Continuing Education (AAACE)

10111 Martin Luther King, Jr. Highway, Suite 200C
Bowie, MD 20720-4200
(301) 459-6261
aaace10@aol.com
http://www.aaace.org

American Association for Health Education (AAHE)

1900 Association Drive
Reston, VA 20191-1598
(800) 213-7193
http://www.aahperd.org/aahe

American Association of Christian Schools (AACS)

602 Belvoir Avenue
East Ridge, TN 37412-2602
(423) 629-4280
lpotter@aacs.org
http://www.aacs.org

American Association of Colleges for Teacher Education

1307 New York Avenue, NW, Suite 300
Washington, DC 20005-4701
(202) 293-2450
http://www.aacte.org

American Association of Collegiate Registrars and Admissions Officers (AACRAO)

One Dupont Circle, NW, Suite 520
Washington, DC 20036-1148
(202) 293-9161
info@aacrao.org
http://www.aacrao.org

American Association of Community Colleges (AACC)

One Dupont Circle, NW, Suite 300
Washington, DC 20036-1188
(202) 728-0200
http://www.aacc.nche.edu

American Association of Family and Consumer Sciences (AAFCS)

400 North Columbus Street, Suite 202
Alexandria, VA 22314-2264
(703) 706-4600
staff@aafcs.org
http://www.aafcs.org

American Association of School Administrators (AASA)

801 North Quincy Street, Suite 700
Arlington, VA 22203-1730
(703) 528-0700
info@aasa.org
http://www.aasa.org

American Association of School Personnel Administrators (AASPA)

11863 West 112th Street, Suite 100
Overland Park, KS 66210-1375
(913) 327-1222

aaspa@aaspa.org
http://www.aaspa.org

American Association of State Colleges and Universities (AASCU)

1307 New York Avenue, NW
Washington, DC 20005-4704
(202) 293-7070
info@aascu.org
http://www.aascu.org

American Association of Teaching and Curriculum (AATC)

c/o Marcella L. Kysilka, Executive Secretary
4240 Yorketowne Road.
Orlando, FL 32812-7958
kysilka@bellsouth.net
http://www.aatchome.org

American Association of University Administrators (AAUA)

PO Box 630101
Little Neck, NY 11363-0101
(347) 235-4822
dking@qcc.cuny.edu
http://www.aaua.org

American Association of University Professors (AAUP)

1012 14th Street NW, Suite 500
Washington, DC 20005-3465
Tel: (202) 737-5900
Email: aaup@aaup.org
http://www.aaup.org

American College Personnel Association (ACPA)

One Dupont Circle, NW, Suite300
Washington, DC 20036-1188
(202) 296-3286
info@acpa.nche.edu
http://www.acpa.nche.edu

American Conference of Academic Deans (ACAD)

1818 R Street, NW
Washington, DC 20009-1692
(202) 884-7419
rzepka@acad-edu.org
http://www.acad-edu.org

American Council on Education (ACE)

One Dupont Circle, NW
Washington, DC 20036-1188
(202) 939-9300
comments@ace.nche.edu
http://www.acenet.edu

American Counseling Association (ACA)

5999 Stevenson Avenue
Alexandria, VA 22304-3304
(800) 347-6647
http://www.counseling.org

American Federation of School Administrators (AFSA)

1101 17th Street, NW, Suite 408
Washington, DC 20036-4720
(202) 986-4209
afsa@AFSAadmin.org
http://www.admin.org

American Federation of Teachers (AFT)

555 New Jersey Avenue, NW
Washington, DC 20001-2029
(202) 879-4400
http://www.aft.org

American Library Association (ALA)

50 East Huron Street
Chicago, IL 60611-2788
(800) 545-2433
library@ala.org
http://www.ala.org

American School Counselor Association (ASCA)
1101 King Street, Suite 625
Alexandria, VA 22314-2957
(703) 683-2722
http://www.schoolcounselor.org

American School Health Association (ASHA)
7263 State Route 43
PO Box 708
Kent, OH 44240-0013
(330) 678-1601
asha@ashaweb.org
http://www.ashaweb.org

American Society for Training and Development (ASTD)
1640 King Street
PO Box 1443
Alexandria, VA 22313-2043
(703) 683-8100
publications@astd.org
http://www.astd.org

Association for Career and Technical Education (ACTE)
1410 King Street
Alexandria, VA 22314-2749
(703) 683-3111
acte@acteonline.org
http://www.acteonline.org

Association for Educational Communications and Technology (AECT)
1800 North Stonelake Drive, Suite 2
Bloomington, IN 47404-1517
(812) 335-7675
aect@aect.org
http://www.aect.org

Association for Supervision and Curriculum Development (ASCD)
1703 North Beauregard Street
Alexandria, VA 22311-1714
(800) 933-2723
Email: member@ascd.org
http://www.ascd.org

Association of American Colleges and Universities (AAU)
1818 R Street, NW
Washington, DC 20009-1604
(202) 387-3760
http://www.aacu.org

Association of School Business Officials International (ASBO)
11401 North Shore Drive
Reston, VA 20190-4232
(866) 682-2729
http://www.asbointl.org

Association of Teacher Educators (ATE)
PO Box 793
Manassas, VA 20113-0793
Tel: (703) 331-0911
Email: info@ate1.org
http://www.ate1.org

College and University Professional Association for Human Resources (CUPA-HR)
1811 Commons Point Drive
Knoxville, TN 37932-1989
(865) 637-7673
http://www.cupahr.org

Council for Advancement and Support of Education (CASE)
1307 New York Avenue, NW, Suite 1000
Washington, DC 20005-4701

(202) 328-2273
MemberServiceCenter@case.org
http://www.case.org

Council of Chief State School Officers (CCSSO)

One Massachusetts Avenue, NW, Suite 700
Washington, DC 20001-1431
(202) 336-7000
info@ccsso.org
http://www.ccsso.org

Distance Education and Training Council (DETC)

1601 18th Street, NW
Washington, DC 20009-2529
(202) 234-5100
rachel@detc.org
http://www.detc.org

National Association For Gifted Children (NAGC)

1707 L Street, NW, Suite 550
Washington, DC 20036-4212
(202) 785-4268
nagc@nagc.org
http://www.nagc.org

National Association For Music Education (MENC)

1806 Robert Fulton Drive
Reston, VA 20191-4341
(800) 336-3768
 info@menc.org
http://www.menc.org

National Board for Professional Teaching Standards (NBPTS)

1525 Wilson Boulevard, Suite 500
Arlington, VA 22209-2451
(800) 228-3224

info@nbpts.org
http://www.nbpts.org

National Association of Elementary School Principals (NAESP)

1615 Duke Street
Alexandria, VA 22314-3406
(800) 386-2377
naesp@naesp.org
http://www.naesp.org

National Association of Independent Colleges and Universities (NAICU)

1025 Conneticut Avenue, NW, Suite 700
Washington, DC 20036-5404
(202) 785-8866
geninfo@naicu.edu
http://www.naicu.edu

National Association of Independent Schools (NAIS)

1620 L Street, NW, Suite 1100
Washington, DC 20036-5695
(202) 973-9700
info@nais.org
http://www.nais.org

National Association of School Psychologists (NASP)

4340 East West Highway, Suite 402
Bethesda, MD 20814-4468
(301) 657-0270
smarshall@naspweb.org
http://www.nasponline.org

National Association of Schools of Music (NASM)

11250 Roger Bacon Drive, Suite 21
Reston, VA 20190-5248
(703) 437-0700
info@arts-accredit.org
http://nasm.arts-accredit.org

National Association of Secondary School Principals (NASSP)
1904 Association Drive
Reston, VA 20191-1537
(703) 860-0200
Email: coneyb@nassp.org
http://www.principals.org

National Association of University Women (NAUW)
1001 E Street, SE
Washington, DC 20003-2847
(202) 547-3967
info@nauw1910.org
http://www.nauw1910.org

National Business Education Association (NBEA)
1914 Association Drive
Reston, VA 20191-1596
(703) 860-8300
nbea@nbea.org
http://www.nbea.org

National Center for Community Education (NCCE)
1017 Avon Street
Flint, MI 48503-2701
(810) 238-0463
info@nccenet.org
http://www.nccenet.org

National Council for Accreditation of Teacher Education
2010 Massachusetts Avenue, NW, Suite 500
Washington, DC 20036-1023
Tel: (202) 466-7496
Email: ncate@ncate.org
http://www.ncate.org

National Education Association (NEA)
1201 16th Street, NW
Washington, DC 20036-3290
Tel: (202) 833-4000
http://www.nea.org

National Head Start Association
1651 Prince Street
Alexandria, VA 22314-2818
Tel: (703) 739-0875
Email: chutchinson@nhsa.org
http://www.nhsa.org

National Middle School Association (NMSA)
4151 Executive Parkway, Suite 300
Westerville, OH 43081-3871
Tel: (800) 528-6672
Email: info@nmsa.org
http://www.nmsa.org

National PTA
541 N Fairbanks Court, Suite 1300
Chicago, IL 60611-3396
Tel: (800) 307-4782
Email: info@pta.org
http://www.pta.org

National School Boards Association (NSBA)
1680 Duke Street
Alexandria, VA 22314-3474
Tel: (703) 838-6722
Email: info@nsba.org
http://www.nsba.org

National School Public Relations Associations
15948 Derwood Road
Rockville, MD 20855
(301) 519-0496
http://www.nspra.org

National Staff Development Council (NSDC)

5995 Fairfield Road, Suite 4
Oxford, OH 45056-1587
Tel: (513) 523-6029
Email: nsdcoffice@nsdc.org
http://www.nsdc.org

ProLiteracy Worldwide

1320 Jamesville Avenue
Syracuse, NY 13210-4224
Tel: (888) 528-2224
Email: info@proliteracy.org
http://www.proliteracy.org

Teacher Education Accreditation Council (TEAC)

c/o Dr. Frank B. Murray .
One Dupont Circle, Suite 320
Washington, DC 20036-0110
Tel: (202) 466-7236
http://www.teac.org

United States Department of Education (USDE)

400 Maryland Avenue, SW
Washington, DC 20202-0001
http://www.ed.gov

APPENDIX II

EDUCATION AND CAREER WEB SITES

The Internet is a premier resource for information, no matter what you need. Surfing the Web can help you locate almost anything you want, from information to services and everything in between.

Throughout the appendices of this book, whenever possible, Web site addresses have been included to help you find information quicker. This listing contains an assortment of various general and education-related career and job Web sites that may be of value to you in your career.

Use this list as a start. More sites are emerging every day. This listing is for your information. The author is not responsible for any site content. Inclusion or exclusion in this listing does not imply any one site is endorsed or recommended over another by the author.

Academic, Educator, and Teaching Jobs
http://www.quintcareers.com/teaching_jobs.html

Academic360.com
http://www.academic360.com

After College Teaching Jobs
http://www.aftercollege.com/jobseekers/teach

Alabama Teaching Jobs
http://www.alsde.edu/html/JobVacancies.asp

Alaska Teacher Placement
http://alaskateacher.org

Arkansas Education Association
http://www.aeaonline.org/members/edu_jobs.asp

Americas Job Bank
http://www.jobbank.com

BioClassroom
http://www.biography.com/classroom

Cablevision-Power To Learn
http://www.powertolearn.com/index.shtml

California.teachers.net
http://california.teachers.net

CareerAge/Academics
http://www.careerage.com/academics

CareerBuilder.com
http://www.careerbuilder.com

Careermag.com
http://www.careermag.com

Careers.org
http://www.careers.org

CoolWorks
http://www.coolworks.com

DC Teaching Fellows
http://www.dcteachingfellows.org

Discovery Education
http://school.discovery.com

Edjoin.org
http://www.edjoin.org

Educating Hawaii's Future
http://www.rrsc.k12.hi.us

Education Jobs
http://www.educationjobs.com

Education Week Job Search
http://www.agentk-12.org

Education World Career Center
http://www.education-world.com/jobs

Educational Placement Service
http://www.educatorjobs.com

ESL Employment
http://www.eslemployment.com

Great Teacher.net
http://www.greatteacher.net

History Channel Classroom
http://www.history.com/classroom/index.html

HotJobs.com
http://www.hotjobs.com

Illinois Association of School Administrators
http://www.illinoiseducationjobbank.org/pages

JobBank USA
http://www.jobbankusa.com

Job.com
http://www.job.com

Kansas Educational Employment Board
http://www.kansasteachingjobs.com

Kentucky Department of Education
http://www.kde.state.ky.us/KDE

K-12 Jobs
http://www.K-12jobs.com

Louisiana Department of Education
http://www.louisianaschools.net

Maine Department of Education
http://www.mainc.info/jobs10.html

Massachusetts Department of Education
http://www.doe.mass.edu/jobs

Michigan School Application Network
http://www.mireap.net

Minnesota Association of School Administrators
http://www.mnasa.org

Mississippi Teacher Center
http://www.mde.k12.ms.us/mtc

Monster.com
http://www.monster.com

NationJob.com
http://www.nationjob.com

Nebraska Education Jobs
http://www.nebraskaeducationjobs.com

New Hampshire Department of Education
http://www.ed.state.nh.us/education/doe/employ.htm

New Jersey Hire
http://www.njhire.com/MainTemp.cfm?page=mainpage.cfm

Ohio Department of Education
http://www.ode.state.oh.us

Oklahoma Teaching Jobs
http://www.oklahomateachingjobs.org

PA-Educators.Net
http://www.pa-educator.net

Professional Education Employee Referral
http://www.doe.state.in.us/peer

Quintessential Careers
http://www.quintcareers.com

Resources for Indispensable Schools and Educators
http://risenetwork.org

Rhode Island Department of Elementary and Secondary Education
http://www.ridoe.net/educatorquality/edjobs.aspx

SchoolShows.com
http://www.schoolshows.com

State Job Banks
http://www.jobbankinfo.org

South Dakota Department of Education Teaching Jobs
http://doe.sd.gov/oatq/teachingjobs/index.asp

Teach Iowa
http://www.iowaeducationjobs.com

Teacher Jobs
http://www.teacherjobs.com

Teach4NC
http://teach4nc.org

Teach In Florida.com
http://www.teachinflorida.com

TeachingJobs
http://www.teachingjobs.com

Teaching Jobs Overseas
http://www.joyjobs.com

Teachers Support Network
http://www.teacherssupportnetwork.com

Teach NYC
http://schools.nyc.gov/teachnyc

Teach Oregon
http://www.teachoregon.com

Teach Virginia
http://www.teachvirginia.org

University Job Bank
http://www.ujobbank.com

Utah State Office of Education Jobs For Educators
http://www.usoe.k12.ut.us/jobs

WA Teach
http://www.wateach.com

West Virginia Department of Education Jobs
http://wvde.state.wv.us/jobs

BIBLIOGRAPHY

A. Books

There are thousands of books on all aspects of education. Sometimes just reading about someone else's success inspires you, motivates you, or just helps you to come up with ideas to help you attain your own dreams.

Books can be a treasure trove of information if you want to learn about a particular aspect of a career or gain more knowledge about how something in the industry works.

The books listed below are separated into general categories. Subjects often overlap. Use this listing as a beginning. Check out your local library, bookstore, or online retailer for other books that might interest you about the industry.

Administration

Cherry, Daniel, and Jeffery M. Spiegel. *Leadership, Myth, & Metaphor: Finding Common Ground to Guide Effective School Change.* Thousand Oaks, Calif.: Corwin Press, 2006.

Cooke, Gwendolyn J. *Keys to Success for Urban School Principals.* Thousand Oaks, Calif.: Corwin Press, 2006.

Sugrue, Ciaran. *Passionate Principalship: Learning from the Life Histories of School Leaders.* New York: Routledge, 2005.

Townsend, Rene S., Gloria L. Johnston, Gwen E. Gross, and Peggy Lynch. *Effective Superintendent-School Board Practices: Strategies for Developing and Maintaining Good Relationships With Your Board.* Thousand Oaks, Calif.: Corwin Press, 2006.

Whitaker, Todd. *What Great Principals Do Differently: Fifteen Things That Matter Most.* New York: Eye On Education, 2003.

Career Opportunities

Echaore-McDavid, Susan. *Career Opportunities In Education and Related Services.* New York: Facts On File, 2006.

Corporate Training

Greeno, Nathan, J. *Corporate Learning Strategies.* Alexandria, Va.: American Society For Training and Development, 2006.

Haskins, Mark E., and James G. S. Clawson. *Teaching Management: A Field Guide for Professors, Consultants, and Corporate Trainers.* New York: Cambridge University Press, 2006.

Rothwell, William, John Lindholm, and William G. Wallick. *What CEOs Expect from Corporate Training: Building Workplace Learning and Performance Initiatives That Advance Organizational Goals.* New York: Amacom, 2003.

College/University Business and Administration

McPhail, Christine Johnson. *Establishing and Sustaining Learning-Centered Community Colleges*. Washington, D.C.: Community College Press, 2005.

Worth, Michael, ed. *New Strategies For Educational Fund-Raising*. Westport, Conn.: Greenwood Publishing Group, 2002.

Wallin, Desna L. *Adjunct Faculty in Community Colleges: An Academic Administrator's Guide to Recruiting, Supporting, and Retaining Great Teachers*. Hoboken, N.J.: John Wiley & Sons, 2007.

Whiteside, Richard. *Student Marketing for Colleges and Universities*. Washington, D.C.: American Association of Collegiate Registrars and Admissions Officers, 2004.

College/University Teaching

Farnsworth, Kent Allen. *A Fieldbook for Community College Online Instructors*. Washington, D.C.: Community College Press, 2007.

Kember, David. *Enhancing University Teaching*. New York: Routledge Press, 2007.

Royse, David D. *Teaching Tips for College and University Instructors: A Practical Guide*. Boston, Mass.: Allyn & Bacon, 2000.

Wallin, Desna L., ed. *Adjunct Faculty in Community Colleges: An Academic Administrator's Guide to Recruiting, Supporting, and Retaining Great Teachers*. Hoboken, N.J.: John Wiley & Sons, 2007.

Education-General

Wilson, Smokey. *What about Rose?: Using Teacher Research to Reverse School Failure*. New York: Teachers College Press, 2007.

Literacy

Rodgers, Adrian. *The Effective Literacy Coach*. New York: Teachers College Press, 2007.

Online Teaching/Podcasting

Ace Staff. *Teaching Strategies in the Online Environment: New Directions for Adult and Continuing Education*. Hoboken, N.J.: John Wiley & Sons, 2003.

Babb, Danielle. *Make Money Teaching Online: How to Land Your First Academic Job, Build Credibility, and Earn a Six-Figure Salary*. Hoboken, N.J.: John Wiley & Son, 2007.

Dawley, Lisa. *The Tools for Successful Online Teaching*. Hershey, Penn.: Idea Group Publishing, 2007.

King, Kathleen, and Mark Gura. *Podcasting for Teachers: Using a New Technology to Revolutionize Teaching and Learning*. Charlotte, N.C.: Information Age Publishing, 2007.

Palloff, Rena M., and Keith Pratt. *Building Online Learning Communities: Effective Strategies for the Virtual Classroom*. Hoboken, N.J.: John Wiley & Sons, 2007.

School/Community

Epstein, Joyce, Mavis G. Sanders, and Karen C. Salinas. *School, Family, and Community Partnerships: Your Handbook for Action*. Thousand Oaks, Calif.: Corwin Press, 2002.

Special Education

Pierangelo, Roger. *The Special Educator's Survival Guide*. Hoboken, N.J.: John Wiley & Sons, 2004.

Student Teaching

Roe, Betty D. D., Elinor P. Ross, and Sandy H. Smith. *Student Teaching and Field Experiences Handbook*. Upper Saddle River, N.J.: Prentice Hall, 2005.

Pelletier, Carol Marra. *Strategies for Successful Student Teaching: A Comprehensive Guide*, 2d edition. Boston, Mass.: Allyn & Bacon, 2003.

Teaching

Airasian, Peter W., and Michael Russell. *Classroom Assessment*. New York: McGraw-Hill, 2007.

Fountas, Irene C. *Classroom Management: Managing The Day—Planning For Effective Teaching*. Portsmouth, N.H.: Heinemann, 2005.

Lovitt, Thomas C. *Promoting School Success: Effective Strategies For Students With Learning Difficulties*. Austin, Texas: PRO-ED, 2007.

Marzano, Robert J. *The Art and Science of Teaching: A Model for Effective Instruction*. Alexandria, Va.: Association for Supervision & Curriculum Development, 2007.

Parks, Jerry. *Teacher Under Construction: Things I Wish I'd Known!: A Survival Handbook for New Middle School Teachers*. Lincoln, Neb.: iUniverse, 2004.

Peltz, William H. *Dear Teacher: Expert Advice for Effective Study Skills*. Thousand Oaks, Calif.: Corwin Press, 2007.

Pitler, Howard. *Using Technology with Classroom Instruction That Works*. Alexandria, Va.: Association for Supervision & Curriculum Development, 2007.

Pollock, Jane E. *Improving Student Learning One Teacher at a Time*. Alexandria, Va.: Association for Supervision & Curriculum Development, 2007.

Pugach, Marleen C. *Because Teaching Matters*. Hoboken, N.J.: John Wiley & Sons, 2006.

Rominger, Lynne Marie, Karen Heisinger, and Natalie Elkin. *Your First Year As an Elementary School Teacher: Making the Transition from Total Novice to Successful Professional*. New York: Crown Publishing Group, 2001.

Rominger, Lynne Marie, Suzanne Packard Laughrea, and Natalie Elkin. *Your First Year As a High School Teacher: Making the Transition from Total Novice to Successful Professional*. New York: Crown Publishing Group, 2001.

Rourke, James. *From My Classroom to Yours: Reflections on Teaching*. Lanham, Md.: Rowman & Littlefield, 2007.

Smith, Rick. *Unlocking the Secrets of Great Teachers-Elementary*. DVD. Salt Lake City, Utah: Linton Professional Development Corporation, 2005.

Stone, Randi. *Best Practices for Teaching Science: What Award-Winning Classroom Teachers Do*. Thousand Oaks, Calif.: Corwin Press, 2007.

Tomal, Daniel R. *Challenging Students To Learn*. Lahnam, Md.: Rowman & Littlefield, 2007.

Wilen, William, Margaret Ishler, Janice Hutchison, and Richard Kindsvatter. *Dynamics of Effective Secondary Teaching*. Boston, Mass.: Allyn & Bacon, 2007.

Williams, R. Bruce. *Higher Order Thinking Skills: Challenging All Students to Achieve*. Thousand Oaks, Calif.: Corwin Press, 2007.

Wootan, Frederick, and Catherine Mulligan. *Not in My Classroom!: A Teacher's Guide to Effective Classroom Management*. Cincinnati, Ohio: Adams Media, 2007.

B. Periodicals

Magazines, newspapers, membership bulletins, and newsletters may be helpful for finding information about a specific job category, finding a job in a specific field, or giving you insight into what certain jobs entail.

This list should serve as a beginning. There are many periodicals that are not listed because of space limitations. The subject matter of some periodicals may overlap with others. Periodicals also tend to come and go. Look in your local library or in the newspaper/magazine shop for other periodicals that might interest you.

Names, addresses, phone numbers, Web sites, and e-mail addresses have been included when available.

ADMINISTRATION

National Forum of Education Administration and Supervision Journal
National Forum Journals
17603 Bending Post Drive
Houston, TX 77095
(281) 550-5700
http://www.nationalforum.com

District Administration
Professional Media Group LLC
488 Main Avenue
Norwalk, CT 06851
(203) 663-0100
(203) 663-0149 (fax)

Education
Project Innovation, Inc.
PO Box 8508
Mobile, AL 36689
(251) 343-1878
http://www.projectinnovation.biz

National Association of Elementary School Principals Resources Catalog
National Association of Elementary School Principals
1615 Duke Street
Alexandria, VA 22314
(703) 684-3345
(703) 548-6021 (fax)
E-mail: naesp@naesp.org
http://naesp@naesp.org

National Forum Journals
17603 Bending Post Drive

Houston, TX 77095
E-mail: wakritsonis@aol.com
http://www.nationalforum.com

Principal Leadership (High School)
National Association of Secondary School Principals
1904 Association Drive
Reston, VA 20191
(703) 860-0200
(703) 476-5432 (fax)
http://www.nassp.org

Principal Leadership (Middle School)
National Association of Secondary School Principals
1904 Association Drive
Reston, VA 20191
(703) 860-0200
(703) 476-5432 (fax)
http://www.nassp.org

ADULT EDUCATION

Adult Basic Education and Literacy Journal
Commission on Adult Basic Education
1320 Jamesville Avenue
Syracuse, NY 13210
(315) 426-0645
(315) 426-422-6369
http://www.coabe.org

BUSINESS EDUCATION

Business Education Forum
National Business Education Association
1914 Association Drive
Reston, VA 20191
(703) 860-8300
(703) 620-4483 (fax)

nbea@nbea.org
http://www.nbea.org

COUNSELING

Intervention in School and Clinic
Sage Publications
2455 Teller Road
Thousand Oaks, CA 91320
(805) 499-0721
(805) 499-0871 (fax)
info@sagepub.com
http://www.sagepub.com

Journal For The School of Professional Counseling
Lindsey Wilson College, School of Professional
Counseling
210 Lindsey Wilson Street
Columbia, KY 42728
(270) 384-2126
(270) 384-8200 (fax)
http://www.schoolcounselor.org

Professional School Counseling
American School Counselor Association
1101 King Street
Alexandria, VA 22314
(703) 683-2722
(703) 683-1619 (fax)
http://www.schoolcounselor.org

CURRICULUM

Classroom Leadership
Association for Supervision and Curriculum
Development
1703 North Beauregard Street
Alexandria, VA 22311
(703) 578-9600
(703) 575-5400 (fax)

E-mail: update@ascd.org
http://www.ascd.org

Curriculum Review
PaperClip Communications
125 Paterson Avenue
Little Falls, NJ 07424
(973) 256-1333
(973) 256-8088 (Fax)
info@paper-clip.com
http://www.paper-clip.com

EDUCATION—GENERAL

American Education Research Journal
Sage Publications
2455 Teller Road
Thousand Oaks, CA 91320
(805) 499-0721
(805) 499-0871 (fax)
info@sagepub.com
http://www.sagepub.com

American Journal of Education
University of Chicago Press
PO Box 37005
Journals Division
Chicago, IL 60637
(773) 753-3347
(773) 753-0811 (fax)
subscriptions@pressuchicago.edu
http://www.journals.uchicago.edu

American Journal of Distance Education
Lawrence Erlbaum Associates, Inc.
325 Chestnut Street
Suite 800
Philadelphia, PA 19106
(215) 625-8900
(215) 625-8914 (fax)

customerservice@taylorandfrancis.com
http://www.leaonline.com

AACE Journal
Association for the Advancement of Computing
in Education
PO Box 1545
Chesapeake, VA 23327
(757) 366-5606
(703) 997-8760 (fax)
info@aace.org
http://www.aace.org

Educational Studies
Lawrence Erlbaum Associates, Inc.
325 Chestnut Street
Suite 800
Philadelphia, PA 19106
(215) 625-8900
(215) 625-8914 (fax)
customerservice@taylorandfrancis.com
http://www.leaonline.com

Basic Education
Council for Basic Education
4000 Cathedral Avenue NW
Apartment 803B
Washington, DC 20016-
(202) 347-4171

Education Digest
Prakken Publications, Inc
832 Phoenix Drive
Ann Arbor, MI 48108
(734) 975-2800
(734) 975-2787 (fax)

Forum For Advancing Basic Education and Literacy
Harvard Institute for International Development
14 Story Street

Cambridge, MA 02138
(617) 495-2161
E-mail: info@hiid.harvard.edu
http://www.hiid.harvard.edu

Education Week
6935 Arlington Road
Bethesda, MD 20814
(301)280-3100
(301)280-3200 (fax)
http://www.edweek.org

Journal of Research in Childhood Education
Association for Childhood Education International
17904 Georgia Avenue
Olney, MD 20832
(301) 570-2111
(301) 570-2212 (fax)
headquarters@acei.org
http://www.acei.org

SCHOOL BOARDS

American School Board Journal
National School Boards Association
1680 Duke Street
Alexandria, VA 22314
(703) 838-6722
(703) 549-6719 (fax)
info@nsba.org
http://www.nsba.org

SCHOOL LIBRARY

School Library Journal
Reed Business Information
360 Park Avenue South
New York, NY 10010
(646) 746-6759
http://www.reedbusiness.com

Teacher Librarian
Scarecrow Press
15200 NBN Way
Blue Ridge Summit, PA 17214
(717) 794-3800
(717 794-3833 (fax)
subs@teacherlibrarian.com
http://www.teacherlibrarian.com

Special Education
National Forum of Special Education Journal
National Forum Journals
17603 Bending Post Drive
Houston, TX 77095
(281) 550-5700
http://www.nationalforum.com

TEACHING

Action In Teacher Education
Association of Teacher Educators
PO Box 793
Manassas, VA 20113
(703) 331-0911
(703) 331-3666 (fax)
ate1@aol.com
http://www.ate1.org

Better Teaching (Elementary Edition)
Teacher Institute
PO Box 397
Fairfax, VA 22039
(703) 503-5413
custsvc@teacher-institute.com
http://www.teacherinstitute.com

Better Teaching (Secondary Edition)
PO Box 397
Fairfax, VA 22039
(703) 503-5413
(703) 323-9173

custsvc@teacher-institute.com
http://www.teacherinstitute.com

Journal For the Association of Teacher Educators
P.O. Box 793
Manassas, VA 20113
(703) 331.0911
(703) 331.3666 (fax)
http://www.ou.edu/action

Language Arts
National Council of Teachers of English
1111 W Kenyon Road
Urbana, IL 61801
(217) 328-3870
(217) 328-9645 (fax)
http://www.ncte.org

School Arts: The Art Education Magazine For Teachers
Davis Publications, Inc
50 Portland Street
Worcester, MA 01608
(508)754-7201
(508) 753-3834
contactus@davis-art.com
http://www.davis-art.com

The Elementary School Journal
University of Chicago Press
PO Box 37005
Chicago, IL 60637
(773)753-3347
(773) 753-0811 (Fax)
subscriptions@press.uchicago.edu
http://www.journals.uchicago.edu

Trends and Issues in Elementary Language Arts
National Council of Teachers of English
1111 W Kenyon Road

Urbana, IL 61801
(217) 328-3870
(217) 328-9645 (fax)
membership@ncte.org
http://www.ncte.org

UNIVERSITIES AND COLLEGES

Academe

American Association of University Professors
1012 14th Street N W
Washington, DC 20005
(202) 737-5900
(202) 737-5526 (fax)
aaupo@aaup.org
http://www.aaup.org

Community College Journal

American Association of Community Colleges
One Dupont Circle, N W
Washington, DC 20036
(202) 728-0200
(202) 223-9390
http://www.aacc.nche.edu

Index